Communications in Computer and Information Science

2675

Series Editors

Gang Li , *School of Information Technology, Deakin University, Burwood, VIC, Australia*
Joaquim Filipe, *Polytechnic Institute of Setúbal, Setúbal, Portugal*
Zhiwei Xu, *Chinese Academy of Sciences, Beijing, China*

Rationale

The CCIS series is devoted to the publication of proceedings of computer science conferences. Its aim is to efficiently disseminate original research results in informatics in printed and electronic form. While the focus is on publication of peer-reviewed full papers presenting mature work, inclusion of reviewed short papers reporting on work in progress is welcome, too. Besides globally relevant meetings with internationally representative program committees guaranteeing a strict peer-reviewing and paper selection process, conferences run by societies or of high regional or national relevance are also considered for publication.

Topics

The topical scope of CCIS spans the entire spectrum of informatics ranging from foundational topics in the theory of computing to information and communications science and technology and a broad variety of interdisciplinary application fields.

Information for Volume Editors and Authors

Publication in CCIS is free of charge. No royalties are paid, however, we offer registered conference participants temporary free access to the online version of the conference proceedings on SpringerLink (http://link.springer.com) by means of an http referrer from the conference website and/or a number of complimentary printed copies, as specified in the official acceptance email of the event.

CCIS proceedings can be published in time for distribution at conferences or as postproceedings, and delivered in the form of printed books and/or electronically as USBs and/or e-content licenses for accessing proceedings at SpringerLink. Furthermore, CCIS proceedings are included in the CCIS electronic book series hosted in the SpringerLink digital library at http://link.springer.com/bookseries/7899. Conferences publishing in CCIS are allowed to use our online conference service (Meteor) for managing the whole proceedings lifecycle (from submission and reviewing to preparing for publication) free of charge.

Publication process

The language of publication is exclusively English. Authors publishing in CCIS have to sign the Springer CCIS copyright transfer form, however, they are free to use their material published in CCIS for substantially changed, more elaborate subsequent publications elsewhere. For the preparation of the camera-ready papers/files, authors have to strictly adhere to the Springer CCIS Authors' Instructions and are strongly encouraged to use the CCIS LaTeX style files or templates.

Abstracting/Indexing

CCIS is abstracted/indexed in DBLP, Google Scholar, EI-Compendex, Mathematical Reviews, SCImago, Scopus. CCIS volumes are also submitted for the inclusion in ISI Proceedings.

How to start

To start the evaluation of your proposal for inclusion in the CCIS series, please send an e-mail to ccis@springer.com

Byung-Gyu Kim · Hiroo Sekiya · Deokwoo Lee
Editors

Multimedia Information Technology and Applications

21st International Conference on Multimedia
Information Technology and Applications,
MITA 2025
Jeju, South Korea, July 21–24, 2025
Proceedings

 Springer

Editors
Byung-Gyu Kim 
Sookmyung Women's University
Seoul, Korea (Republic of)

Hiroo Sekiya
Chiba University
Chiba, Japan

Deokwoo Lee
Keimyung University
Daegu, Korea (Republic of)

ISSN 1865-0929   ISSN 1865-0937 (electronic)
Communications in Computer and Information Science
ISBN 978-981-95-3140-0   ISBN 978-981-95-3141-7 (eBook)
https://doi.org/10.1007/978-981-95-3141-7

Preface

Welcome to the proceedings of the 21st International Conference on Multimedia Information Technology and Applications (MITA 2025). The conference and its associated workshops were hosted and co-organized by the Korea Multimedia Society, South Korea.

MITA is an annual flagship conference of the Korea Multimedia Society and is recognized as one of the largest academic and industrial gatherings in the field of artificial intelligence (AI), multimedia processing technology, and their convergent applications. In 2025, MITA was held in collaboration with the International Workshop on Complex Communication and Multimedia Sciences (CCMS) and the Workshop on Smart Inspection Systems (WSIS), providing a broader platform for the exchange of cutting-edge research and ideas.

The Program Committee carefully selected 19 papers (14 full papers and 5 short papers) out of 94 submissions for publication. Each submission was open-peer reviewed by two or three experts to ensure high-quality contributions. The accepted papers span a variety of topics, including

- Artificial Intelligence for Multimedia
- Multimedia & Intelligent Systems
- Applications of Multimedia
- 3D Multimedia Contents
- Optimization for Multimedia Technology

The final program of MITA 2025, jointly organized with CCMS and WSIS, reflected the culmination of the dedicated efforts of many individuals. We express our sincere gratitude to the authors, whose valuable research enriched the conference program. We also extend our deep appreciation to the members of the Program Committee for their thorough and insightful reviews under a tight schedule. Our heartfelt thanks go to the Korea Multimedia Society for its generous support, to the Organizing Committee and secretariat for their tireless work in coordinating the event, and to Springer for their assistance in ensuring the timely publication of these proceedings.

We hope that all participants found the MITA 2025 conference in Jeju to be both enjoyable and intellectually stimulating.

August 2025
Byung-Gyu Kim
Hiroo Sekiya
Deokwoo Lee

Organization

Organizing Committee

General Chair

Byung-Gyu Kim   Sookmyung Women's University, South Korea

Organizing Committee Co-chairs

Namje Park   Jeju National University, South Korea
Hiroo Sekiya   Chiba University, Japan

Program Committee Co-chairs

Deokwoo Lee   Keimyung University, South Korea
Hidehiro Nakano   Tokyo City University, Japan
Wen-Huang Cheng   National Taiwan University, Taiwan

Plenary Chair

Young-Ho Park   Sookmyung Women's University, South Korea

Tutorial Chairs

Sangoh Park   Chung-Ang University, South Korea
Lu Leng   Nanchang Hangkong University, China

Special Session Co-chairs

Sanghyun Seo   Chung-Ang University, South Korea
Partha Pratim Roy   Indian Institute of Technology, Roorkee, India

Women ICT Session Chair

Hyeyoung Ko   Seoul Women's University, South Korea

Educational Activities Chair

Taewan Kim   Dongduk Women's University, South Korea

Publication Co-chairs

Suk-Hwan Lee   Dong-A University, South Korea
Jiwoo Kang   Sookmyung Women's University, South Korea

Finance Chair

Namje Park   Jeju National University, South Korea

Local Arrangement Chair

Seok Chan Jeong   Dong-Eui University, South Korea

Publicity Chair

Se-Hoon Jung   Sunchon National University, South Korea

Contents

Artificial Intelligence for Multimedia

Retinal Vessel Segmentation Using an Attention-Enhanced U-Net
Architecture 3
    Cheng-Mu Tsai, Shi-Hong Qiu, and Chuan-Wang Chang

A Weighted Ensemble Approach Integrating Large Language Models
for Enhanced Agricultural Knowledge Retrieval 16
    Cyreneo Dofitas Jr, Yong-Woon Kim, and Yung-Cheol Byun

Improving Image Classification Efficiency with Knowledge Distillation
and Channel Attention 28
    Youssef Boulaouane, Jisu Kim, Jimin Park, and Deokwoo Lee

Explainable Graph-Based Retrieval-Augmented Generation
with Landmark-Centric Reasoning Paths 40
    Eu-Tteum Baek

Knowledge Distillation-Based Lightweight Model for Solar Cell Defect
Classification 52
    Hasnain Hyder, Yong-Woon Kim, and Yung-Cheol Byun

Task-Evoked BOLD Contrast and Machine Learning for Schizophrenia
Classification: A DMN-Focused and Whole-Brain Analysis 64
    Akansha Gautam, Indranath Chatterjee, Suruchi Gautam,
    and Naveen Kumar

Edge-Aware Lightweight Network for Medical Image Segmentation 79
    Zhecheng Wu and Lu Leng

Evaluating the Impact of Backbone Networks and Input Resolution
on Forearm Acupoint Localization 86
    V. P. Prathiksha, H. M. K. K. M. B. Herath, Hi-Joon Park,
    Chang-Soo Na, Myunggi Yi, and Byeong-il Lee

Pronoun Matters: A Benchmark for Diagnosing Gender Bias in Emotion
Classification 98
    Qurat Ul Ain Aisha, Yu-Jin Cho, and Byung Gyu Kim

Analyzing Hyperparameter Optimization Methods for Federated Learning
Systems 111
    *Sa Jim Soe Moe, Qazi Waqas Khan, Nguyen Anh Tuan, Misbah Bibi,
    and Dohyeun Kim*

Recognition of Radicals of Guqin Music Notation by YOLOs 118
    *Meguru Hayami, Shun Kuremoto, Mamiko Koshiba, Takashi Kuremoto,
    and Shingo Mabu*

RMSF-ViT: Randomized Multi-scale Fusion Vision Transformer 125
    Yu-Jin Cho, Ah-Hyeon Lee, Byung-Gyu Kim, and Jan Plato

Multimedia System and Applications

Enhancing Traceability and Interpretability of Datasets for RAG
Evaluation: A Context-ID-Aware and Graph-Based Visualization Approach 141
    Beomseok Kim and Jinhong Yang

Intelligent Personality-Aware AR Gait Training Using Smart Glasses:
Personalized Multimodal Feedback for Next-Generation Digital
Rehabilitation 153
    Eunseon Jo and Han-jin Lee

High-Fidelity Synthetic MetaAcuPoint Depth (MAP-d) Dataset
for Acupoint Localization Using MetaHuman Avatars 165
    *Kasunika Guruge, H. M. K. K. M. B. Herath, Hi-Joon Park,
    Chang-Soo Na, Myunggi Yi, and Byeong-il Lee*

Noise-Induced Distributed Scheduling of Message Transmission
of Receiver-Less Nodes in APCMA 178
    *Ryota Yamamoto, Hiroyuki Yasuda, Mikio Hasegawa,
    and Naoki Wakamiya*

AI-Based Health Monitoring System for Old Buildings 185
    Seong Min Jo and Eung Soo Kim

Phase-Specific Gait Characterization and Plantar Load Progression
Analysis Using Smart Insoles 197
    Thathsara Nanayakkara, H. M. K. K. M. B. Herath,
    Hadi Sedigh Malekroodi, Nuwan Madusanka, Myunggi Yi,
    and Byeong-il Lee

A Bilingual App for Campus Wayfinding and Local Cultural Immersion 209
    Chukwuka Chinechebem Yvette and Yoojeong Song

Correction to: A Bilingual App for Campus Wayfinding and Local Cultural
Immersion C1
    Chukwuka Chinechebem Yvette and Yoojeong Song

Author Index 215

Artificial Intelligence for Multimedia

Retinal Vessel Segmentation Using an Attention-Enhanced U-Net Architecture

Cheng-Mu Tsai[1] , Shi-Hong Qiu[1], and Chuan-Wang Chang[2]()

[1] National Chung Hsing University, Taichung, Taiwan
[2] National Chin-Yi University of Technology, Taichung, Taiwan
cwchang@ncut.edu.tw

Abstract. The morphology and variations of retinal blood vessels are crucial indicators for diagnosing various ophthalmic diseases. Therefore, accurate segmentation of retinal vessels holds significant value in assisting clinical diagnosis. However, traditional image analysis methods often rely on manual annotations, which are susceptible to physicians' experience and subjective judgment, thereby limiting segmentation efficiency and consistency. Developing high-performance retinal vessel segmentation techniques has thus become a key challenge. In this study, we propose RSA-UNet, a segmentation model based on the U-Net architecture that integrates ResNet50, a Spatial Channel Block Attention Module (SCBAM), and Atrous Spatial Pyramid Pooling (ASPP) to further enhance segmentation accuracy. The model was evaluated on the publicly available retinal fundus image dataset CHASEDB1. Experimental results demonstrate that RSA-UNet outperforms the traditional U-Net in both segmentation accuracy and stability, highlighting its potential for application in retinal vessel segmentation tasks.

Keywords: Retinal Vessel Segmentation · U-Net · Spatial Channel Block Attention Module · Atrous Spatial Pyramid Pooling

1 Introduction

Retinal vascular diseases, including diabetic retinopathy, glaucoma, and hypertensive retinopathy, are significant causes of vision impairment and blindness. These conditions often involve abnormal vessel morphology—such as narrowing, dilation, tortuosity, and neovascularization—making accurate retinal vessel segmentation essential for early diagnosis and disease monitoring.

Medical imaging, particularly color fundus photography and fluorescein angiography, is vital in evaluating retinal vasculature. However, image interpretation typically depends on manual annotation by ophthalmologists, which is time-consuming and prone to variability. The complexity of retinal vessels, especially in low-contrast or blurred lesion conditions, adds to the difficulty, affecting both model design and diagnostic consistency. Therefore, developing precise automatic segmentation methods is crucial for improving clinical outcomes.

B.-G. Kim et al. (Eds.): MITA 2025, CCIS 2675, pp. 3–15, 2026.
https://doi.org/10.1007/978-981-95-3141-7_1

Automated semantic segmentation has become a key research focus in medical image analysis. Deep learning models—especially encoder-decoder frameworks like U-Net— have shown strong performance. However, traditional U-Nets struggle with capturing detailed vessel structures, handling noisy or low-quality images, and accurately outlining lesion boundaries.

To address these limitations, this paper proposes RSA-UNet, an advanced segmentation framework based on U-Net. It incorporates ResNet50 as the encoder to strengthen feature extraction and network convergence. A Spatial Channel Block Attention Module (SCBAM) is added to enhance lesion saliency and suppress irrelevant background signals. Additionally, an Atrous Spatial Pyramid Pooling (ASPP) module is integrated to capture multi-scale contextual features, improving the model's ability to recognize delicate and large-scale structures.

Combining these innovations, RSA-UNet significantly improves semantic segmentation performance on retinal fundus images. It offers a more accurate and stable automated tool for clinical use, supporting early detection and treatment planning for retinal vascular diseases.

2   Related Work

Medical image segmentation is a core technology in the field of medical image analysis, playing a crucial role in disease diagnosis, lesion annotation, and clinical decision support. With the advancement of deep learning techniques, medical image segmentation has made breakthrough progress, particularly with the adoption of Convolutional Neural Networks (CNNs) due to their powerful feature extraction capabilities, which have been widely applied in medical image processing. For instance, in 2015, Olaf Ronneberger et al. proposed the U-Net [1] model, which utilizes a symmetrical encoder-decoder architecture and skip connections to effectively preserve high-resolution semantic information, making it one of the most mainstream methods in medical image segmentation. However, traditional U-Net still has limited accuracy in thyroid nodule ultrasound imaging. When dealing with complex lesion structures, its segmentation performance remains suboptimal, leaving room for further improvements.

To further enhance the performance of U-Net in medical image segmentation tasks, recent research efforts have increasingly focused on integrating more expressive and deeper feature extraction networks. Among these, ResNet [2] effectively addresses the vanishing gradient problem commonly encountered in deep neural networks by introducing residual connections, thus enabling stable training of deeper network architectures that can capture richer and more abstract feature representations [3].

With the advancement of hardware computational capabilities, attention mechanisms have emerged as another key technology to boost the performance of deep learning models. By employing attention mechanisms, models can assign higher importance to regions or channels within the input feature maps that possess high semantic value, thereby enhancing their selectivity and discriminative ability toward critical features, ultimately improving overall representational power and prediction accuracy [4].

Attention modules that have been widely adopted in image segmentation tasks include the Squeeze-and-Excitation Network (SE) [5], the Efficient Channel Attention

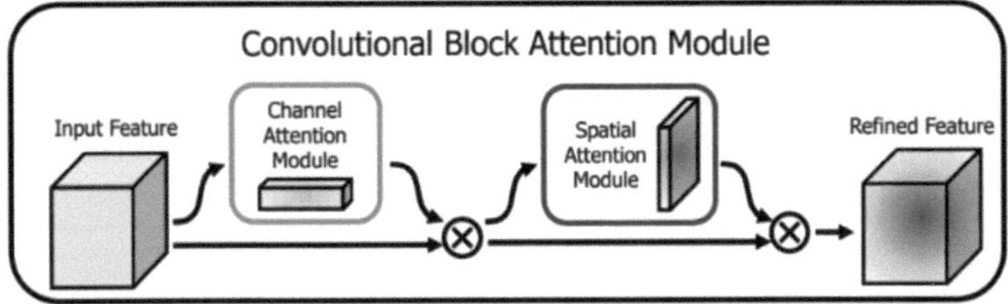

Fig. 1. CBAM Network Architecture [5]

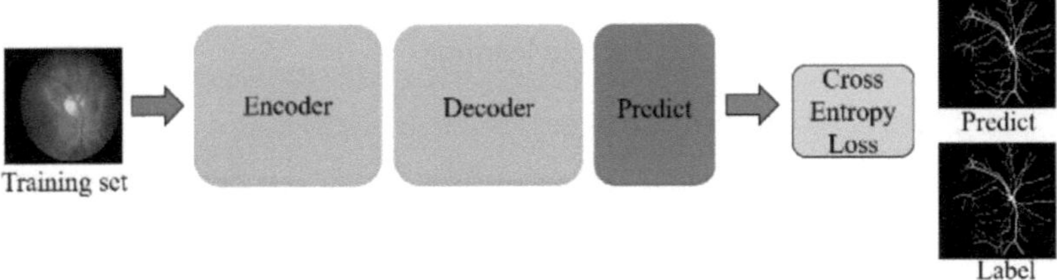

Fig. 2. Schematic Diagram of the RSA-UNet Model for Retinal Vessel Segmentation.

(ECA) module [6], and the Convolutional Block Attention Module (CBAM) [7], as depicted in Fig. 1. These modules not only promote the model's focus on essential channel features but also strengthen its ability to identify important spatial regions within the image, leading to enhanced segmentation boundary details and improved overall accuracy.

Nevertheless, the choice of attention mechanism should be tailored to the specific characteristics of the task and the dataset to achieve optimal model performance and generalization capability. Future research may further explore the integration of multiple attention mechanisms to balance segmentation accuracy and computational efficiency, thereby improving model adaptability across various medical imaging scenarios and facilitating its feasibility for real-world clinical applications.

3   The Proposed Method

In this paper, we propose a retinal vessel image semantic segmentation model named RSA-UNet, which integrates ResNet and U-Net architectures along with multiple attention mechanisms to enhance feature extraction and critical region recognition capabilities. The overall model follows a typical encoder-decoder architecture for its operation, the process is shown in Fig. 2.

The model processes input medical images through an encoder that extracts high-level semantic and contextual features while reducing spatial resolution. A decoder then upsamples the feature maps to reconstruct the original resolution and generate a semantic segmentation map. Skip connections help retain detailed features during decoding. The final prediction layer converts these decoded features into pixel-wise class predictions, completing the segmentation task. The model uses cross-entropy loss to improve classification accuracy and evaluate the difference between predicted labels and ground truth, guiding parameter updates via backpropagation. This training approach optimizes segmentation performance and improves the model's accuracy and stability, especially in retinal vessel segmentation tasks involving color fundus images. The architecture ensures both precision and robustness in medical image analysis.

3.1 Network Architecture

This paper proposes RSA-UNet for semantic segmentation of retinal vessels in color fundus images, as shown in Fig. 3. Based on the U-Net encoder-decoder architecture, RSA-UNet uses ResNet50 as the encoder to enhance feature extraction and avoid vanishing gradients, enabling deeper and more stable learning.

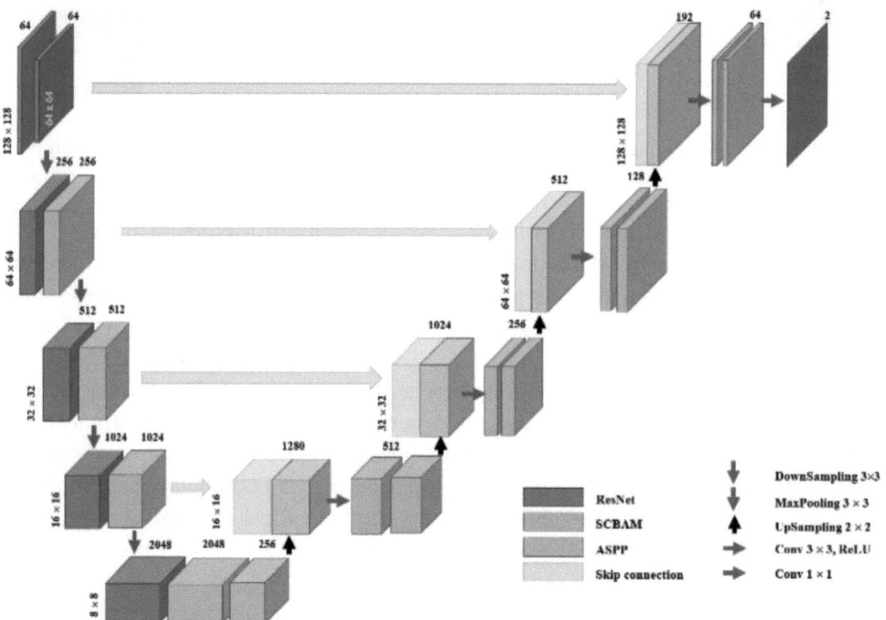

Fig. 3. RSA-UNet Model

A Spatial Channel Block Attention Module (SCBAM) is added after each feature block, skip connections, and upsampling stage to improve the model's focus on critical lesion regions. SCBAM allows the model to highlight important features while suppressing irrelevant information, boosting segmentation accuracy and stability.

Additionally, an Atrous Spatial Pyramid Pooling (ASPP) module is placed at the deepest encoder layer to capture multi-scale and global contextual information, enhancing the model's ability to handle varied lesion sizes and complex vessel structures.

In the decoding stage, RSA-UNet upsamples the feature maps to restore image resolution. A final 1×1 convolution layer produces the pixel-wise classification map, which aligns with the input image size.

With these architectural enhancements, RSA-UNet effectively segments fine and complex retinal vessel structures, demonstrating strong performance and clinical applicability in retinal image analysis.

3.2　Encoder

This paper adopts ResNet50 as the encoder backbone to enhance image feature extraction and improve the model's semantic representation and learning performance. ResNet50 utilizes a residual architecture, where the core unit is the residual block. Each block includes a primary path for nonlinear feature transformation and an identity mapping that passes input features directly to the output. This structure helps overcome the gradient decent problem in deep networks, ensuring stable training and effective deep feature learning.

To address the degradation problem that arises as network depth increases, ResNet employs an identity mapping design, allowing the network to learn a direct "input equals output" mapping under certain conditions. This mechanism significantly enhances the trainability of deep networks, not only preventing performance degradation as network depth increases but also facilitating stable gradient propagation. Through the residual architecture, networks can stack more layers without encountering issues such as vanishing or exploding gradients, thereby enabling deeper models to converge successfully while achieving stronger feature representation capabilities.

3.3　Spatial Channel Block Attention Module (SCBAM)

The Spatial Channel Block Attention Module (SCBAM) is integrated into RSA-UNet to enhance important features and suppress irrelevant information to improve model accuracy and stability. SCBAM increases the network's sensitivity to critical regions and reduces background interference that could affect segmentation results. It is strategically applied after feature extraction in each encoder layer—before forming skip connections—and after each upsampling step in the decoder. This multi-level integration strengthens feature representation throughout the network, enabling more accurate and robust segmentation of retinal vessel structures in medical images.

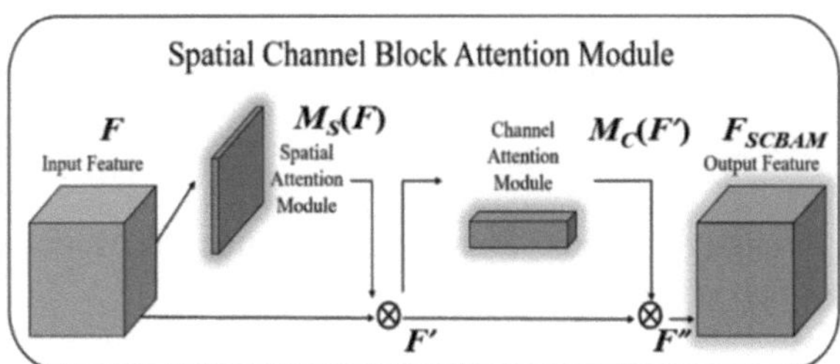

Fig. 4. SCBAM Attention Module.

As illustrated in Fig. 4, SCBAM integrates both a Spatial Attention Module and a Channel Attention Module to improve the discriminative capability of feature representations. This enhancement ultimately leads to better accuracy and stability in image segmentation tasks. Given an input feature map $F \in R^{1 \times H \times W}$, SCBAM sequentially applies channel and spatial attention mechanisms to perform weighted feature refinement.

Spatial Attention Module
This module focuses on identifying discriminative spatial regions within the input feature map. It outputs a spatial attention map $M\_s \in R^{\wedge}(1 \times H \times W)$, which is used to weight the spatial features at each location. The computation process is described in Eq. (1):

$$M_s(F) = \sigma \left(f^{7 \times 7} \left(\left[AvgPool(F); MaxPool(F) \right] \right) \right) \tag{1}$$

- $f^{7 \times 7}$: Represents a 7×7 convolution operation.
- [;]: Denotes concatenation along the channel dimension.
- σ: Refers to the Sigmoid function, which is used to compress the weights into the range [0, 1].

The final spatially weighted feature is given by:

$$F' = M_s(F) \otimes F \tag{2}$$

where $\otimes$ denotes element-wise multiplication.

Channel Attention Module
This module focuses on identifying features with higher semantic value across different channels. The channel attention map $M_C \in R^{C \times 1 \times 1}$ is generated based on the information obtained from both average pooling and max pooling operations applied to the feature map.

$$M_C(F) = \sigma(MLP(AvgPool(F)) + MLP(MaxPool(F))) \tag{3}$$

- AvgPool and MaxPool operations reduce the feature map to $R^{C \times 1 \times 1}$.
- MLP: A two-layer fully connected neural network with shared weights.

The channel-weighted result is given by:

$$F'' = M_C(F') \otimes F' \tag{4}$$

After passing through the Spatial Channel Block Attention Module (SCBAM), the final output feature map is obtained as follows:

$$F_{SCBAM} = M_C(M_{S(F)} \otimes F) \otimes (M_S(F) \otimes F) \tag{5}$$

The spatial attention mechanism focuses on identifying key regions within the feature map, applying weights to spatial areas that exhibit high semantic relevance. Meanwhile, the channel attention mechanism is designed to automatically learn the importance of different feature channels, thereby enhancing the responses of channels with strong semantic significance.

By incorporating the SCBAM module, RSA-UNet dynamically adjusts the attention distribution at various levels of both the encoder and decoder stages. This integration enhances the network's ability to perceive retinal vessel lesions, particularly improving segmentation accuracy and feature selection performance when dealing with images characterized by blurred boundaries or low contrast.

3.4 Atrous Spatial Pyramid Pooling (ASPP)

In semantic segmentation tasks, achieving strong performance requires capturing both local details and global contextual information. As network depth increases, the receptive field expands, allowing the model to learn higher-level semantic features. However, simply stacking more convolutional layers can significantly raise computational costs and increase the risk of losing fine-grained information—an especially critical issue in medical imaging, where small lesions may be missed. The proposed model integrates an Atrous Spatial Pyramid Pooling (ASPP) module at the deepest encoder layer to address this challenge, as shown in Fig. 5. The ASPP module applies parallel atrous convolutions with different dilation rates to the same feature map. It expands the receptive field without adding parameters, enhancing semantic understanding while preserving high-resolution details, ultimately improving segmentation accuracy for medical images.

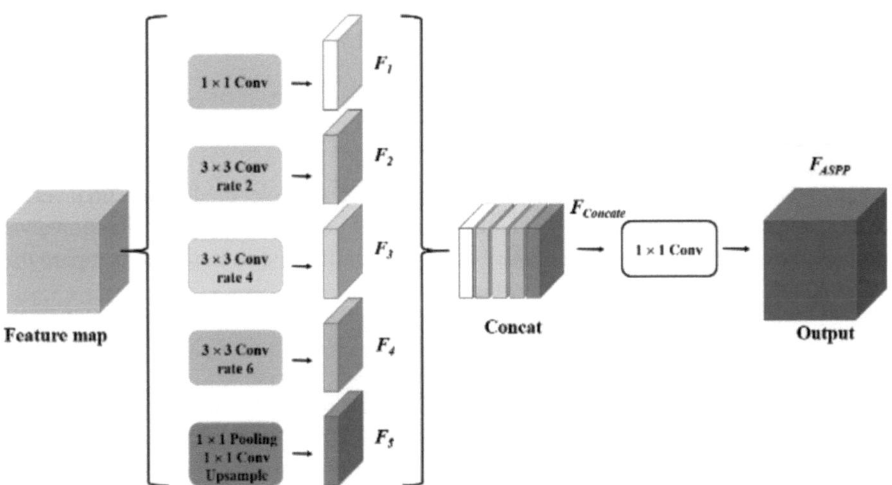

Fig. 5. The ASPP Structure [8]

The ASPP structure consists of the following four main components:

- 1×1 Standard Convolution Layer: Responsible for extracting local features and adjusting the channel dimensions.
- Three Atrous Convolution Branches: Utilizing different dilation rates (2, 4, and 6) to capture multi-scale regional features.

- Global Average Pooling (GAP) Branch: Helps the model integrate global contextual information across the entire image. The feature map obtained through GAP is further processed by a 1×1 convolution and then upsampled to match the original feature map size.
- Feature Fusion and Channel Compression: The five feature maps generated from the previous branches are concatenated, followed by a 1×1 convolution to integrate features and compress channel dimensions.

3.5 Loss

To enhance the segmentation performance of the RSA-UNet model during training, this study adopts the cross-entropy loss function, which is widely used in classification and semantic segmentation tasks, as defined in Eq. (6):

$$H(y, p) = -\left[\sum_{i=1}^{N} \sum_{j=1}^{N_{cls}} y_j^i log(p_j^i) \right] \tag{6}$$

- (y, p) = Cross Entropy Loss.
- N = Total number of pixels.
- N_{cls} = Number of classes.
- y_j^i = The ground truth label indicating that the i-th pixel belongs to the j-th class.
- p_j^i = The predicted probability that the i-th pixel belongs to the j-th class.

The cross-entropy loss effectively quantifies the discrepancy between the model's predictions and the ground truth labels. Through the backpropagation mechanism, it guides the updating of model parameters, thereby improving the accuracy of the segmentation results.

4   Experiments and Results

To verify the segmentation capability of the proposed RSA-UNet model for retinal vessel segmentation and to evaluate its potential for clinical decision support applications, we conducted experiments using a retinal vessel color fundus image dataset to compare the performance of RSA-UNet with that of other models.

4.1   Experimental Environment

To assess the practicality and effectiveness of the proposed semantic segmentation method, we performed model training and testing in a high-performance experimental environment. The overall experimental configuration is summarized in Table 1.

4.2   Dataset

In this study, we utilized the publicly available color fundus image dataset CHASEDB1 (Child Heart and Health Study in England Database 1), which consists of 537 high-resolution retinal fundus images, as shown in Fig. 6. For the experiments, all images were resized to 512×512 pixels, and subsequently split into training and testing sets at a ratio of **9:1** through random sampling.

Table 1. Experimental Environment and Hardware Specifications

Software/Hardware	Specification
CPU	Intel Xeon Gold 6230R
RAM	512 GB
Graphics	NVIDIA RTX A6000
Operating System	Windows Server 2019 Standard 64bit
Deep Learning Framework	Tensorflow 2.4.0

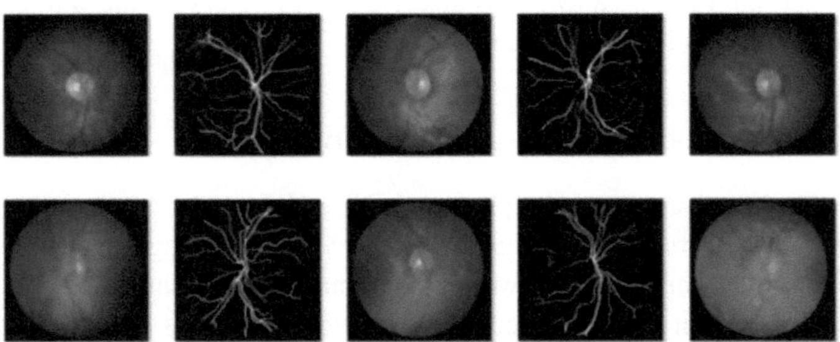

Fig. 6. Retinal Vessel Image Samples and Annotations from the Dataset

4.3 Evaluation Metrics

To assess the proposed RSA-UNet's performance in detecting retinal vessel lesions from color fundus images, we used the confusion matrix as the primary evaluation tool. While typically used in classification, confusion matrices are also effective for semantic segmentation, allowing pixel-level assessment of lesion versus non-lesion regions. The confusion matrix reveals classification accuracy and consistency by comparing predictions with ground truth annotations. This analysis helps verify RSA-UNet's effectiveness in retinal vessel segmentation and demonstrates its potential for reliable clinical application in ophthalmic diagnostics.

We adopted multiple evaluation metrics to comprehensively assess the model's segmentation accuracy and stability from different perspectives.

$$IoU = \frac{TP}{FN + TP + FP} \tag{7}$$

$$mIoU = \frac{(IoU_1 + IoU_2 + \cdots + IoU_{N_{cls}})}{N_{cls}} \tag{8}$$

$$Dsc = \frac{2TP}{2 \times TP + FP + FN} \tag{9}$$

$$Accuracy = \frac{TP + TN}{TP + TN + FP + FN} \tag{10}$$

$$Precision = \frac{TP}{TP + FP} \tag{11}$$

$$Specificity = \frac{TN}{TN + FP} \tag{12}$$

$$Recall = \frac{TP}{TP + FN} \tag{13}$$

In the confusion matrix, TP (True Positive) represents the number of cases correctly classified as retinal vessels, TN (True Negative) represents the number of cases correctly classified as healthy regions, FP (False Positive) refers to the number of cases incorrectly classified as retinal vessels, and FN (False Negative) refers to the number of cases incorrectly classified as healthy regions.

4.4 Model Performance Comparison and Analysis

To evaluate the effectiveness of the proposed RSA-UNet model in semantic segmentation, experiments were conducted using a retinal vessel image dataset. RSA-UNet was compared with several well-known medical image segmentation models, including UNet++ [9], DenseUNet [10], PSPNet [11], AttUNet [12], Trans UNet [13], and CENet [14]. All models were trained and tested under identical conditions for fair comparison. As shown in Table 2, RSA-UNet achieved the highest performance across all evaluation metrics. It outperformed other models' overall segmentati on accuracy while maintaining strong stability, sensitivity, and specificity in lesion detection, demonstrating its effectiveness and reliability for medical image segmentation tasks.

Table 2. Performance Comparison between RSA-UNet and Other Semantic Segmentation Models

| Method | Retinal Vessel | | | | | | |
| | Color Fundus Imaging | | | | | | |
	mIoU	DSC	Accuracy	Recall	Precision	Specificity	#.Param.
Unet [1]	88.27	93.49	98.15	93.15	93.83	93.15	24.9M
UNet++ [9]	90.74	94.97	98.62	93.23	96.88	93.23	24.9M
DenseNet [10]	91.14	95.21	98.63	95.22	95.20	95.22	35.0M
PSPnet [11]	90.87	95.05	98.62	94.06	96.09	94.06	**57.6M**
AttUNet [12]	92.02	95.72	98.79	95.22	**96.23**	95.22	22.5M
TransUNet [13]	92.35	95.91	98.84	95.68	96.13	95.68	35.4M
CENet [14]	91.98	95.69	98.78	95.31	96.08	95.31	34.3M
RSA-UNet	**92.77**	**96.15**	**98.90**	**96.25**	96.05	**96.25**	52.7M

4.5 Visual Comparison and Analysis of Retinal Vessel Semantic Segmentation

To evaluate model performance in retinal vessel segmentation, this study employed visual heatmap analysis using Gradient-weighted Class Activation Mapping (Grad-CAM). This method highlights areas where the model focuses during prediction, with red indicating strong attention and blue indicating weak attention. As shown in Fig. 7, RSA-UNet's attention heatmaps concentrate on actual lesion regions, confirming that the SCBAM attention mechanism effectively guides the model to focus on semantically important features.

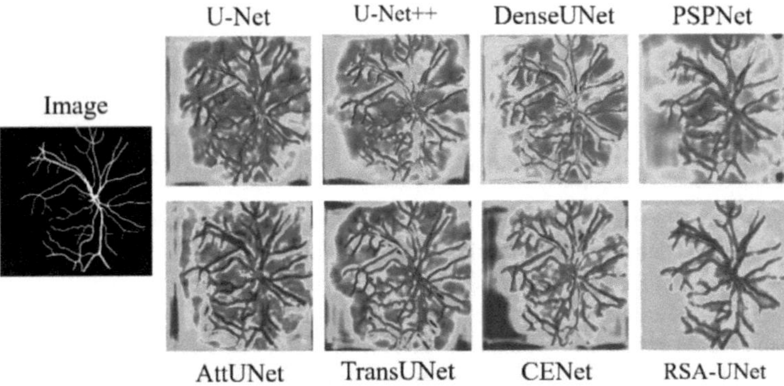

Fig. 7. Attention Response Heatmaps Generated by Different Models

In contrast, heatmaps from other models show scattered or misplaced attention, often focusing on non-lesion areas, which can lead to inaccurate segmentation and classification errors. This suggests that without SCBAM, models are more prone to errors in identifying lesion boundaries.

This study also used segmentation boundary overlap maps, which—along with the Grad-CAM results—demonstrate that RSA-UNet enhances boundary recognition and significantly improves attention allocation to critical regions. These visual analyses confirm that the SCBAM module is key in boosting segmentation accuracy. Overall, RSA-UNet performs better than mainstream models, offering more precise and reliable retinal vessel segmentation.

5 Conclusion

This paper proposes RSA-UNet, a deep learning model for semantic segmentation of retinal vessels in color fundus images. It addresses key challenges in medical imaging, such as data heterogeneity, manual annotation difficulties, blurred lesion boundaries, and the complex morphology of small vessels. RSA-UNet integrates a ResNet50-based encoder, a Spatial Channel Block Attention Module (SCBAM), and an Atrous Spatial Pyramid Pooling (ASPP) module to enhance feature extraction and focus on clinically relevant lesion areas while retaining global context.

Experimental results show that RSA-UNet outperforms several benchmark models, achieving an mIoU of 92.77%, DSC of 96.15%, accuracy of 98.90%, recall of 96.25%, precision of 96.05%, and specificity of 96.25%. Compared to UNet++, DenseUNet, PSPNet, AttUNet, TransUNet, and CENet, RSA-UNet demonstrates superior accuracy, stability, and interpretability.

Acknowledgments. This work was supported by the National Science and Technology Council (NSTC 112-2221-E-167 -022 -MY2).

Disclosure of Interests. The authors have no competing interests to declare that are relevant to the content of this article.

References

1. Ronneberger, O., et al.: U-net: convolutional networks for biomedical image segmentation. In: Medical Image Computing and Computer-Assisted Intervention–MICCAI 2015, Proceedings, part III 18, pp. 234–241 (2015)
2. He, K., et al.: Deep residual learning for image recognition. In: Proceedings of the IEEE Conference on Computer Vision and Pattern Recognition, pp. 770–778 (2016)
3. Szegedy, C., et al.: Rethinking the inception architecture for computer vision. In: Proceedings of the IEEE Conference on Computer Vision and Pattern Recognition, pp. 2818–2826 (2016)
4. Vaswani, A.: Attention is all you need. Adv. Neural Inf. Process. Syst. (2017)
5. Hu, J., et al.: Squeeze-and-excitation networks. In: Proceedings of the IEEE Conference on Computer Vision and Pattern Recognition, pp. 7132–7141 (2018)
6. Wang, Q., et al.: ECA-Net: efficient channel attention for deep convolutional neural networks. In: Proceedings of the IEEE/CVF Conference on Computer Vision and Pattern Recognition, pp. 11534–11542 (2020)
7. Woo, S., et al.: CBAM: convolutional block attention module. In: Proceedings of the European Conference on Computer Vision (ECCV), pp. 3–19 (2018)
8. Chen, L.C., et al.: DeepLab: semantic image segmentation with deep convolutional nets, atrous convolution, and fully connected CRFs. IEEE Trans. Pattern Anal. Mach. Intell. **40**(4), 834–848 (2017)
9. Zhou, Z., et al.: Unet++: a nested u-net architecture for medical image segmentation. In: Deep Learning in Medical Image Analysis and Multimodal Learning for Clinical Decision Support: 4th International Workshop, pp. 3–11 (2018)
10. Li, X., et al.: H-DenseUNet: hybrid densely connected UNet for liver and tumor segmentation from CT volumes. IEEE Trans. Med. Imaging **37**(12), 2663–2674 (2018)
11. Zhao, H., et al.: Pyramid scene parsing network. In: Proceedings of the IEEE Conference on CVPR, pp. 2881–2890 (2017)
12. Oktay, O., et al.: Attention U-Net: Learning where to look for the pancreas. arXiv preprint arXiv:1804.03999 (2018)
13. Chen, J., et al.: TransUNet: Transformers make strong encoders for medical image segmentation arXiv:2102.04306 (2021)
14. Cheng, H.X., et al.: CENet: toward concise and efficient LiDAR semantic segmentation for autonomous driving. In: 2022 IEEE International Conference on Multimedia and Expo (ICME), pp. 01–06 (2022)

A Weighted Ensemble Approach Integrating Large Language Models for Enhanced Agricultural Knowledge Retrieval

Cyreneo Dofitas Jr[1], Yong-Woon Kim[2], and Yung-Cheol Byun[3(✉)]

[1] Department of Electronic Engineering, Institute of Information Science Technology, Jeju National University, Jeju 63243, South Korea
`cdofitas@stu.jejunu.ac.kr`
[2] Department of Computer Engineering, Institute of Information Science Technology, Jeju National University, Jeju 63243, South Korea
`ywkim@jejunu.ac.kr`
[3] Department of Computer Engineering, Major of Electronic Engineering, Institute of Information Science Technology, Jeju National University, Jeju, South Korea
`ycb@jejunu.ac.kr`

Abstract. Knowledge retrieval plays an essential role in decision-making, and it becomes a challenge for farmers due to the complexity of farming data. In this work, an ensemble model that integrates general-purpose and domain-specific LLMs (BERT-base uncased, Agricultural-BERT and LLaMA 3.1) to enhance response correctness and appropriateness for agricultural questions. Using domain-specific data and a weighted voting scheme, our ensemble model demonstrates significant effectiveness in improving response accuracy, achieving approximately 94.6% accuracy, a BLEU score of 54.7, and a ROUGE-1 score of 0.73, as confirmed by performance evaluation. Results demonstrate that this system can assist farmers by providing actionable insights, especially for agricultural management and crop health. This ensemble model represents a better solution for advancing agriculture knowledge retrieval by integrating powerful but general LLM with domain-specific knowledge to tackle its unique challenges.

Keywords: Ensemble Learning · Agricultural NLP · Large Language Models · Knowledge Retrieval · Domain Adaptation

1 Introduction

Large language models are complex algorithms built to read and write in human language, showing significant potential to enhance agricultural knowledge discovery through natural language processing (NLP) [1]. While specialized models trained on agricultural datasets provide domain-specific guidance to farmers and experts, they leverage word order and contextual relationships from input data

© The Author(s) 2026
B.-G. Kim et al. (Eds.): MITA 2025, CCIS 2675, pp. 16–27, 2026.
https://doi.org/10.1007/978-981-95-3141-7_2

to predict outcomes through probability distributions. Large language models demonstrate significant promise in addressing critical agricultural challenges and enhancing productivity [2,3]. Employing advanced technology like large language models (LLMs) and natural language processing (NLP), significant potential is created to provide practical insights that tackle important issues and improve agricultural output [4].

While the transformative capability of Large Language Models (LLMs) can provide unprecedented support for agriculture, flexible agricultural knowledge retrieval often faces challenges with single-model approaches due to high variation and diverse complexity levels. Agricultural questions cover wide-ranging topics from crop health and pest control to soil quality evaluation and climate adaptation measures, demanding both general language understanding capabilities and specialized domain knowledge [5].

Previous research has primarily focused on implementing individual LLMs in agricultural applications, with limited exploration of model combination approaches [6]. While natural language processing enables effective LLM fine-tuning through expert ensemble methods and demonstration selection, these approaches face substantial challenges in agriculture. These challenges include insufficient domain-specific training data, language barriers, and high deployment costs. These include insufficient domain-specific training data, language barriers, and high deployment costs [7,8].

BERT and LLaMA are exemplary models, performing well on a wide range of natural language tasks such as machine translation, automatic summarization, and data-to-text (D2T) that generate natural language text from semistructured data [9]. Nonetheless, they need a complicated hyperparameter tuning process that causes non-reliable performance. To overcome these limitations, we present a new weighted voting ensemble that feeds general agriculture LLM with weights sourced from their domain models. Combining a set of specialized models for focused areas makes this method no longer bound to one model and provides context-aware accuracy in answering complex agricultural questions.

This study aims to create a new agricultural knowledge retrieval system by implementing an ensemble model over large language models(LLM) and federated domain-specific data that enhances the capability of resolving agricultural queries. Our contributions to the proposed model are:

- Designing an intuitive, farmer-centered LLM and ensemble-powered interface gives farmers access to actionable insights, predictive mechanisms, and user support.
- Improving agricultural productivity by providing farmers with a functional system to diagnose diseases, respond to their crop production questions, and agricultural sector development.
- Fine-tune the ensemble of LLMs on text-text data to accurately diagnose crop symptoms and provide suitable recommendations to minimize the possibility of misdiagnosis.

2   Related Works

Developing reliable knowledge retrieval methods presents several key challenges, including enhancing LLM question-answering capabilities, evaluating source reliability, extracting relevant information from extensive datasets, and maintaining system stability as knowledge evolves. This section examines the current state of LLM development and analyzes existing research solutions addressing these fundamental challenges.

Different transformer models using BERT and XLNet and their variants are extensively utilized in Natural Language Generation (NLG) tasks, including GPT-based applications. The attention mechanisms that drive these models have revolutionized recent research, demonstrating superior performance on challenges that were previously limitations for traditional architectures like RNN and LSTM, which struggled with the vanishing gradient problem. These advanced algorithms have proven particularly effective in agricultural applications, efficiently processing and synthesizing information from diverse sources to generate relevant, domain-specific responses [10].

Current agricultural applications have leveraged GPT-4's capabilities, though primarily through systematic reviews of existing literature without generating novel insights. While LLMs have demonstrated promising results in crop disease diagnosis, previous approaches were limited to single-model implementations. Our ensemble method addresses these limitations by combining multiple models' strengths and enhancing their collective performance through domain-specific knowledge integration and real-time query processing [11,12]. Recent research on LLM and ensemble learning techniques has shown significant advances in various applications. Studies have explored the identification and attribution of AI-generated content, while other research has investigated aggregation techniques that combine multiple LLM for improved text categorization. These experiments consistently demonstrate enhanced performance through the integration of numerous pre-trained models. Additionally, research focusing on specialized applications of transformer models like RoBERTa and BERT has shown promising results in improving accuracy and relevance for complex tasks [13].

3   Methodology

Our study focuses on enhancing agricultural knowledge retrieval by integrating pre-trained large language models (LLM) and ensemble learning techniques. This methodology is designed to efficiently process agricultural queries, extract relevant domain-specific knowledge, and deliver optimized responses addressing farmers needs (Fig. 1).

The data collection methodology involved compiling a dataset comprising agricultural question-answer pairs structured in a single-choice format, with an 80–20 split between training and testing sets. The dataset initially contained 22,684 samples and was enriched through multiple sources.

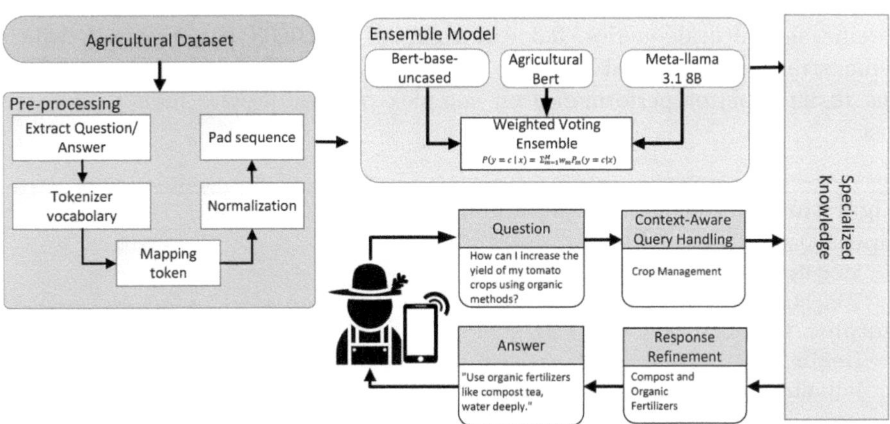

Fig. 1. Work flow of a weighted ensemble approach integrating large language models for enhanced agricultural knowledge retrieval.

The pre-processing pipeline applied different tokenization methods appropriate to each model architecture. The system uses WordPiece tokenization, with a vocabulary of 30,522 tokens for BERT-based models (BERT-base-uncased and Agricultural-BERT), specifically augmented with agricultural domain terminology. LLaMA 3.1 uses SentencePiece to tokenize with a specially increased vocabulary size of 32,000 tokens. After starting with the extraction and cleaning of question-answer pairs, the pipeline adds architecture-specific unique tokens: [CLS]/[SEP] for BERT models and [BOS]/[EOS] for LLaMA. Sequence normalization adheres to the properties of the model; BERT models have a limit of 512 tokens, while LLaMA 3.1 allows for up to 4096 tokens; padding and truncation are done accordingly. This final step translates the tokens into numerical indices with model-specific dictionaries to best match each architecture's needs.

A set of hyperparameters optimized for agricultural domain adaptation was carefully selected for the model training process. We used a learning rate of 2e-5 with linear decay for stable convergence and a batch size of 32 to balance efficiency during training and stability across the training session for 20 epochs. We used the AdamW optimizer. To prevent overfitting and improve model generalization, we implemented a dropout rate of 0.1. All these hyperparameters were selected empirically to maximize the model's overall performance on agricultural knowledge retrieval problems with minimal computation time. The model training process was conducted on NVIDIA 4080 GPU using mixed-precision training for computational efficiency.

The architecture for implementation encompasses three domain-dependent models, including BERT-based uncased for the generic language understanding, Agriculture-BERT for specialized agricultural context, and Meta-Llama 3.18B complicated queries processing model. A simple grid search on the validation set determined these model weights(0.5, 0.3, 0.2). The maximum weight of 0.5 was assigned to Agriculture-BERT based on its relative performance on domain-specific agricultural queries. 0.3 was assigned to BERT-base-uncased, which demonstrates solid general language capabilities, and 0.2 for Meta-Llama 3.18B due to its superior performance on complex queries, despite higher inference costs).

Algorithm 1. Weighted Voting Ensemble

Input: Query Q,
   Models $M = M1, M2, M3$,
   Weights $W = w1, w2, w3$
Output: Train ensemble model M
  Begin
  Initialize empty prediction vector P

  for each model Mi in M : **do**
     Generate prediction pi $= Mi(Q)$
     Scale prediction: $pi_scaled =$ wi * pi
  end for
  return P
  End

The query processing technique employs specialized domain filters and context-aware mechanisms to analyze agricultural inquiries accurately. Through systematic identification and processing of essential agricultural concepts, including crop rotation, soil health, pest control, and irrigation methodologies, the system decomposes queries into fundamental components to target the most relevant aspects for response generation. This serves as the primary framework to process data from agricultural practitioners, who can then be effectively directed on challenges as diverse as the management of their water resources and how to gain maximal crop yields. Output refinement aligns the output with user-specific needs, improving precision. It infuses geographic review, local farm practices, and modern agricultural techniques to provide scientifically correct and socially relevant solutions. When a farmer asks the system about the optimal soil for growing cassava, information is combined on the quality tests of soils with regional variations to identify questions that are factually correct and relevant to local farming conditions.

Our method implements a weighted voting ensemble that amalgamates the predictions of various independent models, each attending to particular aspects of agriculture information processing. Through a complex weighting process, the ensemble assigns weights to predictions from individual models according to performance measures and reliability criteria. Combined, these produce holistic responses beyond the capacity of any single model. As shown in the Eq. 1, a weighted average gives higher accuracy by multiplying weights with individual predictions and normalizing using the total weight sum.

$$\hat{y}_{\text{ensemble}} = \sum_{i=1}^{N} w_i \cdot \hat{y}_i \tag{1}$$

In equation where $\hat{y}_{\text{ensemble}}$ represents the ensemble prediction, $\hat{y}_i$ denotes the prediction of the ith base prediction, and w_i signifies the weight assigned to the ith prediction. The weights w_i were established by evaluating each base classifier's performance on a validation set, with the goal of prioritizing classifiers that exhibit better individual accuracies.

The framework that we propose to assess system outputs in agricultural situations, uses BLEU and ROUGE metrics as our evaluation methods. Using BLEU scores computed with the sacreBLEU library comparing system outputs against human reference answers in key agricultural domains (irrigation, pest control and crop production), Instead of basic textual and semantic similarity, which is often tried with cosine similarity and euclidean distances, this metric measures the precision of n-gram matches between generated text tokens and reference text tokens, a good exercise on how it provides information about response accuracy, as shown in Eq. 2.

$$\text{BLEU} = \text{BP} \times \exp\left(\sum_{n=1}^{N} w_n \log P_n\right) \tag{2}$$

The ROUGE metric evaluates generated content against references based on n-gram overlap and longest common subsequence, taking into account both coverage (recall) and precision. Together, these complementary metrics give a holistic assessment of model performance for accuracy and recall of methodologically rigorous agricultural domain-specific responses.

$$f(s)_i = \frac{e^{s_i}}{\sum_{j=1}^{C} e^{s_j}} \tag{3}$$

A vector of scores $s=[s1,s2,...,s_C]$ is transformed by the softmax function into a probability distribution, where each $f(s)$ represents the probability of the $i-th$ class. IThe resulting distribution is valid as the sum of all probabilities equals 1, as shown in Eq. 3.

$$CE = -\sum_{i=1}^{C} t_i \log(f(s)_i) \tag{4}$$

In this Eq. 4, the summary goes over all types i from 1 to C, and the negative log-likelihood is calculated for the correct class i, weighted by the true label t_i. The objective is to minimize the cross-entropy loss, which means making the predicted probability for the correct class as close to 1 as possible.

4   Results

The model's performance on agricultural domain answer generation tasks is impressive, achieving a BLEU score of 54.7, shown in Table 1 and high ROUGE scores at (Rouge-1: 0.73, Rouge-2: 0.54, Rouge-l: 0.63) as shown in Table 2. These quantitative results confirm the ability of the model to produce accurate and domain-specific answers that behave like standard reference texts. The model's improved accuracy with key agricultural words or phrases is reflected in the BLEU score. Similarly, low ROUGE scores indicate insufficient coverage of relevant information. The ensemble tackles complex agricultural queries by outputting accurate and contextually relevant responses, leveraging the distinct strengths of each model in the component system being BERT-base uncased, Agriculture-BERT and Meta-llama 3.18B (Fig. 2).

Table 1. Summary our approach using in Bleu

Model	Bleu Score
BERT-base-uncased	44.4
Agricultural-BERT	48.1
LlaMA 3.1 (8B)	52.5
Ensemble Model	54.7

Table 2. Summary our approach using in Rouge Score

Model	ROUGE-1	ROUGE-2	ROUGE-L
BERT-base-uncased	0.64	0.43	0.55
Agricultural-BERT	0.66	0.47	0.56
LlaMA 3.1 (8B)	0.70	0.52	0.59
Ensemble Model	0.73	0.54	0.63

Figure 3 illustrates the model's probability distribution for crop recommendations in sandy soil conditions. The model assigns the highest confidence score of 0.85 to a comprehensive list of suitable crops: "Crop protection refers to methods and practices used to prevent damage to crops from pests, diseases, and weeds." Two alternative predictions receive lower confidence scores: "Crop protection includes pesticides, biological controls, and cultural practices to safeguard crops." at 0.10 and "Crop protection involves methods like crop rotation and Integrated Pest Management (IPM) to maintain crop health." at 0.04. The model assigns the lowest probability of 0.01 to "Crop protection aims to maximize crop yield by reducing losses.", indicating minimal confidence in this option. This hierarchical probability distribution demonstrates the model's sophisticated decision-making process in agricultural recommendations, effectively differentiating between optimal and suboptimal crop choices for sandy soil conditions.

To further investigate each model's contribution within the ensemble, we performed an ablation study by selectively removing individual models. As shown in Table 3, removing Agricultural-BERT caused the largest drop in accuracy, highlighting its essential role in domain-specific agricultural tasks. This supports

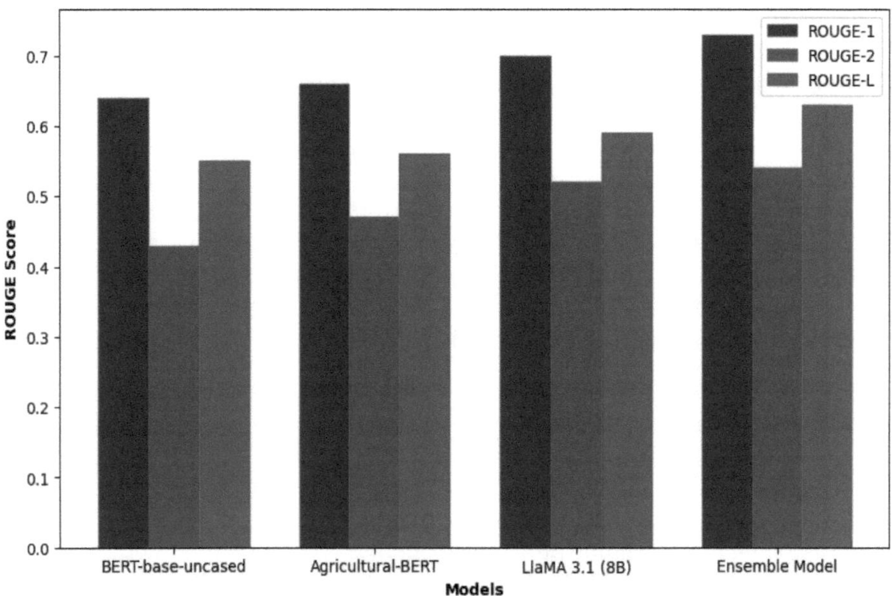

Fig. 2. Comparison of ROUGE Scores across different models.

```
──────────────────── Context ────────────────────
Crop protection refers to the various methods used to protect crops from pests, diseases, and other threats


──────────────────── Question ────────────────────
what is crop protection?


──────────────────── Answer ────────────────────
Crop protection refers to methods and practices used to prevent damage to crops from pests, diseases, and
weeds. | Probability: 0.85
Prediction: Crop protection includes pesticides, biological controls, and cultural practices to safeguard
crops. | Probability: 0.10
Prediction: Crop protection involves methods like crop rotation and Integrated Pest Management (IPM) to
maintain crop health. | Probability: 0.04
Prediction: Crop protection aims to maximize crop yield by reducing losses. | Probability: 0.01
```

Fig. 3. Context-based predictions for crops suited to sandy soil, with probability scores assigned to each prediction, highlighting the first prediction as the most accurate response with the highest confidence score.

Table 3. Ablation Study: Impact of Model Removal on Ensemble Accuracy

Model Removed from Ensemble	Accuracy (%)
Our Ensemble Model	**94.6**
LLaMA 3.1	91.2
Agricultural-BERT	89.5
BERT-base-uncased	90.3

the hypothesis that combining general-purpose and domain-adapted LLMs yields superior performance.

To showcase real-world applicability, consider a farmer in querying the ensemble system with: "Why are my cassava leaves yellowing despite regular watering?" The ensemble model processes this through domain-specific filters and weighted voting. It identifies symptoms associated with magnesium deficiency and suggests soil testing, followed by crop rotation with legumes. Additionally, local pest data is retrieved using retrieval-augmented generation (RAG), pointing to spider mite outbreaks. This result demonstrates how the ensemble LLM can synthesize regionally grounded, actionable insights, thereby assisting farmers in diagnosing and solving crop health issues.

5   Discussion

This analysis evidences that our proposed weighted voting ensemble method is effective for agricultural information retrieval based on LLM. By leveraging the strengths of high-performing pre-trained models, the ensemble model outperformed individual models in both accuracy and contextual relevance, achieving an accuracy score of 94.6%. This improvement stems from the ensemble's voting mechanism, which assigns higher weights to models that exhibit better individual performance, thereby enhancing the overall precision of output. Table 4 shows that while models specializing in sub-domains (e.g., AgroGPT and KITA) perform well within specific areas, the ensemble generalizes better across diverse agricultural queries.

Despite these promising results, several limitations require further discussion. First, when constituent models produce conflicting outputs, the current ensemble resolves these conflicts using static, pre-assigned weights. This may not always yield optimal answers, especially for ambiguous or context-dependent queries. Incorporating confidence-based dynamic weighting or decision arbitration strategies could improve the consistency. Second, while the ensemble demonstrates strong quantitative results, a qualitative analysis of edge cases would provide deeper insights, such as ambiguous questions like "How to manage soil health in varying climates?", would offer deeper insight into model behavior. These scenarios sometimes trigger divergent responses among models, highlighting the need for further interpretability analysis. Lastly, the use of LLaMA 3.1 introduces a latency of approximately 1.8 s per query, which may limit deployment in resource-constrained environments. To address this, future work will explore model distillation, pruning, and quantization techniques to reduce inference cost while maintaining prediction quality.

Table 4.

Reference	Year	Model	Accuracy
[14]	2025	AgroGPT	89%
[15]	2024	Bert Based	81%
[16]	2023	Flan-T5	79%
[17]	2024	GPT4	80%
Our Ensemble Model	–	–	94.6%

The high BLEU and ROUGE scores further validate the model's ability to deliver accurate, contextually relevant responses, closely matching reference answers. While BLEU emphasizes n-gram overlap and the model's accuracy in replicating key phrases, ROUGE highlights content coverage and underscores the model's suitability for agricultural knowledge retrieval.

6   Conclusion

We present a novel ensemble-based framework for agricultural query resolution, integrating multiple LLMs using a weighted voting mechanism. This study contributes novel deployment evaluations and model scalability considerations. The ensemble outperformed individual models in both linguistic metrics and prediction reliability, achieving a 94.6% accuracy with strong BLEU and ROUGE scores. By combining strengths across models and optimizing practical constraints, our approach serves as a viable solution for intelligent agricultural support systems. Although the ensemble achieves improved accuracy, it introduces a latency of 1.8 s per query. We aim to reduce this via model pruning and distillation.

7   Future Works

Extending the ensemble's utility through model distillation and pruning to reduce inference latency. We also aim to implement multilingual adaptation to support region-specific agricultural dialects and incorporate RAG-based (retrieval-augmented generation) pipelines for real-time access to external agronomic documents. Additionally, we plan to distill the ensemble into a compact transformer model optimized for mobile and low-resource deployments.

Further directions include integrating Explainable AI (XAI) techniques such as SHapley Additive exPlanations(SHAP values) or attention-based visualization to improve transparency and trust in recommendations. Incorporating structured knowledge graphs can also enhance semantic reasoning. Moreover, coupling LLM responses with satellite imagery and sensor-based farm data opens the path for multimodal learning in precision agriculture. These enhancements can drive robust, scalable, and context-aware decision-making for real-world farming environments.

Acknowledgments. This work was supported by the National Research Foundation of Korea(NRF) grant funded by the Korea government(MSIT) (No. RS-2024-00405278) and this work was supported by the National Research Foundation(NRF), Korea, under project BK21 FOUR.

Disclosure of Interests. The authors have no competing interests to declare that are relevant to the content of this article.

References

1. Zhao, X., et al.: Implementation of large language models and agricultural knowledge graphs for efficient plant disease detection. Agriculture **14**(8), 1359 (2024)
2. Sapkota, R., et al.: Multi-modal LLMs in agriculture: A comprehensive review. Authorea Preprints (2024)
3. Bengio, Y., Ducharme, R., Vincent, P.: A neural probabilistic language model. Adv. Neural Inf. Process. Syst. **13** (2000)
4. Hadi, M.U., et al.: A survey on large language models: applications, challenges, limitations, and practical usage. Authorea Preprints (2023)
5. Mienye, I.D., Swart, T.G.: A comprehensive review of deep learning: architectures, recent advances, and applications. Information **15**(12), 755 (2024)
6. Shaikh, T.A., Rasool, T., Veningston, K., Yaseen, S.M.: The role of large language models in agriculture: harvesting the future with LLM intelligence. Progress Artif. Intell. 1–48 (2024)
7. Wang, J.: LLM-based fine-tuning data generation for relation triplet extraction with expert ensemble and demonstration selection. In: 2024 IEEE 12th International Conference on Intelligent Systems (IS), pp. 1–7. IEEE (2024)
8. Zhao, B., Jin, W., Ser, J., Yang, G.: ChatAgri: exploring potentials of ChatGPT on cross-linguistic agricultural text classification. Neurocomputing **557**, 126708 (2023)
9. Topal, M., Bas, A., van Heerden, I.: Exploring transformers in natural language generation: GPT, BERT, and XLNet. arxiv 2021. arXiv preprint arXiv:2102.08036(2021)
10. Yang, S., Yuan, Z., Li, S., Peng, R., Liu, K., Yang, P.: GPT-4 as evaluator: Evaluating large language models on pest management in agriculture. arXiv preprint arXiv:2403.11858 (2024)
11. Yadav, S., Kaushik, A., Sharma, M., Sharma, S.: Disruptive technologies in smart farming: an expanded view with sentiment analysis. AgriEngineering **4**(2), 424–460 (2022)
12. Imbert, B., Kreplak, J., Flores, R.G., Aubert, G., Burstin, J., Tayeh, N.: Development of a knowledge graph framework to ease and empower translational approaches in plant research: a use-case on grain legumes. Front. Artif. Intell. **6**, 1191122 (2023)
13. Kumar, B.P., Sadanandam, M.: A fusion architecture of BERT and RoBERTa for enhanced performance of sentiment analysis of social media platforms. Int. J. Comput. Digital Syst. **15**(1), 51–67 (2024)
14. Awais, M., Alharthi, A.H.S.A., Kumar, A., Cholakkal, H., Anwer, R.M.: AgroGPT: efficient agricultural vision-language model with expert tuning. In: 2025 IEEE/CVF Winter Conference on Applications of Computer Vision (WACV), pp. 5687–5696. IEEE (2025)

15. Chang, Y., et al.: A survey on evaluation of large language models. ACM Trans. Intell. Syst. Technol. **15**(3), 1–45 (2024)
16. Zhao, B., Jin, W., Ser, J., Yang, G.: ChatAgri: exploring potentials of ChatGPT on cross-linguistic agricultural text classification. Neurocomputing **557**, 126708 (2023)
17. Luo, Y., Cai, X., Qi, J., Guo, D., Che, W.: FPGA–accelerated CNN for real-time plant disease identification. Comput. Electron. Agric. **207**, 107715 (2023)

Improving Image Classification Efficiency with Knowledge Distillation and Channel Attention

Youssef Boulaouane[1]([✉])[iD], Jisu Kim[2][iD], Jimin Park[1][iD], and Deokwoo Lee[2][iD]

[1] Keimyung University, Daegu, South Korea
y.boulaouane11@gmail.com
[2] University of Nebraska-Lincoln, Lincoln, NE, USA
jkim73@huskers.unl.edu, dwoolee@kmu.ac.kr

Abstract. Image classification is a fundamental task in computer vision, with convolutional neural networks (CNNs) being the state-of-the-art approach for this task. However, CNNs can be large and computationally expensive, which limits their deployment on resource-constrained devices. To address this issue, model optimization and compression techniques such as knowledge distillation and channel attention have been proposed. In this paper, we propose a modified version of the skip-connection knowledge distillation method, which integrates the efficient channel attention module. Our experiments on the CIFAR-10 dataset show that this approach improves the performance of both large teacher-small student and self-distillation scenarios, and also leads to smaller model sizes. We also visualize the intermediate feature maps to understand the learning process of the network. Our results demonstrate the effectiveness of combining knowledge distillation and channel attention for improving the performance and efficiency of CNNs.

Keywords: Image classification · Convolutional neural networks · Knowledge distillation · Channel attention · Model optimization · Model compression

1 Introduction

This paper proposes a novel method that combines knowledge distillation and efficient channel attention to optimize image classification neural networks in terms of accuracy and efficiency. Knowledge distillation transfers knowledge from a large teacher model to a smaller student model, enabling model compression while maintaining performance [1–3]. In addition, channel attention mechanisms focus on the most informative features by computing inter-channel relationships, further improving CNN performance [8,9].

B.-G. Kim et al. (Eds.): MITA 2025, CCIS 2675, pp. 28–39, 2026.
https://doi.org/10.1007/978-981-95-3141-7_3

1.1 Overview

Model optimization aims to improve performance by increasing accuracy and reducing loss. While traditional optimization algorithms adjust weights and learning rates, knowledge distillation offers an alternative by transferring learned knowledge from teacher to student models [1]. Originally introduced for model compression, it allows smaller models to achieve comparable performance to larger models, which is particularly valuable for resource-constrained devices [4].

Beyond classical teacher-student frameworks, self-knowledge distillation enables models to refine their own representations, treating the model itself as both teacher and student [5–7]. Figure 1 illustrates the general knowledge distillation framework.

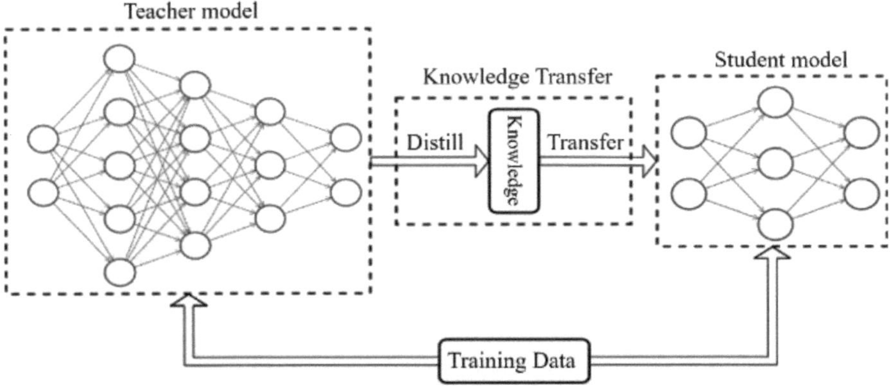

Fig. 1. Overview of the generic Knowledge Distillation teacher-student framework.

Channel attention mechanisms, such as the Channel Attention Module [8,9], enhance CNNs by emphasizing critical feature channels while suppressing less informative ones. As shown in Fig. 2, attention maps are generated by applying global pooling (max and average), followed by shared Multi-Layer Perceptrons (MLPs) [10], and merged through summation and sigmoid activation to form the final attention weights.

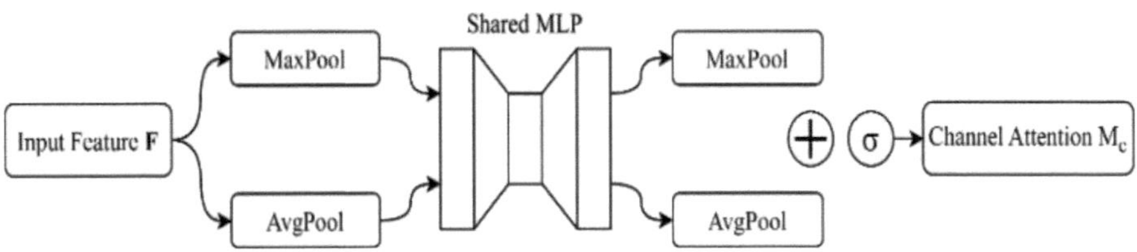

Fig. 2. Diagram of a channel attention module

However, conventional channel attention may increase model complexity. Efficient Channel Attention (ECA) [8], based on Squeeze-and-Excitation Networks (SENet) [11], mitigates this by using lightweight local cross-channel interactions without dimensionality reduction, preserving both efficiency and performance.

1.2   Problem Statement

While knowledge distillation and channel attention have shown significant success in improving image classification models, further performance gains are still possible. This paper investigates the combination of multiple knowledge distillation strategies and channel attention techniques to enhance both accuracy and efficiency.

We propose a modified skip-connection knowledge distillation framework integrated with efficient channel attention. Our method is evaluated in both teacher-student distillation and self-distillation scenarios. Additionally, we utilize intermediate feature map visualizations to analyze and better understand the learning process. The proposed approach demonstrates improved performance and offers potential for broader applications in efficient neural network optimization.

2   Related Works

2.1   Convolutional Neural Networks for Image Classification

Image classification has long been a key problem in computer vision [12]. Early approaches relied on hand-crafted features such as BRIEF, SIFT, and SURF [13], which required manually selecting relevant features [14].

The field shifted dramatically in 2012 with the success of deep convolutional neural networks (CNNs), notably SuperVision, on the ImageNet dataset [14]. Despite initial skepticism towards neural networks [14], CNNs have since become the dominant architecture for object recognition [15], driven by advances in network design, computing resources, and large-scale datasets. The landmark ImageNet paper has been cited over 100,000 times, reflecting CNNs' major impact [14].

2.2   Residual Networks (ResNet)

Residual Networks (ResNet) were introduced by He et al. in 2016 to address vanishing and exploding gradients in deep networks [16]. By introducing residual blocks, ResNet allows layers to learn residual mappings instead of directly learning the full transformation [17].

In a residual block, the input x is combined with the output of stacked layers to form the mapping:

$$F(x) := H(x) - x, \quad \text{so that} \quad H(x) = F(x) + x. \tag{1}$$

This structure enables training of very deep networks, such as the original 152-layer ResNet [16]. Figure 3 illustrates a basic residual block.

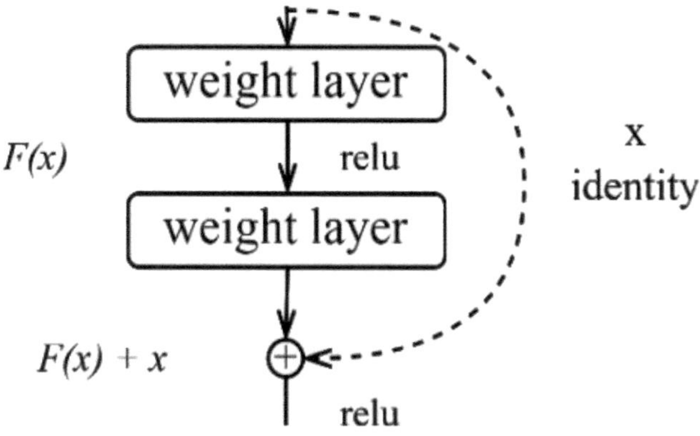

Fig. 3. The architecture of a residual block.

2.3 Knowledge Distillation

Deep learning models have grown increasingly large, posing challenges for deployment due to high computational cost [15]. Knowledge Distillation (KD) addresses this by transferring knowledge from a high-capacity teacher to a smaller student model [1,4,18].

KD methods include response-based and feature-based approaches. In response-based KD, the student mimics the teacher's final output logits [2], as illustrated in Fig. 4. The loss is defined as:

$$L_{RBD}(R_t, P_s) = \mathcal{L}_R(P_t, P_s),\tag{2}$$

where P_t and P_s denote teacher and student predictions, respectively. Predictions are computed using softmax:

$$P = softmax(a_i) = \frac{exp(a_i)}{\sum_j exp(a_j)},\tag{3}$$

and temperature scaling [1]:

$$P_{t/s}^T = softmax\left(\frac{a_{t/s}}{T}\right),\tag{4}$$

where T controls the smoothness of the soft targets. The full loss combines Kullback-Leibler divergence [19] and cross-entropy loss.

Feature-based KD transfers intermediate representations, enabling student models to benefit from teacher's hierarchical feature learning [3,4,20]. Fit-Nets [21] introduced this by guiding student layers to match selected teacher layers. Proper selection of hint layers is crucial to avoid over-regularization and optimize student performance.

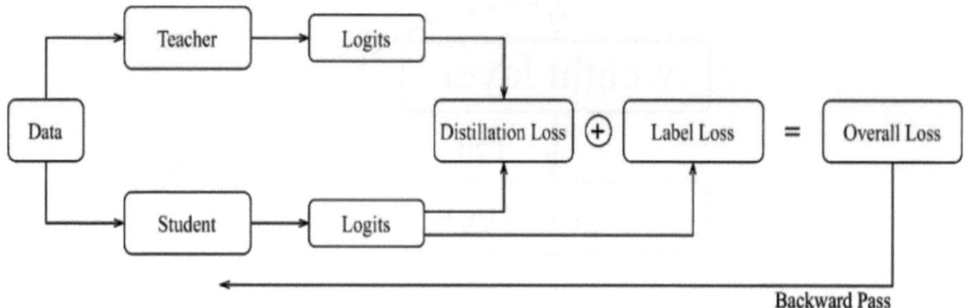

Fig. 4. Generic response-based knowledge distillation scheme.

2.4 Channel Attention

Channel attention enhances CNN performance by focusing on informative feature channels. Squeeze-and-Excitation Networks (SE-Net) [11] introduced a three-part SE-block consisting of squeeze (global average pooling), excitation (fully connected layers with ReLU), and scaling (sigmoid activation). This generates attention weights applied via element-wise multiplication. Figure 5 illustrates the SE-block architecture.

While SE-Net improves accuracy, it increases model complexity due to dimensionality reduction [8]. To address this, Efficient Channel Attention (ECA-Net) [8] eliminates dimensionality reduction by directly applying 1D convolution across channel neighbors, preserving both efficiency and performance [9,23,24].

As shown in Fig. 6, ECA applies global average pooling followed by a fast 1D convolution of kernel size k (typically $k = 3$). The attention weights are computed as:

$$\omega = \sigma(C1D_k(y)), \tag{5}$$

where σ is a sigmoid function and $C1D_k$ represents 1D convolution with kernel size k.

3 Proposed Method

We explore model optimization by combining response-based knowledge distillation with skip connections in ResNet [25], and integrating Efficient Channel Attention (ECA) both in residual blocks and exportable base blocks.

3.1 Skip Connection Knowledge Distillation

We modify ResNet to extract skip-connection outputs before the final average pooling. The identity mapping x from the skip connection is saved as an additional output for distillation (Fig. 7).

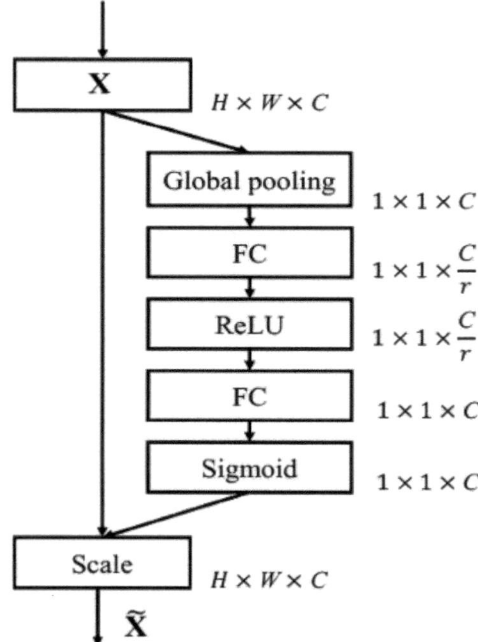

Fig. 5. Architecture of a squeeze-and-excitation module.

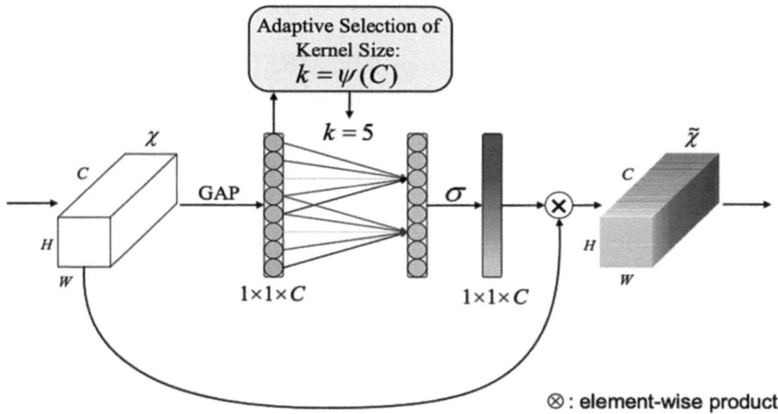

Fig. 6. Architecture of the efficient channel attention module.

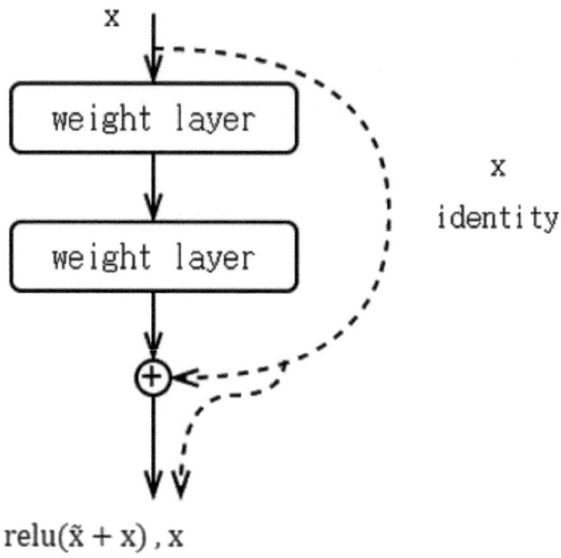

Fig. 7. Architecture of the custom exportable based block.

The distillation loss combines cross-entropy loss and Mean Squared Error (MSE) between teacher and student skip-connection outputs:

$$\mathcal{L}_R = H(P_s, targets) + \alpha \cdot MSE(P_s, P_t), \tag{6}$$

where $H(P_s, targets)$ is the cross-entropy loss, $MSE(P_s, P_t)$ is the mean squared error between teacher and student, and α controls the balance between losses [1]. Providing both output and hidden feature guidance allows the student to better approximate teacher knowledge. The full architecture is shown in Fig. 8.

3.2   Custom Efficient Channel Attention Module

The Efficient Channel Attention (ECA-Net) module [8] was integrated into the proposed model in two configurations. First, ECA was added in parallel with the initial residual blocks of ResNet, following its original design (Fig. 6).

The second approach combined ECA with the custom exportable base block, enabling the distillation process to utilize both channel attention outputs and skip-connection identity mappings from the teacher model.

Experimental results showed that integrating ECA into the exportable base block, alongside the proposed knowledge distillation framework, yielded superior performance compared to applying ECA in early residual blocks.

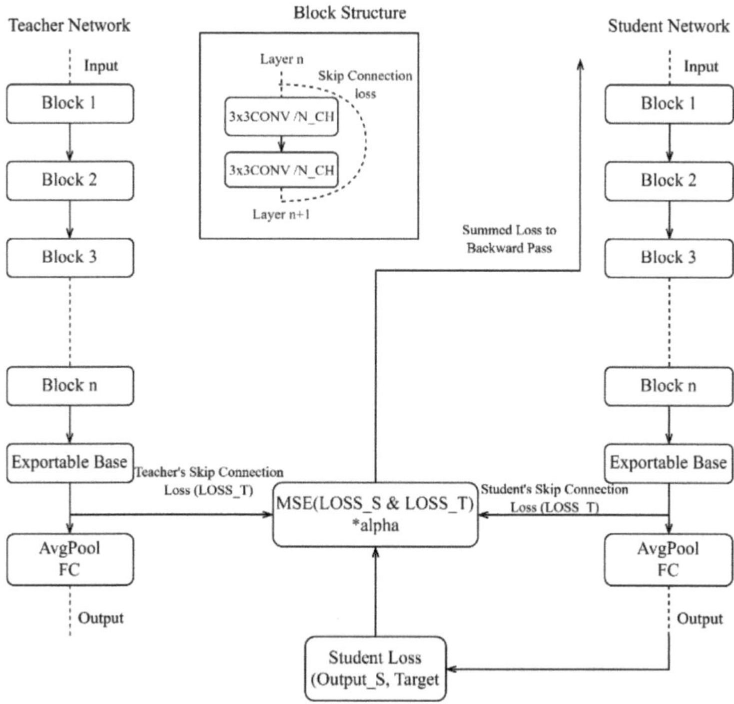

Fig. 8. Diagram of the custom response-based knowledge distillation applied on a ResNet model.

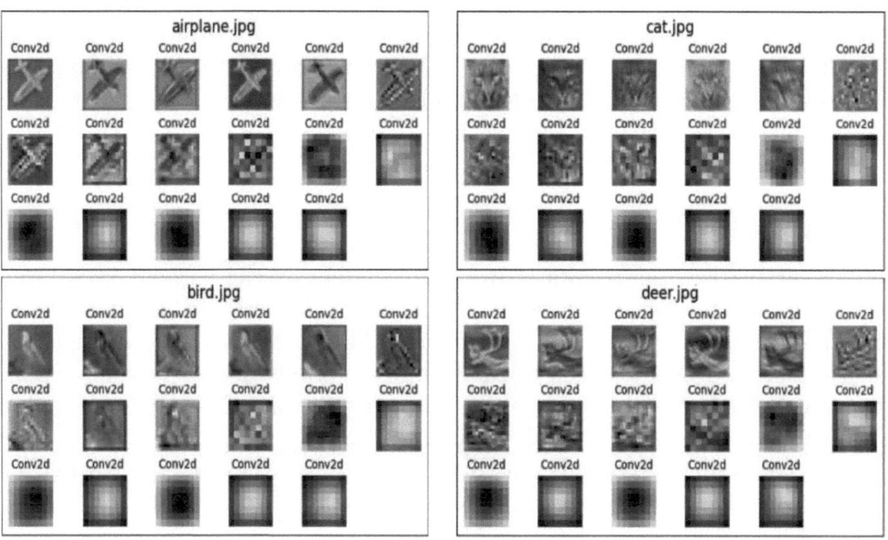

Fig. 9. Visualization of intermediate convolution layers feature maps for four images from different classes.

3.3 Feature Visualization

Visualizing intermediate feature maps helps interpret how the model learns class-specific features [26]. As shown in Fig. 9, the self-distilled ResNet18 model highlights relevant patterns such as edges and object parts (e.g., airplane wings or deer antlers). These visualizations provide insights into feature extraction, aiding model understanding and refinement during training.

3.4 Hardware and Software Setup

All experiments were conducted on a Windows machine using PyTorch [27], Torchvision [28], and CUDA [29]. The detailed hardware and software specifications are summarized in Table 1.

Table 1. Implementation and experimental environment.

Category	Component	Specification
Hardware	CPU	Intel Core i7 6700 @ 3.40GHz
	GPU	NVIDIA TITAN Xp
	RAM	8GB DDR4 @ 1064MHz
Software	OS	Windows 10 Pro
	Framework	Python 3.8, PyTorch 1.12.0, CUDA 11.6, Torchvision 0.13.0
	IDE	PyCharm, Jupyter Notebook

3.5 Dataset

We conducted experiments using the CIFAR-10 dataset [28], which contains 60,000 color images (32×32 pixels) evenly distributed across 10 classes. The dataset is split into 50,000 training and 10,000 test samples. CIFAR-10 is a subset of the larger 80 million tiny images dataset [30].

3.6 Experiments

Table 2 summarizes the results of ResNet18 and ResNet34 without knowledge distillation. For ResNet18, integrating ECA into the exportable base block (proposed method) achieved the best performance. This suggests that applying channel attention to deeper abstract features improves representation learning [9,20]. In contrast, ResNet34 showed lower performance on CIFAR-10 due to possible overfitting on this relatively small dataset [31,32].

Next, we evaluate knowledge distillation where ResNet34 acts as teacher for ResNet18. Table 3 shows that our proposed method improves accuracy by 2.96% over baseline distillation approaches [25].

Finally, self-distillation results are shown in Table 4. The proposed method again achieves the highest accuracy, demonstrating its effectiveness for fine-tuning lightweight models.

Table 2. Performance results without knowledge distillation.

Backbone	Methods	Accuracy (%)	CrossEntropyLoss
ResNet18	Baseline [16]	94.12	0.208
	ECA-Net [8]	92.53	0.297
	ECA-Net Module in last block (**proposed**)	**94.0**	**0.182**
ResNet34	Baseline [16]	91.27	0.407
	ECA-Net [8]	**92.61**	**0.337**
	ECA-Net Module in last block (**proposed**)	91.13	0.422

Table 3. Performance of ResNet18 distilled from ResNet34.

Backbone	Methods	Accuracy (%)	Distillation Loss
ResNet18 distilled from ResNet34	Baseline [16]	92.62	0.349
	ECA-Net [8]	92.73	0.296
	Proposed Method	**93.83**	**0.216**

Table 4. Self-distillation results on ResNet18.

Backbone	Methods	Accuracy (%)	Distillation Loss
Self-distilled ResNet18	Baseline [16]	94.14	0.217
	ECA-Net [8]	92.36	0.304
	Proposed Method	**95.07**	**0.171**

4 Conclusion

We proposed a modified skip-connection knowledge distillation framework integrated with efficient channel attention to improve neural network accuracy and efficiency. The method demonstrated superior performance in both teacher-student and self-distillation scenarios. Intermediate feature visualization further provided insights into the learning process. Future work includes extending the approach to other datasets and architectures, and exploring deployment on edge devices.

Acknowledgments. This research was supported by Basic Science Research Program through the National Research Foundation of Korea(NRF) funded by the Ministry of Education(NO.2022R1I1A3069352) and was results of a study on the "Convergence and Open Sharing System" Project, supported by the Ministry of Education and National Research Foundation of Korea.

Disclosure of Interests. The authors declare no conflict of interest.

References

1. Hinton, G., Vinyals, O., Dean, J.: Distilling the Knowledge in a Neural Network. arXiv arXiv:1503.02531 (2015)
2. Zhang, G., Xie, J., Wang, Q., Li, P.: Global second-order pooling convolutional networks. In: Proceedings of IEEE/CVF Conference on Computer Vision and Pattern Recognition (CVPR), pp. 3024–3033 (2019)
3. Urban, O., Yunfei, L., Yunlong, L.: What Knowledge Gets Distilled in Knowledge Distillation?. arXiv arXiv:2205.16004 (2022)
4. Gou, J., Yu, B., Maybank, S.J., Tao, D.: Knowledge distillation: a survey. Int. J. Comput. Vision **129**(6), 1789–1819 (2021). https://doi.org/10.1007/s11263-021-01453-z
5. Kim, K., Byun, J., Dong, Y., Seo, H.: Self-knowledge distillation with progressive refinement of targets. In: Proceedings of IEEE/CVF International Conference on Computer Vision (ICCV), pp. 6567–6576 (2021)
6. Yuan, L., Tay, F., Geng, L., Wang, T., Feng, J.: Revisiting knowledge distillation via label smoothing regularization. In: Proceedings of IEEE/CVF Conference on Computer Vision and Pattern Recognition (CVPR), pp. 3903–3911 (2020)
7. Sohn, S., Park, J., Kim, K., Seo, J.: Regularizing class-wise predictions via self-knowledge distillation. In: Proceedings of IEEE/CVF Conference on Computer Vision and Pattern Recognition (CVPR), pp. 13876–13885 (2020)
8. Wang, Q., Wu, B., Zhong, P., Li, P., Zhou, W., Huang, Q.: ECA-Net: efficient channel attention for deep convolutional neural networks. In: Proceedings of IEEE/CVF Conference on Computer Vision and Pattern Recognition (CVPR), pp. 11534–11542 (2020)
9. Woo, S., Park, J., Lee, J., Kweon, I.S.: CBAM: convolutional block attention module. In: Proceedings of European Conference on Computer Vision (ECCV), pp. 3–19 (2018)
10. Sahu, A., Chauhan, P.: Energy-efficient edge-based real-time healthcare support system. Adv. Comput. **117**, 339–368 (2020)
11. Hu, J., Shen, L., Sun, G.: Squeeze-and-excitation networks. In: Proceedings of IEEE Conference on Computer Vision and Pattern Recognition (CVPR), pp. 7132–7141 (2018)
12. Wang, S., Zhu, S.: Metamorphic Testing for Object Detection Systems. arXiv arXiv:1912.12162 (2019)
13. Nogueira, O., et al.: Deep learning vs. traditional computer vision. Proc. Comput. Vis. Conf. (CVC) **11**, 128–144 (2020)
14. Krizhevsky, A., Sutskever, I., Hinton, G.: ImageNet classification with deep convolutional neural networks. Commun. ACM **60**(6), 84–90 (2017)
15. Voulodimos, A., Doulamis, N., Doulamis, A., Protopapadakis, E.: Deep learning for computer vision: a brief review. Comput. Intell. Neurosci. (2018)
16. He, K., Zhang, X., Ren, S., Sun, J.: Deep residual learning for image recognition. In: Proceedings of IEEE Conference on Computer Vision and Pattern Recognition (CVPR), pp. 770–778 (2016)
17. pawangfg. Residual Networks (ResNet) - Deep Learning. GeeksforGeeks (2020). https://www.geeksforgeeks.org/residual-networks-resnet-deep-learning/
18. Bucil, C., Caruana, R., Niculescu-Mizil, A.: Model compression. In: Proceedings of ACM SIGKDD International Conference on Knowledge Discovery and Data Mining (KDD), pp. 535–541 (2006)

19. Kullback, S., Leibler, R.A.: On information and sufficiency. Ann. Math. Stat. **22**(1), 79–86 (1951)
20. Bengio, Y., Courville, A., Vincent, P.: Representation learning: a review and new perspectives. IEEE Trans. Pattern Anal. Mach. Intell. **35**(8), 1798–1828 (2013)
21. Romero, A., et al.: FitNets: Hints for Thin Deep Nets. arXiv arXiv:1412.6550 (2014)
22. Nair, V., Hinton, G.: Rectified linear units improve restricted Boltzmann machines. In: Proceedings of International Conference on Machine Learning (ICML), pp. 807–814 (2010)
23. Gao, J., Xie, J., Wang, Q., Li, P.: Global second-order pooling convolutional networks. In: Proceedings of IEEE/CVF Conference on Computer Vision and Pattern Recognition (CVPR), pp. 3024–3033 (2019)
24. Hu, J., Shen, L., Albanie, S., Sun, G., Vedaldi, A.: Gather-excite: exploiting feature context in convolutional neural networks. In: Advance Neural Information Processing Systems, vol. 31 (2018)
25. Gwak, M.: A Study on a Convolutional Neural Network Model with Knowledge Distillation and Post-Training Quantization. Master's thesis. Kyungpook Nat. Univ., Daegu, South Korea (2022)
26. Yosinski, J., Clune, J., Nguyen, A., Fuchs, T., Lipson, H.: Understanding Neural Networks Through Deep Visualization. arXiv arXiv:1506.06579 (2015)
27. Paszke, A., et al.: PyTorch: an imperative style, high-performance deep learning library. In: Advance Neural Information Processing Systems, vol. 32 (2019)
28. Krizhevsky, A., Hinton, G.: Learning Multiple Layers of Features from Tiny Images (2019)
29. Nickolls, J., Buck, I., Garland, M., Skadron, K.: Scalable parallel programming with CUDA. Queue **6**(2), 40–53 (2008)
30. Torralba, A., Fergus, R., Freeman, W.: 80 million tiny images: a large data set for nonparametric object and scene recognition. IEEE Trans. Pattern Anal. Mach. Intell. **30**(11), 1958–1970 (2008)
31. Bishop, C.M.: Pattern Recognition and Machine Learning: All "Just the Facts 101". Cram101 (2013)
32. IRIC Bioinformatics Platform. Overfitting and Regularization. https://bioinfo.iric.ca/overfitting-and-regularization/. Accessed 11 Mar 2022

Explainable Graph-Based Retrieval-Augmented Generation with Landmark-Centric Reasoning Paths

Eu-Tteum Baek[✉]

Department of Computer Engineering Andong, Andong-si, Republic of Korea
eutteum@gknu.ac.kr

Abstract. Retrieval-Augmented Generation (RAG) enhances the answer quality of language models by incorporating external knowledge. However, most RAG systems do not clearly explain how evidence is retrieved, and can be slow with large-scale databases. This paper proposes a novel graph-based RAG method that selects landmark nodes using K-means clustering and constructs a sparse graph for efficient and interpretable retrieval. Text passages are embedded using Sentence-BERT, and the centroid of each cluster serves as a landmark. During inference, queries are mapped to the nearest landmark, and relevant evidence is identified by traversing the landmark graph linked to stored embeddings. The proposed approach enables users to understand how evidence is retrieved within RAG, and provides richer input information for the prompt, which in turn improves the answer quality of generative AI models.

Keywords: Retrieval-Augmented Generation (RAG) · explainability · K-means clustering

1 Introduction

Large language models (LLMs) have demonstrated impressive capabilities in natural language understanding and generation tasks. However, they are often limited by their inability to access up-to-date external knowledge and their tendency to produce hallucinated or unverified content. Retrieval-Augmented Generation (RAG) addresses these limitations by grounding model outputs in external documents [1]. By integrating retrieval mechanisms with language generation models, RAG systems enhance factual accuracy, scalability, and domain adaptability.

Despite these benefits, conventional RAG frameworks primarily rely on vector similarity search techniques such as FAISS to identify relevant passages. While effective in finding semantically similar documents, these methods often lack transparency in their retrieval process. Users and practitioners remain unable to interpret how and why specific evidence was selected, hindering trust and explainability, especially in safety-critical applications such as healthcare, legal AI, and scientific research assistance. Furthermore, as dataset sizes increase, the computational costs associated with exhaustive vector search become prohibitively high, motivating the need for more efficient alternatives.

B.-G. Kim et al. (Eds.): MITA 2025, CCIS 2675, pp. 40–51, 2026.
https://doi.org/10.1007/978-981-95-3141-7_4

In this paper, we propose a novel graph-based RAG framework that enhances both the efficiency and explainability of retrieval processes by incorporating landmark-centric reasoning paths. Our approach leverages K-means clustering to select representative landmarks that serve as nodes in a sparse semantic graph, enabling structured multi-hop traversal during inference. Queries are mapped to their nearest landmarks, and evidence is retrieved through interpretable reasoning paths within the graph. This design not only reduces retrieval costs by limiting searches to semantically clustered regions but also provides human-understandable justifications for the selected evidence. The contributions of this work are threefold:

1 We introduce a landmark-based sparse graph retrieval mechanism that encodes document relationships efficiently while enabling explainable multi-hop evidence selection.
2 We implement an end-to-end graph-based RAG system that integrates dense text embeddings, clustering-based landmark selection, and semantic graph traversal to produce grounded and interpretable outputs.
3 By applying the proposed method to the SQuAD 2.0 dataset [2], we demonstrate the reasoning basis for its retrieval explanations.

2 Related Work

Retrieval-Augmented Generation was introduced as a paradigm to enhance language model outputs by incorporating relevant external knowledge retrieved from large corpora [1]. Early RAG systems employed dense vector retrieval techniques such as FAISS [3], which leveraged pre-trained embedding models (e.g., BERT [4], Sentence-BERT [5]) to map queries and passages into a shared semantic space for similarity-based retrieval. However, these methods are inherently black-box, providing little transparency into how specific documents were selected, limiting their applicability in domains requiring traceable reasoning.

Graph structures have been explored in information retrieval to model document relationships, improve search efficiency, and enable multi-hop reasoning. Works such as GraphRetriever [6] utilize knowledge graphs to enhance question answering by reasoning over entity connections. Similarly, knowledge graph-based RAG systems integrate structured triples to support factual consistency [7]. However, these approaches often require pre-built knowledge graphs, which are domain-dependent and expensive to maintain.

Clustering techniques have been employed to improve interpretability in retrieval tasks by grouping semantically similar documents and selecting cluster centroids as representatives [8]. For example, cluster-based retrieval frameworks reduce search space and provide hierarchical explanations of retrieved results. K-means clustering, in particular, has been widely adopted due to its simplicity and effectiveness in high-dimensional embedding spaces.

Recent research has emphasized the need for explainability in NLP systems to build user trust and ensure accountability [9, 10]. Approaches include attention-based explanations [11], counterfactual reasoning [12], and path-based explanations in graph-structured data [13]. However, the integration of explainable graph-based reasoning within RAG remains underexplored.

This paper addresses this gap by proposing a landmark-centric sparse graph framework that combines the benefits of clustering-based representation, graph-based multi-hop reasoning, and retrieval-augmented generation to achieve interpretable, efficient, and high-quality evidence retrieval for language models.

3   Methodology

This work proposed a retrieval-augmented generation framework that leverages graph-based reasoning to enhance interpretability. This method consists of five key components: (1) constructing a database of dense text embeddings using a pre-trained language model, (2) selecting representative landmark nodes via K-means clustering, (3) building a sparse similarity graph that captures semantic relationships among these landmarks and connects documents to their assigned clusters, (4) performing multi-hop, explainable retrieval by traversing the graph based on query similarity, and (5) providing the retrieved evidence and reasoning path as input to a generative language model to produce answers. The following sections detail each component of the proposed system.

3.1   Database Construction Using Text Embedding Models

To facilitate efficient semantic retrieval, we first preprocess the entire corpus by embedding all context passages into dense vector representations. This preprocessing step ensures that each textual passage is transformed into a form suitable for vector similarity computations. Specifically, we utilize a pre-trained BERT model to encode each passage into a fixed-dimensional embedding vector. BERT, being a bidirectional transformer-based model, captures rich contextual dependencies, which is crucial for accurately representing the semantic meaning of each passage. The embedding process involves passing the tokenized passage through the BERT encoder and extracting the final hidden state corresponding to the [CLS] token as the representation for that passage.

Through this embedding process, we construct a comprehensive vector database (DB), where each passage in the corpus is associated with a unique embedding vector. To ensure consistent similarity calculations during subsequent retrieval operations, all embedding vectors are L2-normalized prior to storage. L2 normalization scales each vector to have a unit norm, which is essential for cosine similarity-based comparisons, as it ensures that similarity computations depend solely on the angle between vectors rather than their magnitudes.

3.2   Landmark Selection via K-means Clustering

Based on the embedding matrix constructed from all passages, we then apply K-means clustering to partition the dataset into K clusters [14], where K is a tunable hyperparameter that controls the granularity of the clustering. The purpose of clustering is to group semantically similar passages together, thereby enabling the construction of a higher-level abstraction of the corpus. K-means clustering operates by iteratively assigning each embedding to the nearest cluster centroid and updating centroids as the mean of their assigned embeddings until convergence.

Formally, the centroid c_k of each cluster is computed as the element-wise average of all embeddings assigned to that cluster, according to the formula:

$$c_k = \frac{1}{|C_k|} \Sigma_{x_i \in c_k} x_i \tag{1}$$

where c_k denotes the centroid of the k k-th cluster, C_k is the set of embeddings belonging to cluster k, and x_i is the embedding of passage i. The landmark for each cluster is then defined as the stored embedding that is closest to the centroid in Euclidean distance:

$$l_k = \arg\min_{x_i \in C_k} \|x_i - c_k\|_2 \tag{2}$$

where l_k is the landmark embedding for cluster k. These landmark vectors provide a high-level abstraction of the semantic space and serve as nodes in the subsequent retrieval graph.

3.3 Sparse Landmark Graph Construction

To capture global semantic relationships while maintaining efficiency, we construct a sparse, undirected graph among the landmark nodes. For each landmark l_i, we compute pairwise cosine similarities with all other landmarks l_i as follows:

$$\text{sim}(l_i, l_j) = \frac{l_i \cdot l_j}{\|l_i\|_2 \|l_j\|_2} \tag{3}$$

This similarity computation captures the semantic relatedness between landmarks, with higher similarity scores indicating closer semantic proximity.

Each landmark then retains edges only to the top-N most similar landmarks (where N is a design parameter), as well as to those whose similarity exceeds a threshold τ τ. The set of edges E is defined as:

$$E = \left\{ (l_i, l_j) \mid l_j \in N_i \text{ or } \text{sim}(l_i, l_j) \geq \tau \right\} \tag{4}$$

where N_i denotes the set of top-N most similar landmarks to l_i l_i. This sparsification ensures that the graph encodes only meaningful semantic neighborhoods, avoiding the combinatorial overhead of full connectivity.

In addition to landmark-to-landmark edges, we establish landmark-to-document connections by linking each passage to the landmark of its assigned cluster. This hybrid graph structure, consisting of dense BERT-encoded passages and sparse landmark centroids, as shown in Fig. 1, enables efficient reasoning and retrieval. Each passage is thus reachable via its cluster's landmark node, anchoring the document within the higher-level semantic graph.

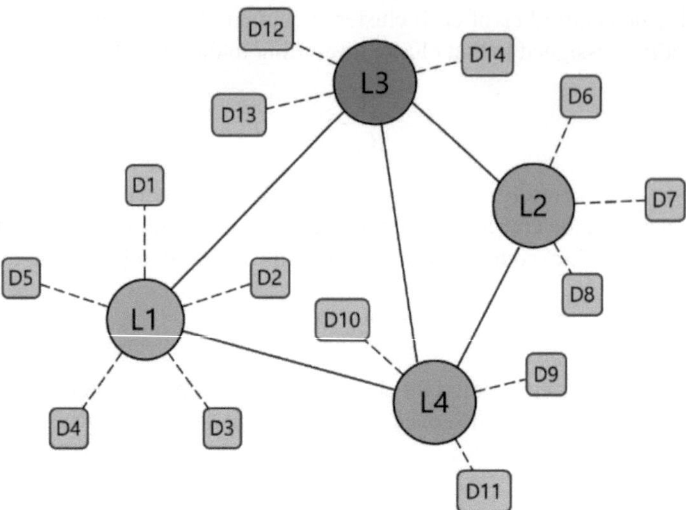

Fig. 1. Example of Sparse Landmark-Document Graph Structure. (This diagram illustrates a hybrid graph consisting of four landmark nodes (L1–L4, colored circles) and fourteen document nodes (D1–D14, gray squares). Landmark nodes are sparsely interconnected based on semantic similarity (solid lines), while each document node is exclusively connected to the landmark representing its assigned cluster.)

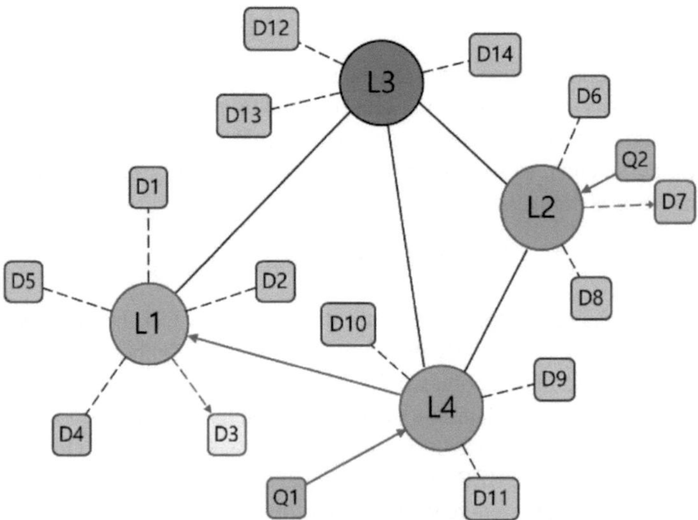

Fig. 2. Example of Explainable Path Reasoning over a Sparse Landmark-Document Graph for RAG. This figure demonstrates how two example queries (Q1 and Q2, yellow squares) traverse a sparse landmark-document graph to retrieve supporting evidence. Each query is first assigned to its closest landmark node (L1 for Q1, L2 for Q2; colored circles), then a multi-hop path (highlighted in red) is followed via connected landmarks and associated documents (D3 for Q1, D7 for Q2) to reach relevant evidence.

3.4 Landmark Path Reasoning with Graph Traversal

At inference time, when a user query is given, the system first encodes the query using the same BERT model applied during database construction. The query embedding is then compared to all landmark embeddings, and the most similar landmark is selected as the starting node for graph traversal. Next, the system utilizes DB vector search to retrieve the top-k nearest document embeddings to the query. Each of these retrieved documents is mapped to its corresponding landmark cluster, resulting in one or more target landmarks. For each candidate target landmark, the shortest path from the starting landmark to the target is computed within the sparse landmark graph, as illustrated in Fig. 2. To ensure computational efficiency, we utilize Dijkstra's shortest path algorithm [15], which is a classic graph search algorithm that efficiently finds the minimum cost path between nodes in a weighted graph by iteratively selecting the unvisited node with the smallest tentative distance and updating its neighbors accordingly. Specifically, given a graph $G = (V, E)$ with non-negative edge weights $w(u, v)$, Dijkstra's algorithm computes the shortest path distance $d(s, v)$ from a source node s to every other node $v \in V$ by maintaining a priority queue of nodes sorted by their current tentative distance estimates[16]. In our implementation, Dijkstra's algorithm is applied exclusively on the graph comprising landmark nodes to efficiently determine the semantic reasoning path. Subsequently, the reasoning path is constructed by connecting the query node to the starting landmark and linking the target landmark to its associated document node. This approach effectively generates a multi-hop, explainable reasoning chain through the semantic space, enabling both transparent and interpretable retrieval for the given query.

3.5 Generative Model to Answer the Question

For each query, the system aggregates the evidence passages corresponding to the top-k retrieved documents. These passages, together with the explicit reasoning path generated over the landmark graph, are combined to form the context section of the prompt provided to the generative model. This allows the language model to not only ground its answer in factual evidence but also to leverage a reasoning process that is interpretable by humans. Finally, the assembled prompt is fed into a large language model. The language model then generates an answer by attending to both the retrieved evidence and the given reasoning path, thereby producing responses that are both factually grounded and explainable.

4 Experimental Results

To evaluate the effectiveness and interpretability of our proposed graph-based RAG framework, we conducted a series of comprehensive experiments. All evaluations were performed using the SQuAD 2.0 dataset, which consists of context, question, and answer triples. For passage embedding, we used the all-MiniLM-L6-v2 variant of Sentence-BERT [3] to balance accuracy and computational efficiency. Clustering was performed with the K-means algorithm (K = 50) from the scikit-learn library. The sparse landmark graph was constructed by connecting each landmark node to its top five neighbors based on cosine similarity, with an additional similarity threshold of 0.1 applied for further filtering. All passage embeddings were indexed and stored as DB vectors using the FAISS library. For retrieval, we evaluated system performance by testing the top-1, top-3, and top-5 document retrievals for each query. Answer generation was handled by the Gemini 1.5 model [15].

To further illustrate the interpretability and structure of our system, Table 1 shows an example prompt generated for the question, "When did Beyoncé start becoming popular?" This example includes both the multi-hop landmark graph reasoning path and the context provided to the generative model. Figure 3 shows the list of extracted landmark nodes along with their decoded textual descriptions. Using the textual descriptions provided in Fig. 3, we can interpret the reasoning path presented in Table 1.

Table 1. Example of Generated Prompt and Reasoning Path

Component	Content
Context	Beyoncé Giselle Knowles-Carter is an American singer, songwriter, and actress. She rose to fame in the late 1990s as the lead singer of Destiny's Child…
Reasoning Path	**Query** → **Landmark_14**: "Destiny's Child is a female vocal group that debuted in Houston, Texas in the late 1990s…" → **Landmark_7**: "Beyoncé became widely recognized after her group's global success in the late 1990s." → **Landmark_3**: "Solo debut album 'Dangerously in Love' was released in 2003 and was a commercial hit." → **Doc_56**
Question	When did Beyoncé start becoming popular?
Instruction	Answer in a single word or short phrase. Do not explain.

To qualitatively evaluate the explainability of the proposed method, we submit several queries and generate prompts that include the retrieved context. Table 2 shows qualitative results for a sample query. For each example, we present the input question, the ground-truth answer, the corresponding reasoning path through landmark nodes, and a GPT-generated explanation of how the reasoning path leads to the final answer. As shown, the reasoning path offers interpretable. As illustrated in Table 2, for each representative query, we display the corresponding answer, the detailed reasoning path, and an explanation generated by GPT-4. As shown in the table, the reasoning path explicitly reveals why each document was retrieved.

```
Landmark_0: Many districts and landmarks in New York City have become well known, and the city received a r
Landmark_1:
 India: Due to concerns about pro-Tibet protests, the relay through New Delhi on April 17 was cut to just 2
Landmark_2: Beyoncé further expanded her acting career, starring as blues singer Etta James in the 2008 mus
Landmark_3: The cardinal protodeacon, the senior cardinal deacon in order of appointment to the College of
Landmark_4: One rescue team reported only 2,300 survivors from the town of Yingxiu in Wenchuan County, out
Landmark_5: For his second album, Late Registration (2005), he collaborated with film score composer Jon Br
Landmark_6: The Noble Eightfold Path-the fourth of the Buddha's Noble Truths-consists of a set of eight int
Landmark_7: At the age of 21 he settled in Paris, Thereafter, during the last 18 years of his life, he gave
Landmark_8: With the example of the Ming court's relationship with the fifth Karmapa and other Tibetan lead
Landmark_9: This unified institution consists of sea, land, and air elements referred to as the Royal Canad
Landmark_10: Buddhism /ˈbudɪzəm/ is a nontheistic religion[note 1] or philosophy (Sanskrit: धर्म dharma; Pali
Landmark_11: There were 13 finalists this season, but two were eliminated in the first result show of the f
Landmark_12: During this time, Link also helps Midna find the Fused Shadows, fragments of a relic containin
Landmark_13: In the United States and Canada, the film opened on 6 November 2015, and in its opening weeken
Landmark_14: The area north of the Congo River came under French sovereignty in 1880 as a result of Pierre
Landmark_15: The development of new technologies has made it dramatically easier and cheaper to do sequenci
Landmark_16: Comprehensive schools are primarily about providing an entitlement curriculum to all children,
Landmark_17: American Idol is an American singing competition series created by Simon Fuller and produced b
Landmark_18: Solar energy is radiant light and heat from the Sun harnessed using a range of ever-evolving t
Landmark_19: The torch was lit at a park outside at AT&T Park at about 1:17 pm PDT (20:17 UTC), briefly hel
Landmark_20: Native Alabamian Allen Barra sharply criticized Lee and the novel in The Wall Street Journal c
Landmark_21: Bond disobeys M's order and travels to Rome to attend Sciarra's funeral, That evening he visit
Landmark_22: Beyoncé participated in George Clooney and Wyclef Jean's Hope for Haiti Now: A Global Benefit
Landmark_23: Domestic dogs have been selectively bred for millennia for various behaviors, sensory capabili
Landmark_24: On April 9, 2007, it was announced that Apple had sold its one-hundred millionth iPod, making
Landmark_25: Symbiotic relationships include those associations in which one organism lives on another (ect
Landmark_26: The Wayback Machine is a digital archive of the World Wide Web and other information on the In
Landmark_27: The Legend of Zelda: Twilight Princess (Japanese: ゼルダの伝説 トワイライトプリンセス, Hepburn
Landmark_28: New York City is the most-populous city in the United States, with an estimated record high of
Landmark_29: Mendes revealed that production would begin on 8 December 2014 at Pinewood Studios, with filmi
Landmark_30: Raised in Chicago, West briefly attended art school before becoming known as a producer for Ro
Landmark_31: The Iranian languages or Iranic languages form a branch of the Indo-Iranian languages, which i
Landmark_32: When talking about genome composition, one should distinguish between prokaryotes and eukaryot
Landmark_33: In several countries, like Germany, the Netherlands, Switzerland and Turkey, institutes of tec
Landmark_34: In September 2006, the iTunes Store began to offer additional games for purchase with the laun
Landmark_35: On December 13, 2013, Beyoncé unexpectedly released her eponymous fifth studio album on the iT
Landmark_36:
 Thailand: The April 18 relay through Bangkok was the Olympic flame's first visit to Thailand, The relay co
Landmark_37: In 1582 the United Provinces invited Francis, Duke of Anjou to lead them; but after a failed a
Landmark_38: In parliamentary systems fashioned after the Westminster system, the prime minister is the pre
Landmark_39: In season eight, Latin Grammy Award-nominated singer-songwriter and record producer Kara DioGu
Landmark_40: The region was dominated by Bantu-speaking tribes, who built trade links leading into the Cong
Landmark_41: All of Chopin's compositions include the piano, Most are for solo piano, though he also wrote
Landmark_42: The iPod is a line of portable media players and multi-purpose pocket computers designed and m
Landmark_43: Spectre (2015) is the twenty-fourth James Bond film produced by Eon Productions, It features D
Landmark_44: New York City traces its roots to its 1624 founding as a trading post by colonists of the Dutc
Landmark_45: Strong aftershocks continued to strike even months after the main quake, On May 25, an aftersh
Landmark_46: There is disagreement about the origin of the term, but general consensus that "cardinalis" fr
Landmark_47: While West had encountered controversy a year prior when he stormed out of the American Music
Landmark_48: In January 2013, Destiny's Child released Love Songs, a compilation album of the romance-theme
Landmark_49: Beyoncé has received numerous awards, As a solo artist she has sold over 15 million albums in
```

Fig. 3. Example of Explainable Path Reasoning over a Sparse Landmark-Document Graph for RAG. This figure demonstrates how two example queries (Q1 and Q2, yellow squares) traverse a sparse landmark-document graph to retrieve supporting evidence. Each query is first assigned to its closest landmark node (L1 for Q1, L2 for Q2; colored circles), then a multi-hop path (highlighted in red) is followed via connected landmarks and associated documents (D3 for Q1, D7 for Q2) to reach relevant evidence.

5 Conclusion

In this paper, we proposed a landmark-based reasoning framework to enhance the explainability of retrieval-augmented generation (RAG) systems. By incorporating multi-hop reasoning paths through interpretable landmark nodes, our approach enables transparent and stepwise justification for retrieved answers. Experimental results, including both quantitative metrics and qualitative analysis with GPT-generated explanations, demonstrate the effectiveness of the proposed method in providing human-understandable evidence. Future work will focus on further improving retrieval accuracy and extending the framework to broader domains and modalities.

Table 2. Qualitative Examples of Explainable Reasoning Paths and GPT-4 Generated Explanations

Query	Answer	Reasoning Path	GPT4-generated Explanation of the Reasoning Path
Beyonce along with Jay Z met with whom's family after their death?	Freddie Gray	Query → Landmark_35 → Landmark_22 → Doc_392	For this query, the system traverses through Landmark_35 and Landmark_22, which provide contextual information about Beyoncé and Jay Z's collaborations and their active involvement in social issues. By following this reasoning path, the system ultimately reaches Doc_392, which states that after the death of Freddie Gray, Beyoncé and Jay Z met with his family, thereby providing the correct answer, "Freddie Gray."

(continued)

Table 2. (*continued*)

Query	Answer	Reasoning Path	GPT4-generated Explanation of the Reasoning Path
Beyonce signed a letter with who in 2015?	the ONE Campaign	Query → Landmark_22 → Doc_380	For this query, the system first moves through Landmark_22, which summarizes Beyoncé's charitable activities and participation in various social campaigns. This intermediate step ensures that the reasoning process focuses on evidence related to her philanthropic work. The system then reaches Doc_380, which specifically mentions that in 2015, Beyoncé signed an open letter with the ONE Campaign, thereby providing the correct answer, "the ONE Campaign."

(*continued*)

Table 2. (*continued*)

Query	Answer	Reasoning Path	GPT4-generated Explanation of the Reasoning Path
What song did Beyoncé perform at the 2009 inauguration of Obama?	America the Beautiful	Query → Landmark_48 → Landmark_22 → Doc_361	For this query, the reasoning path begins at Landmark_48, which summarizes Beyoncé's major public performances, including her participation in presidential inaugurations and national events. The path then proceeds to Landmark_22, which provides further context about Beyoncé's involvement in high-profile social and charitable activities. By following this sequence, the system ultimately retrieves Doc_361, where it is explicitly stated that Beyoncé performed "America the Beautiful" at the 2009 pre-inaugural events for President Obama, thereby directly supporting the correct answer.

References

1. Lewis, P., et al.: Retrieval-augmented generation for knowledge-intensive NLP tasks. In: Advance Neural Information Processing Systems, Vol. 33, pp. 9459–9474 (2020)
2. Rajpurkar, P., Jia, R., Liang, P.: Know what you don't know: Unanswerable questions for SQuAD. arXiv preprint arXiv:1806.03822 (2018)
3. Douze, M., et al.: The faiss library. arXiv preprint arXiv:2401.08281 (2024)
4. Devlin, J., Chang, M. W., Lee, K., Toutanova, K.: BERT: pre-training of deep bidirectional transformers for language understanding. In: Proceedings of the 2019 Conference of the North American Chapter of the Association for Computational Linguistics: Human Language Technologies, vol. 1 (long and short papers) (pp. 4171–4186) (2019)
5. Reimers, N., Gurevych, I.: Sentence-BERT: Sentence embeddings using Siamese BERT-networks. arXiv preprint arXiv:1908.10084, 2019
6. Asai, A., Hashimoto, K., Hajishirzi, H., Socher, R., Xiong, C.: Learning to retrieve reasoning paths over wikipedia graph for question answering. arXiv preprint arXiv:1911.10470 (2019)
7. Xu, T., et al.: NodeRAG: Structuring graph-based rag with heterogeneous nodes. arXiv preprint arXiv:2504.11544 (2025)
8. Djenouri, Y., et al.: Cluster-based information retrieval using pattern mining. Appl. Intell. **51**(4), 1888–1903 (2021)
9. Zhao, H., et al.: Explainability for large language models: a survey. ACM Trans. Intell. Syst. Technol. **15**(2), 1–38 (2024)
10. Lyu, Q., Apidianaki, M., Callison-Burch, C.: Towards faithful model explanation in NLP: a survey. Comput. Linguist. **50**(2), 657–723 (2024)
11. Chrysostomou, G., Aletras, N.: Improving the faithfulness of attention-based explanations with task-specific information for text classification. arXiv preprint arXiv:2105.02657 (2021)
12. McAleese, S., Keane, M.: A Comparative Analysis of Counterfactual Explanation Methods for Text Classifiers. arXiv preprint arXiv:2411.02643 (2024)
13. Chang, H., et al.: Path-based explanation for knowledge graph completion. In: Proceedings of the 30th ACM SIGKDD Conference on Knowledge Discovery and Data Mining (2024)
14. Hartigan, J.A., Wong, M.A.: A k-means clustering algorithm. J. Roy. Stat. Soc. Ser. C (Appl. Stat.) **28**(1), 100–108 (1979)
15. Dijkstra, E.W.: A note on two problems in connexion with graphs. In: Edsger Wybe Dijkstra: his life, work, and legacy (pp. 287–290) (2022)
16. Cormen, T.H., Leiserson, C.E., Rivest, R.L., Stein, C.: Introduction to algorithms. MIT Press (2022)
17. Google Team, et al.: Gemini: A family of highly capable multimodal models. arXiv. preprint arXiv:2312.11805 (2023)

Knowledge Distillation-Based Lightweight Model for Solar Cell Defect Classification

Hasnain Hyder[1], Yong-Woon Kim[2], and Yung-Cheol Byun[3(✉)]

[1] Department of Electronic Engineering, Institute of Information Science and Technology, Jeju National University, Jeju 63243, Korea
[2] Department of Computer Engineering, Jeju National University, Jeju-si 63243, South Korea
ywkim@jejunu.ac.kr
[3] Department of Computer Engineering, Major of Electronic Engineering, Jeju National University, Institute of Information Science Technology, Jeju 63243, South Korea
ycb@jejunu.ac.kr

Abstract. The rapid expansion of photovoltaic (PV) systems underscores the need for efficient defect classification frameworks to ensure their reliable and uninterrupted operation. Although Vision Transformer (ViT) have demonstrated exceptional performance in image classification tasks, their high computational complexity makes them unsuitable for real-time deployment on resource-constrained edge devices commonly found in PV systems. To address this limitation, we propose a lightweight knowledge distillation (KD) framework tailored for multi-class solar cell defect classification. In this approach, a compact MobileNetV3 student model learns from a powerful ViT-B-8 teacher, effectively transferring knowledge to achieve high classification performance with minimal resource requirements. The distilled MobileNetV3 achieves a test accuracy of 97.9% and a validation accuracy of 97.54%, closely matching the teacher's performance. Moreover, it reduces the number of parameters by 93.62%, inference time by 79.01%, and GFLOPs by 92.16%, highlighting its efficiency. The framework's effectiveness was validated through metrics including accuracy, precision, recall, F1-score, and inference speed. These results demonstrate that the proposed KD framework offers an excellent trade-off between accuracy and computational efficiency, making it highly suitable for real-time defect monitoring in PV systems deployed on edge devices.

Keywords: Photovoltaic (PV) · Solar Cell Defect Classification · Vision Transformer (ViT) · Lightweight Deep Learning · Knowledge Distillation (KD)

1 Introduction

The global shift to renewable energy has driven widespread deployment of photovoltaic (PV) systems across residential, commercial, and utility sectors [1,2].

© The Author(s) 2026
B.-G. Kim et al. (Eds.): MITA 2025, CCIS 2675, pp. 52–63, 2026.
https://doi.org/10.1007/978-981-95-3141-7_5

Ensuring their long-term efficiency requires early detection of common defects such as microcracks and interconnection failures, which can degrade performance and cause financial losses [3]. This highlights the need for accurate and timely defect detection frameworks to support predictive maintenance.

Recent advances in deep learning have enabled powerful image-based defect classification systems [4]. While ViTs offer high accuracy by capturing complex spatial patterns, their high computational cost limits deployment on edge devices [5,6]. In contrast, lightweight CNN like MobileNet are efficient and edge-friendly [7], but often lack the precision of heavier models when trained independently.

To bridge this gap, we propose a lightweight KD framework for multi-class solar cell defect classification. A ViT-B/8 teacher transfers knowledge to a MobileNetV3 student, enhancing accuracy while preserving computational efficiency.

Extensive evaluation shows that the KD student achieves 97.92% test accuracy closely matching the ViT teacher, while reducing parameters by 93.62%, inference time by 79.01%, and GFLOPs by 92.16%. These results demonstrate the framework's suitability for real-time defect detection in edge-based PV monitoring systems.

The key contributions of this work can be summarized as follows:

- Develop a lightweight knowledge distillation framework that effectively transfers knowledge from a robust ViT Base-8 teacher to a MobileNetV3 student, used for multi-class solar cell defect classification.
- The distilled student model achieves high classification performance while maintaining a minimal resources, making it ideal for deployment on edge devices.
- We present a thorough evaluation highlighting substantial reductions in model size, inference time, and computational requirements, enabling real-time, on-site PV system health monitoring.

2   Literature Review

In recent years, substantial progress has been made in the automated detection and classification of solar cell defects using deep learning techniques [8]. This surge in interest is driven by the growing demand for accurate, scalable, and efficient inspection systems for PV modules. A range of deep learning models have been developed, each utilizing distinct methodologies with varying success in addressing classification challenges. This section provides an overview of recent innovations, highlighting their methodological strengths, performance, and existing limitations in real-world PV deployments.

2.1   Deep Learning Approaches for Solar Cell Defect Classification

Deep learning has emerged as a powerful tool in solar cell defect classification, enabling automated feature extraction, resilience to image variability, and higher accuracy than traditional methods. Research has increasingly focused on both binary and multi-class classification using imaging modalities such as EL and infrared (IR).

Tang et al. [9] introduced TLDR-CNN, a transfer learning model with a multi-scale feature extraction (MSFE) module replacing standard convolutions. Using VGG16 as baseline, they reduced depth with minimal accuracy loss and achieved a 0.9% accuracy and 6.89% F1 improvement, though the model remained moderately sized. To tackle data scarcity, Demirci et al. [10] combined GAN-based augmentation (GAN, cGAN, WGAN-GP) with a weighted CNN, boosting accuracy to 94.11% and recall to 96.70%, but at high computational cost. Al-Otum et al. [11] proposed a light-depth CNN (CNN-ILD) with geometric augmentation, reaching 98.05% accuracy in 8-class tasks and 11 fps—suggesting further gains via generative or KD methods. Khosa et al. [12] used handcrafted features (GLCM, LBP) and shallow CNNs/ANNs for lightweight classification, achieving 94.3% binary and 83.5% multiclass accuracy with 1.3M parameters and fast convergence. Thomsen et al. [13] integrated conformal prediction with VGG-13 for uncertainty-aware learning, improving macro F1 from 0.44 to 0.63 with minimal expert review, albeit at higher computational cost. Li et al. [14] presented a multi-model framework for GaAs solar cells using MobileNetV2 and decoupled heads, achieving 95.64% AP and 100% binary accuracy at 13.29 FPS, highlighting the future potential of unifying such designs via KD or attention mechanisms.

Table 1. Summary of Deep Learning Approaches for Solar Cell Defect Classification

Ref.	Year	Dataset	Model	Performance	Limitations
(9)	2024	PV IR	TLDR-CNN with MSFE on VGG16	94.1% acc., 95.7% F1 Score	Moderate size; not optimized for edge
(10)	2024	ELPV, EL	Weighted CNN with GAN, cGAN, WGAN-GP	94.1% acc, 96.7% recall	High compute cost for GAN training
(11)	2023	ELPV	CNN-ILD vs. ResNet18, ShuffleNet	98.05% acc (8-class), 11 fps	Relies on geom. aug.; suggests KD/gen.
(12)	2023	EL	Shallow CNN with GLCM, LBP, ANN	94.3% bin acc, 83.5% multi, 23× faster	Simple aug., shallow design limits advanced
(13)	2023	EL	VGG-13 + Conformal pred.	Macro F1: 0.44 to 0.63, 9.4% flagged	More compute due to multi-net cross-val
(14)	2024	GaAs data	MobileNetV2, YOLOv5s (K-means)	95.6% AP (mismatch), +11.3 mAP, 100% at 13.3 FPS	Multi-stage; needs KD/attention

Despite advances in deep learning for PV defect classification, challenges remain, particularly data imbalance, high computational costs, and the scarcity of lightweight models suited for resource-limited deployment. Notably, few studies explore KD to transfer the rich representations of large models like ViT into efficient architectures. To address this gap, this study proposes a KD framework that distills feature knowledge from a ViT teacher to a MobileNetV3 student, aiming to maintain high classification accuracy while ensuring low computational overhead for real-time PV inspection.

2.2   Using Knowledge Distillation for Computer Vision Tasks

KD has emerged as a widely adopted technique for reducing model complexity by transferring the learned representations from a large, well-trained teacher network to a more compact student model [15]. Its effectiveness has been demonstrated across diverse domains, including image classification [17] and natural language processing [18], where KD consistently enhances the performance of lightweight models without incurring significant computational costs.

Salamah et al. [19] propose coded knowledge distillation (CKD), introducing an adaptive JPEG compression layer before the teacher to mitigate overconfident outputs and improve generalization. Tested on ImageNet, CIFAR-100, and fine-grained datasets, CKD outperforms standard KD and adversarial methods, but increases complexity due to adaptive encoding. Building on the idea of enhancing student learning via richer teacher guidance, Fu et al. [20] propose Interactive Knowledge Distillation (IAKD), where teacher blocks are dynamically swapped into the student network during training. Unlike Salamah coded KD that modifies logits, IAKD uses direct feature transformation, improving classification without extra distillation losses or hyperparameter tuning. Chen et al. [21] appliedKD with lightweight CNN to cervical cell classification, using soft targets from an Inception-ResNetV2 teacher to improve MobileNet and Xception performance. Their hybrid loss enhanced accuracy under limited resources, demonstrating KD potential for medical image tasks, though requiring careful teacher design and hyperparameter tuning.

2.3   Research Gap and Motivation

Recent advances in deep learning have improved PV defect classification, yet practical deployment remains constrained by reliance on heavy architectures and extensive augmentation, limiting use on edge devices like drones and IoT systems. Lightweight models with high accuracy under efficiency constraints are still lacking. In contrast, KD has proven effective in computer vision, enabling compact models to approach the performance of larger ones through techniques like coded KD [19], interactive distillation [20], and hybrid KD for medical imaging [21]. However, KD remains underexplored for transferring ViT global representations into efficient CNNs for PV defect tasks. To address this gap, we propose a KD framework where a ViT-B-8 teacher distills knowledge into a MobileNetV3 student, aiming for high classification accuracy with low computational cost-supporting real-time, edge-friendly PV inspection.

3 Methodology

This section outlines the proposed knowledge distillation framework for multi-class solar cell defect classification, as illustrated in Fig. 1. The process begins with data collection, cleaning, augmentation, and balanced splitting to improve model robustness. At the core of the framework is the transfer of knowledge from a high-capacity teacher model (ViT Base, 8×8 patch size) to a lightweight student model (MobileNetV3) using both soft and hard distillation losses. The final phase involves evaluating the model's performance in terms of accuracy, precision, recall, F1-score, inference time, and model size, demonstrating that the student model can closely match the teacher's performance while offering improved efficiency for real-world deployment.

3.1 Dataset Collection

This study utilizes the publicly available PVEL-AD dataset [22], which contains near-infrared EL images of PV cells. Originally designed for binary anomaly detection, we restructured the dataset for multi-class classification, focusing on eight common defect types: Crack, Finger Interruption, Star-Crack, Thick Line, Short Circuit, Horizontal Dislocation, Vertical Dislocation, and Black-Core. This reformulation enables detailed defect characterization and supports the development of models capable of detecting multiple defect classes simultaneously enhancing diagnostic precision for PV system maintenance and quality control.

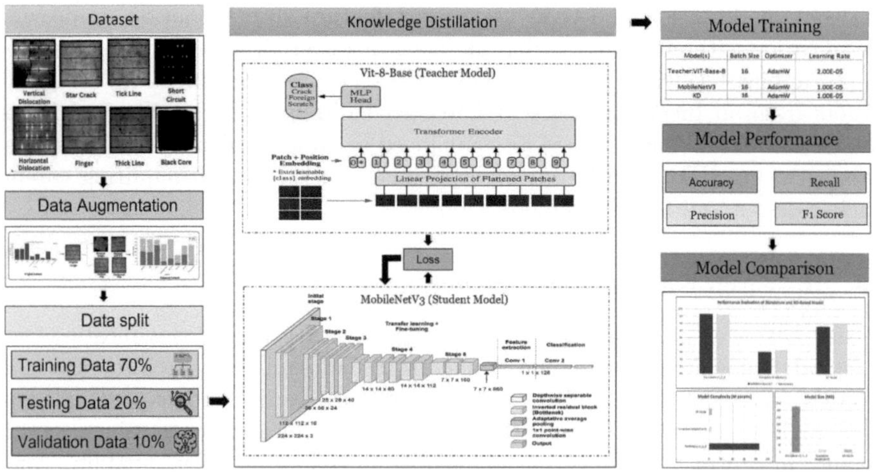

Fig. 1. Proposed Architecture for knowledge distillation framework for multi-class solar cell defect classification.

3.2   Data Augmentation

To address class imbalance and enhance generalization, this study applied data augmentation using geometric transformations such as random rotations, tilting, and horizontal/vertical flips [23,24]. These augmentations increased sample diversity and generated additional examples for underrepresented defect classes [25,26], resulting in a more balanced and comprehensive dataset. As shown in Fig. 2, these methods were key to improving the model's performance in multi-class defect classification.

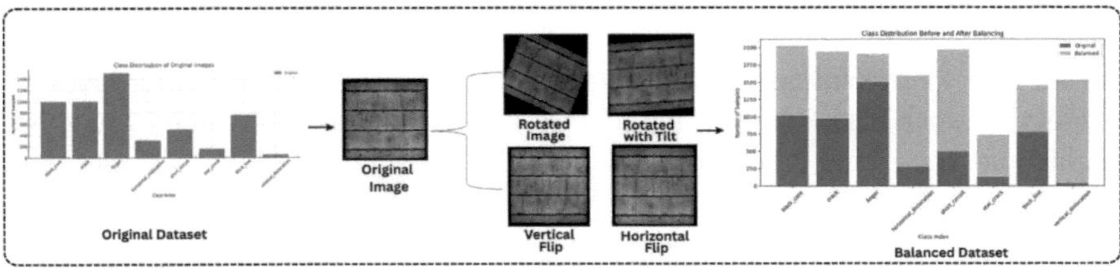

Fig. 2. Visualization of data augmentation and balancing process.

3.3   Proposed Lightweight Knowledge Distillation Framework

In this section, we present a compact knowledge distillation framework that transfers knowledge from a high-capacity (complex) teacher model to a compact student model, enabling efficient multi-class solar cell defect classification. This approach significantly reduces computational and memory requirements while maintaining competitive accuracy, making it ideal for edge deployments in smart manufacturing environments.

ViT Base 8-Patch (Teacher Model). In this study, we used the ViT as our teacher model, specifically the ViT-Base architecture with an 8-pixel patch size (ViT-B-8). The ViT processes an input image $x \in \mathbb{R}^{H \times W \times C}$ by first splitting it into a sequence of flattened patches. Given patch size $P = 8$, the image is divided into $N = \frac{HW}{P^2}$ patches.

Each patch is then linearly projected into a D-dimensional embedding space, with positional information added:

$$z_0^i = E \, \text{flatten}(x_p^i) + p_i \tag{1}$$

where $E \in \mathbb{R}^{(P^2 C) \times D}$ is the learnable projection matrix, x_p^i denotes the i-th patch, and p_i is its positional encoding.

The input sequence, including a learnable class token $z_0^{[CLS]}$, becomes:

$$Z_0 = [z_0^{[CLS]}, z_0^1, z_0^2, \ldots, z_0^N] \in \mathbb{R}^{(N+1) \times D} \tag{2}$$

This sequence is then processed by $L = 12$ identical transformer encoder layers. Each layer applies multi-head self-attention (MHSA) and a feed-forward network (MLP), formulated as:

$$Z'_\ell = \text{MHSA}(\text{LN}(Z_{\ell-1})) + Z_{\ell-1} \tag{3}$$

$$Z_\ell = \text{MLP}(\text{LN}(Z'_\ell)) + Z'_\ell \tag{4}$$

for each layer $\ell = 1, \ldots, L$, where LN denotes layer normalization and the residual connections stabilize learning.

Finally, classification is performed using the output of the class token through a linear head:

$$\hat{y} = \text{Softmax}(W_{\text{head}} \, z_L^{[CLS]} + b_{\text{head}}) \tag{5}$$

where $z_L^{[CLS]}$ is the transformed class token after the final transformer layer.

For this work, the ViT-B/8 model was initialized with pretrained ImageNet weights and fine-tuned on our balanced multi-class solar cell defect dataset. ViT Base achieves high accuracy due to its global attention mechanism and rich feature representations, but its performance comes at the cost of increased computational complexity and memory usage (approximately 86 million parameters and 17.56 GFLOPs), making it more suitable for server-side inference.

MobileNetV3 (Student Model). This study employs MobileNetV3-Large as the student model, a lightweight CNN optimized for efficient inference on resource-constrained devices. Its design incorporates depthwise separable convolutions, squeeze-and-excitation (SE) modules, and hard-swish activations to balance accuracy and efficiency, making it ideal for real-time PV inspection on drones, mobile devices, and IoT sensors.

Among lightweight alternatives such as ShuffleNet, EfficientNet-Lite, SqueezeNet, MobileNetV3 was chosen due to its superior ImageNet performance, NAS derived optimizations, strong edge deployment support, and proven efficiency in low-power environments [27–31]. However, when trained alone on our eight-class defect dataset, it showed limited accuracy due to reduced representational capacity.

Its lightweight nature, nonetheless, makes MobileNetV3 an ideal candidate for knowledge distillation. By learning from a ViT-B/8 teacher, it can gain richer feature representations and improve defect classification performance while retaining the low computational cost required for real-time deployment.

Knowledge Distillation Loss and Training Framework. The KD framework integrates outputs from the ViT teacher and the MobileNetV3 student. The student is trained using a composite loss:

$$\mathcal{L}_{\text{total}} = \alpha\mathcal{L}_{\text{hard}} + \beta\mathcal{L}_{\text{soft}} + \gamma\mathcal{L}_{\text{feature}} \tag{6}$$

where $\mathcal{L}_{\text{hard}}$ is the standard cross-entropy loss on ground truth labels, $\mathcal{L}_{\text{soft}}$ measures divergence between the student and teacher logits (e.g., using Kullback-Leibler divergence), and $\mathcal{L}_{\text{feature}}$ encourages alignment of intermediate feature maps. The hyperparameters α, β, and γ balance these objectives.

By combining these losses, the framework guides the lightweight student to learn not only the final class predictions but also intermediate representations, thereby effectively inheriting the ViT's rich feature extraction capabilities.

4 Results

We evaluate the proposed knowledge distillation framework, in which a lightweight MobileNetV3-Small student learns from a high-capacity ViT-Base-8 teacher. This framework enables the student model to inherit the rich feature representations of the transformer while maintaining computational efficiency. Compared to baseline models, including ViT-Base variants with different patch sizes and ResNet-50, the distilled MobileNetV3-Small achieves competitive classification performance while offering significantly lower inference time, reduced parameter count, and minimal memory consumption. These results highlight the effectiveness of the KD approach in delivering a balanced solution for real-time, resource-constrained PV defect inspection tasks.

4.1 Training Dynamics of KD Framework

Figure 3 illustrates the training behavior of the MobileNetV3 student under the KD framework. Training and validation losses steadily decrease, converging below 0.02 by epoch 80, indicating stable optimization. The loss decomposition shows soft loss dominates early as the student absorbs knowledge from the ViT teacher, then declines over time. Hard and feature losses remain low and stable, supporting accurate learning. Accuracy curves for both training and validation rise steadily and converge near 98.8%, confirming strong generalization.

Figure 4 compares the final model performances. The KD-based MobileNetV3 achieves 98.8% validation and 98.6% test accuracy—closely approaching the ViT-B/8 teacher (99.2%) and outperforming the standalone MobileNetV3 (94.0%). With only 4.85M parameters and a 23 MB model size, it maintains a lightweight profile ideal for real-time edge deployment.

Table 2 further quantifies this trade-off. ViT-B/8 achieves the highest F1-score (99.10%) but requires 17.56 GFLOPs and 0.00873 s per image. The standalone MobileNetV3 is highly efficient (0.22 GFLOPs, 0.00049 s), but lags in performance (F1: 89.80%). The KD-enhanced MobileNetV3 achieves a strong balance, boosting F1-score to 94.90% with only a slight increase in compute (0.28 GFLOPs), validating the KD framework's effectiveness in improving accuracy while maintaining deployment efficiency.

These results highlight the effectiveness of the proposed KD framework. By distilling both soft logits and intermediate features from the ViT teacher, the MobileNetV3 student gains enhanced discriminative power-achieving an F1-score within 4% of the teacher while reducing parameters and GFLOPs by over 60×. It also outperforms the standalone student by nearly 5%.

As shown in Fig. 3, minimal gap between training and validation accuracy suggests that KD acts as an implicit regularizer, improving generalization. With

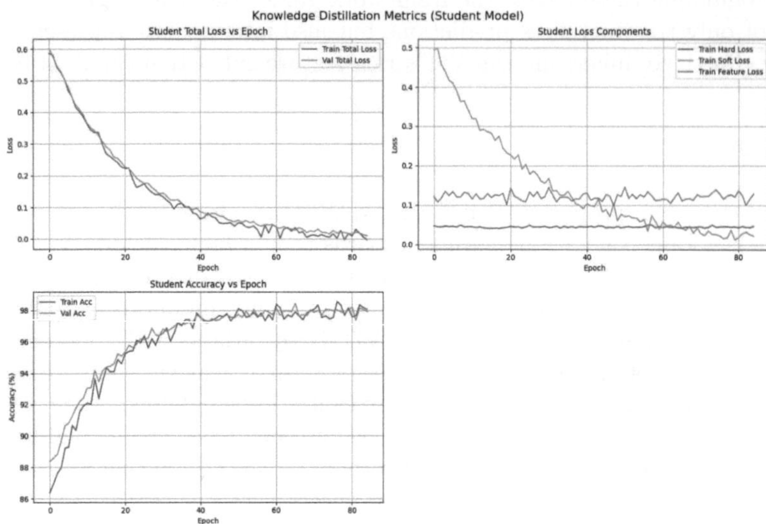

Fig. 3. Knowledge distillation training dynamics of the MobileNetV3 student model.

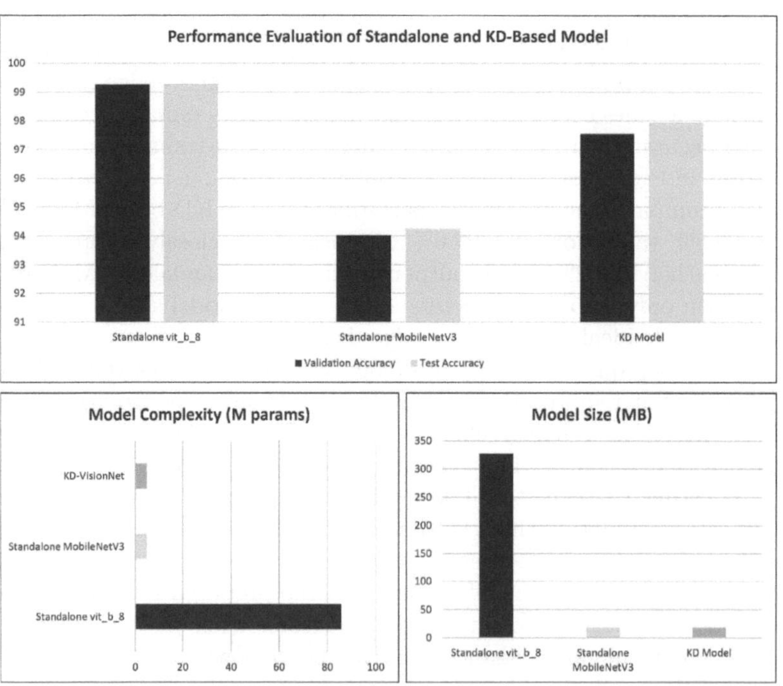

Fig. 4. Performance and complexity comparison of standalone models and the KD-based approach.

Table 2. Comparison of classification performance and computational efficiency among the standalone ViT-B/8 teacher, standalone MobileNetV3 student, and the proposed KD-based MobileNetV3 model.

Model	Precision	Recall	F1-Score	Inference (s/image)	GFLOPs
ViT-B-8	99.20	99.00	99.10	0.00873	17.56
MobileNetV3	90.20	89.50	89.80	0.00049	0.22
KD Model (Ours)	95.10	94.70	94.90	0.00049	0.28

its compact size (23 MB), low compute (0.28 GFLOPs), and fast inference (0.49 ms/image), the KD student is well-suited for real-time, edge-based PV inspection. Overall, this demonstrates KD's potential to enhance lightweight models for robust and scalable defect monitoring.

5   Conclusion

This study presents a lightweight KD framework for multi-class solar cell defect classification, using the powerful ViT-B-8 teacher model to guide a compact MobileNetV3 student model. Through soft and hard distillation, the student inherits rich feature representations, enabling it to achieve 98.6% test accuracy, 0.949 F1-score, and significantly reduced model complexity. Compared to the standalone MobileNetV3, the KD model improves accuracy by over 4%, while retaining fast inference speed (0.49 ms/image) and low computational cost (0.28 GFLOPs). Our findings show that knowledge distillation successfully narrows the performance gap between large, high-performing models and compact models, making it a viable approach for real-time solar panel monitoring on edge-based systems. The proposed approach achieves a strong trade-off between accuracy and efficiency, outperforming several baseline architectures.

Acknowledgments. This work was supported by the National Research Foundation of Korea (NRF) grant funded by the Korea government (MSIT) (No. RS-2024-00405278), and by the National Research Foundation (NRF) of Korea under the project BK21 FOUR.

References

1. Kapsalis, V., et al.: Bottom-up energy transition through rooftop PV upscaling: remaining issues and emerging upgrades towards NZEBs at different climatic conditions. Renew. Sustain. Energy Transit. 100083 (2024)
2. Abdulla, H., Sleptchenko, A., Nayfeh, A.: Photovoltaic systems operation and maintenance: a review and future directions. Renew. Sustain. Energy Rev. **195**, 114342 (2024)
3. Shaban, W.M.: Detection and classification of photovoltaic module defects based on artificial intelligence. Neural Comput. Appl. **36**(27), 16769–16796 (2024)

4. Abdelsattar, M., AbdelMoety, A., Ismeil, M.A., Emad-Eldeen, A.: Automated defect detection in solar cell images using deep learning algorithms. IEEE Access (2025)

5. Pratt, L.: Deep learning models for defect detection in electroluminescence images of solar PV modules. PhD thesis, University of the Witwatersrand (2024)

6. Yunusa, H., Qin, S., Chukkol, A.H.A., Yusuf, A.A., Bello, I., Lawan, A.: Exploring the synergies of hybrid CNNs and ViTs architectures for computer vision: a survey. arXiv preprint arXiv:2402.02941 (2024)

7. Xu, Y., Khan, T.M., Song, Y., Meijering, E.: Edge deep learning in computer vision and medical diagnostics: a comprehensive survey. Artif. Intell. Rev. 58(3), 1–78 (2025)

8. Demirci, M.Y., Beşli, N., Gümüşçü, A.: An improved hybrid solar cell defect detection approach using generative adversarial networks and weighted classification. Expert Syst. Appl. 252, 124230 (2024)

9. Tang, R., Ren, Z., Ning, S., Zhang, Y.: Fault classification of photovoltaic module infrared images based on transfer learning and interpretable convolutional neural network. Sol. Energy 276, 112703 (2024)

10. Demirci, M.Y., Beşli, N., Gümüşçü, A.: An improved hybrid solar cell defect detection approach using Generative Adversarial Networks and weighted classification. Expert Syst. Appl. 252, 124230 (2024)

11. Al-Otum, H.M.: Deep learning-based automated defect classification in Electroluminescence images of solar panels. Adv. Eng. Inform. 58, 102147 (2023)

12. Khosa, I., et al.: Fault-level grading of photovoltaic cells employing lightweight deep learning models. Comput. Intell. Neurosci. 2023, 2663150 (2023)

13. Thomsen, V.B., Mantel, C., dos Reis Benatto, G.A., Engsig-Karup, A.P., Forchhammer, S.: Improving deep learning-based defect classification in solar cells using conformal prediction. In: Proceedings of 50th IEEE Photovoltaic Specialists Conference (PVSC), pp. 1–6 (2023)

14. Li, Z., Zhang, S., Qu, C., Zhang, Z., Sun, F.: Research on multi-defects classification detection method for solar cells based on deep learning. PLoS ONE 19(6), e0304819 (2024)

15. Park, I., Kim, W.H., Ryu, J.: Style-KD: class-imbalanced medical image classification via style knowledge distillation. Biomed. Signal Process. Control 91, 105928 (2024)

16. Ma, Y., Zou, X., Pan, Q., Yan, M., Li, G.: Target-embedding autoencoder with knowledge distillation for multi-label classification. IEEE Trans. Emerg. Top. Comput, Intell (2024)

17. Belinga, A.G., Tekouabou Koumetio, C.S., Haziti, M., Hassouni, M.: Knowledge distillation in image classification: the impact of datasets. Computers 13(8), 184 (2024)

18. Mei, T., Zi, Y., Cheng, X., Gao, Z., Wang, Q., Yang, H.: Efficiency optimization of large-scale language models based on deep learning in natural language processing tasks. In: 2024 IEEE 2nd Internation Conference on Sensors, Electronics and Computer Engineering (ICSECE), pp. 1231–1237. IEEE (2024)

19. Salamah, A.H., Hamidi, S.M., Yang, E.-H.: A coded knowledge distillation framework for image classification based on adaptive JPEG encoding. Pattern Recogn. 158, 110966 (2025)

20. Fu, S., Li, Z., Liu, Z., Yang, X.: Interactive knowledge distillation for image classification. Neurocomputing 449, 411–421 (2021)

21. Chen, W., Gao, L., Li, X., Shen, W.: Lightweight convolutional neural network with knowledge distillation for cervical cells classification. Biomed. Signal Process. Control **71**, 103177 (2022)
22. Binyisu, P.: Photovoltaic electroluminescence anomaly detection dataset. GitHub repository (2022). https://github.com/binyisu/PVEL-AD
23. Hwang, D., Kim, J.-J., Moon, S., Wang, S.: Image augmentation approaches for building dimension estimation in street view images using object detection and instance segmentation based on deep learning. Appl. Sci. **15**(5) (2025)
24. Han, J., Kim, J., Kim, S., Wang, S.: Effectiveness of image augmentation techniques on detection of building characteristics from street view images using deep learning. J. Constr. Eng. Manag. **150**(10), 04024129 (2024)
25. Rathod, V.M., Patil, A.M., Motekar, H.S., Usmani, M., Solavande, V.D., Rathod, S.B.: Automatic face recognition based on enhanced VGGFace-16 model in an unconstrained environment using transfer learning. Multimed. Tools Appl. 1–23 (2025)
26. Chaari, A., Fourati Kallel, I., Kammoun, S., Frikha, M.: Hybrid data augmentation strategies for robust deep learning classification of corneal topographic map. Express, Biomed. Phys. Eng (2025)
27. Das, S.R., Salih, A., Sulaiman, R.B., Farhan, M.: Enhancing lung cancer classification with MobileNetV3 and EfficientNetB7: a transfer learning approach. In: 2024 International Conference on Computer and Applications (ICCA), pp. 1–8. IEEE (2024)
28. Qin, D., et al.: MobileNetV4: universal models for the mobile ecosystem. In: European Conference on Computer Vision (ECCV), pp. 78–96. Springer (2024)
29. Mahto, I.C., Mathew, J.: Compact deep learning models for leaf disease classification and recognition in precision agriculture. Neural Comput. Appl. 1–21 (2025)
30. Islam, M., Azad, A.K.M., Arman, S.E., Alyami, S.A., Hasan, M.M.: PlantCareNet: an advanced system to recognize plant diseases with dual-mode recommendations for prevention. Plant Methods **21**(1), 52 (2025)
31. Kaviani, N.: Track geometry monitoring using measured data from commercial trains towards predictive maintenance. Technical report, Università degli Studi di Roma "La Sapienza" (2024)

Task-Evoked BOLD Contrast and Machine Learning for Schizophrenia Classification: A DMN-Focused and Whole-Brain Analysis

Akansha Gautam[1], Indranath Chatterjee[2(✉)], Suruchi Gautam[3], and Naveen Kumar[1]

[1] Department of Computer Science, University of Delhi, Delhi 110007, India
[2] Department of Computing and Mathematics, Manchester Metropolitan University, Manchester M1 5GD, UK
i.chatterjee@mmu.ac.uk
[3] Department of Computer Science, Rajdhani College, University of Delhi, Delhi 110015, India

Abstract. Machine learning methods are now widely used to study fMRI data in schizophrenia. One commonly studied brain network is the Default Mode Network (DMN), but its usefulness in tasks like classification is still not fully known. In this work, we tested if brain activity patterns from DMN regions, during an auditory oddball task, can help separate schizophrenia patients from healthy controls. We used data from the FBIRN Phase 2 3T dataset (25 schizophrenia and 25 controls). From the DMN areas defined by the Yeo atlas, we took voxel-wise contrast values (deviant > standard), and after selecting features and applying PCA, we trained logistic regression models. Models using only DMN features gave around 50% accuracy, close to chance. But models using whole-brain data performed better, with accuracy up to 80% and average cross-validated accuracy of 67.5%. Interpretation using SHAP showed that most useful voxels were not in the DMN but in visual and cerebellar areas. This suggests that DMN alone may not be enough for schizophrenia classification in task-based fMRI. Future work should focus on combining multiple brain networks.

Keywords: Schizophrenia · Default Mode Network · Functional MRI · Machine Learning · Principal Component Analysis · SHapley Additive exPlanations

1 Introduction

Schizophrenia is a complex psychiatric disorder that typically emerges in late adolescence or early adulthood, marked by positive symptoms (hallucinations, delusions), negative symptoms (anhedonia, apathy), and cognitive impairments (attention and working memory deficits). Its heterogeneous presentation and variable course suggest it is a spectrum disorder. Neuroimaging studies reveal structural and functional abnormalities, including dysconnectivity in major networks. Schizophrenia is associated with significant alterations in brain function and connectivity patterns, which tend to worsen with age and can be effectively studied using advanced neuroimaging techniques (Chatterjee

© The Author(s) 2026
B.-G. Kim et al. (Eds.): MITA 2025, CCIS 2675, pp. 64–78, 2026.
https://doi.org/10.1007/978-981-95-3141-7_6

et al., 2020). The Default Mode Network (DMN) shows reduced task-induced deactivation, while the Salience and Central Executive Networks show hyper- and hypoactivity, respectively. Recent reviews have pointed out the disconnect between major brain systems in schizophrenia. They highlight abnormalities present in both resting states and during tasks (Colizzi & Baselli, 2023). Dong et al. (2018) reported widespread alterations in resting-state functional connectivity across core intrinsic brain networks.

The Default Mode Network (DMN) is a large brain network that shows more activity during rest and less during tasks that require focus. It helps with internal processes like self-reflection, memory retrieval, and mental simulation. Key regions include the medial prefrontal cortex, posterior cingulate cortex, precuneus, and angular gyri—these interconnected hubs support introspection, memory retrieval, and perspective-taking, forming the core of the DMN. The DMN includes several brain regions, such as the left and right angular gyrus (lAG and rAG), the posterior cingulate cortex (PCC), and the medial prefrontal cortex (mPFC). It is known to have a negative correlation with task-positive activity, leading to the idea of a "default state" (Marino, M., et al., 2022). Good cognitive function depends on switching between the DMN and task-positive networks. This process can be disrupted in mental health conditions. In schizophrenia, problems with DMN deactivation and unusual connectivity contribute to symptoms like hallucinations and disorganized thinking (Menon, 2023). Disrupted functional connectivity (FC) of the default mode network (DMN) may play a role in the development of schizophrenia (Sasabayashi, D., et al., 2023).

The Default Mode Network (DMN) is important for executive functions and accurate responses. It deactivates during hard tasks, which lets other networks like the frontoparietal control network focus on attention and cognitive control. In schizophrenia, the DMN often shows unusually high activity, even when at rest. Sendi et al. (2021) found that patients spend more time in hyperconnected DMN states, which are connected to more severe symptoms. These patterns might disrupt the brain's ability to switch from focusing inward to processing relevant tasks. This disruption can indirectly lead to cognitive and functional impairments. Additionally, problems with DMN activation during tasks that require response inhibition relate to trouble switching focus between internal and external stimuli. This contributes to cognitive inflexibility and attention issues frequently seen in schizophrenia (Krakowski et al., 2024).

The auditory oddball paradigm is a key method in cognitive neuroscience. Researchers use it to study how the brain reacts to unexpected sounds. This approach usually features common standard tones, which are interrupted by rare deviant tones that vary in pitch or duration. These deviant tones trigger the P300 event-related potential (ERP), a known neural marker of attention and working memory updates. Changes in the P300 response have been seen in people with schizophrenia. These changes are being investigated as possible biomarkers for psychosis risk or heritable traits that link genetic factors to clinical symptoms (Hamilton et al., 2024). The auditory oddball paradigm reliably evokes neural responses in schizophrenia, with recent large-scale fMRI studies showing robust hypoactivation in the left frontal pole, precuneus, hippocampus, and thalamus in patients compared to controls, correlating with both cognitive deficits and elevated polygenic risk scores (Nakahara et al., 2023).

The growing complexity of neuroimaging data has led to increased use of machine learning (ML) in psychiatric research, especially for schizophrenia. Techniques such as univariate feature selection and logistic regression help identify the most informative brain regions while reducing dimensionality. Interpretability has become a major focus in clinical applications, with tools like SHAP offering insights into model decisions at the voxel level. Schnack and Kahn (2016) pointed out that having a sufficient sample size is crucial for detecting strong neuroimaging biomarkers. Durstewitz et al. (2019) emphasized the need for explainable ML in psychiatry. Recent work shows multi-view deep learning models that combine imaging and behavioral data while keeping interpretability intact through new frameworks (Munroe et al., 2024). Various machine learning and deep learning techniques have demonstrated effectiveness in analyzing fMRI data to identify functional brain alterations, as shown in recent neuroimaging research (Chatterjee et al., 2023).

The DMN has been widely studied in schizophrenia, mainly through resting-state analyses. However, this data may not show how the brain responds during cognitive tasks. New research suggests that schizophrenia patients often do not deactivate the DMN when focusing on tasks outside themselves. This indicates they struggle to shift their attention from internal thoughts to external stimuli (Krakowski et al., 2024). Disruptions in DMN connectivity during task engagement have been observed in schizophrenia using EEG-based paradigms (Guha et al., 2024). Tools like SHAP help pinpoint specific areas that contribute to classification decisions (Chen et al., 2018). Also, clear models improve clinical relevance and transparency (Doshi-Velez & Kim, 2017).

This research is based on the hypothesis that contrast features obtained solely from the DMN when engaged with tasks might lack enough discriminatory power to correctly classify schizophrenia patients from healthy controls. Since neurobiological dysfunction in schizophrenia is widespread and heterogeneous, it is expected that models using whole-brain information would perform better than those limited to DMN alone. But determining the unique contribution of the DMN during cognitive load is still significant, especially with its recognized role in self-referential processing and task-evoked deactivation. Thus, the primary research question motivating this inquiry is: "Are machine learning algorithms trained on task-evoked BOLD contrast patterns in DMN regions able to distinguish schizophrenia patients from healthy subjects reliably?" This question seeks not only to evaluate the predictive power of DMN features but also investigate their interpretability considering established cognitive and clinical disturbances of the disorder.

2   Materials and Methods

2.1   Participants and Data Acquisition (FBIRN Phase 2 Dataset)

A. Participants

Twenty-five patients who were diagnosed with schizophrenia based on DSM-IV criteria were selected. All the patients were clinically stable at scanning time and were recruited from several imaging sites which were involved in the FBIRN Phase 2 study. There were standardized scanning protocols used at all the sites to maintain data consistency. The control group included twenty-five individuals who did not present any known psychiatric or neurological disorder. The same demographic makeup in relation to age and gender was ensured between the two groups. All the subjects at all sites were scanned using the same imaging parameters and protocols (as shown in Table 1).

In the FBIRN Phase II auditory oddball dataset, the subgroup scanned on 3 T (3T) MRI scanners included 25 schizophrenia patients and 25 healthy control participants. These 3T subjects were adults aged between 18 and 70 years old. On average, both groups were in their mid-30s, with mean ages of about 37 years for patients and 35 years for controls; there was no significant age difference between the groups. The gender makeup was also similar across the groups, with more male participants in each. For example, in the overall Phase II oddball cohort, about 70 to 78% of participants were male in both the schizophrenia and control groups, showing a similar male majority in the 3T subset.

B. Auditory Oddball Task Paradigm

In the auditory oddball (AUD) task, participants listened to a continuous flow of tones. This included frequent standard tones at 1000 Hz, making up 95% of the sounds, and rare deviant tones at 1200 Hz, which accounted for 5%. Each tone lasted 100 ms. Participants had to focus on a central fixation cross shown on a gray screen and press a button when they heard a deviant tone. The task started and ended with 15 s of silence. Deviant tones appeared every 6 to 15 s. The FBIRN ran this task for 280 s in each session, collecting 140 brain scans per session with a repetition time (TR) of 2 s.

C. fMRI Data Preprocessing

Preprocessing was performed using Statistical Parametric Mapping (SPM8) toolbox, including motion correction, slice timing, spatial normalization to MNI space, resampling to $3 \times 3 \times 3$ mm^3, and smoothing with a 9 mm FWHM Gaussian kernel.

D. First-Level Analysis

The General Linear Model (GLM) analyzed the preprocessed fMRI data to create subject-level activation maps for the auditory oddball (AUD) task. For each participant, the 4D time-series data were modeled to produce a single 3D contrast map. This map shows the difference in BOLD activation between deviant and standard tones. Each voxel in the map reflects the contrast evoked by the task, with higher or lower values indicating increased or decreased activation. No statistical thresholding was used at this stage, so the maps kept the raw contrast values across all brain voxels (about 153,594). To ensure reliability, the contrast maps from four runs per subject were averaged to create one mean contrast map for each individual. These spatial maps were then applied in downstream machine learning processes, including both DMN-constrained and whole-brain voxel analyses.

2.2 DMN Definition and Feature Extraction.

A. Identifying DMN Regions of Interest (Using Yeo 7-network Atlas)

In order to delineate areas related to the DMN, we used the Yeo 7-network parcellation, an accepted functional atlas derived from large resting-state datasets. The atlas divides the cerebral cortex into seven known functional networks, one being the DMN. By mapping the parcellation onto the brain volume, we created a binary mask labeling voxels assigned to the DMN. To add anatomical precision and remove extraneous non-brain space, the DMN mask was intersected with a standard whole-brain mask, leaving only voxels that were in both categories. This left us with a refined set of spatial coordinates labeling specifically DMN-related brain areas. The voxels preserved formed the foundation of further analysis, allowing us to extract task-related BOLD contrast features (deviant > standard) within the network for further machine learning use.

B. Extraction of Task-Evoked BOLD Contrast Values (Deviant > Standard) Within DMN

From each participant's deviant versus standard contrast map, obtained after GLM analysis, voxel-wise BOLD values were extracted to create two different sets of features for later analysis. In the first method, values were limited to voxels within the Yeo 7-network DMN mask. This produced about 8,337 voxels, or features, per participant. The values were then processed using Principal Component Analysis (PCA) without any pre-statistical filtering. The second method used a whole-brain approach. It included contrast values from all available brain voxels, which totaled around 153,594, based on the brain mask provided by Nilearn. To eliminate features that had no variability among participants, we removed all voxels that were constant across the group. This step resulted in a refined feature set of around 78,000 voxels, preserving meaningful variation. These high-dimensional features were then reduced through PCA, and SHAP values were applied to the trained model to pinpoint the most important voxels for classifying schizophrenia.

2.3 Machine Learning Pipeline

A. Feature Selection Within DMN

Several studies include machine learning (ML) and deep learning algorithms to automate the diagnosis of this mental disorder (Alves, C. L., et al., 2023). In our study, to address the high dimensionality of the fMRI BOLD contrast data (deviant > standard) relative to the sample size, two distinct feature engineering strategies were employed prior to classification: a DMN-constrained analysis and a whole-brain analysis. In the DMN-constrained analysis, approximately 8,337 voxels within the predefined Yeo 7-network DMN mask were directly utilized. These raw contrast values were passed to PCA without prior statistical filtering, thus preserving the spatial integrity of the DMN. For the whole-brain analysis, the initial dataset of approximately 153,594 voxels was first reduced to about 78,000 features by removing voxels with zero variance across participants. In both conditions, PCA was applied to project the high-dimensional data into a lower-dimensional space, retaining the top 10 components that explained the maximum variance across participants. These principal components served as input features for the classification models, a strategy crucial for mitigating overfitting and alleviating the curse of dimensionality. While no univariate statistical filtering was performed before classification, interpretability was conducted post-hoc using SHAP (SHapley

Additive exPlanations) to identify the most discriminative features. A summary of the PCA dimensionality reduction is provided in Table 1.

Table 1. PCA Dimensionality Reduction

Experiment	Initial Features	After Preprocessing	Number of Principal Components Used
DMN-Only	8,337 voxels	8,337 voxels	10
Whole-Brain	153,594 voxels	~78,000 voxels	10

B. Classification Model Training and Validation

Following dimensionality reduction, we constructed a logistic regression classifier from principal component scores of DMN-exclusive and whole-brain feature sets. The data were randomly divided into training and testing subsets with an 80–20 stratified split to maintain class balance. For assessing the model's generalizability and robustness, we applied 5-fold cross-validation on the training subset. Logistic regression was employed because of its interpretability and compatibility with small-sample neuroimaging sets (Chatterjee, I. 2021).

2.4 Interpretability Analysis

A. SHAP (SHapley Additive ExPlanations) for Feature Importance

It is essential to comprehend the rationale behind a model's particular prediction in the context of clinical neuroimaging application. To explain the forces behind classification, we performed a post hoc interpretability analysis based on voxel-wise SHAP values. This allowed us to measure the influence of every voxel feature on the model's decision-making process and investigate the spatial significance of functional abnormality. Once the logistic regression classifier was trained on the entire-whole brain feature set, SHAP values were calculated for every voxel for all subjects. They represent the average marginal contribution of each feature to the model's prediction over a large number of perturbed samples. The 10 voxels with the highest SHAP values are considered. The voxels were ranked by the average importance over the dataset. The most discriminative voxels were not in the DMN, but some were in the visual network (e.g., Occipital Fusiform Gyrus), and some mapped onto non-DMN background areas, showing the extensive network involvement in task-induced schizophrenia classification.

B. Mapping Important Features to Anatomical Locations and DMN Sub-regions

To put the model's results into perspective, we spatially mapped the highest SHAP-ranked voxels onto two of the most widely used atlases, Yeo 7-network atlas. The mapping outcomes showed that a single voxel coincided with the visual network (Yeo label), whereas the remaining voxels were labeled as "background" or "unknown" as they were located outside of standard cortical templates. This pattern was observed in both atlases, suggesting that the voxels ranked as most influential for classification did not belong to the standard DMN composition as per Yeo label 7.

3 Results and Discussions

3.1 Classification Performance

A. Comparison of Feature Selection Strategies

Two separate classification pipelines were developed to explore how different voxel selection strategies can support diagnosis: Pipeline A: DMN-Constrained Voxel Selection. In this approach, we extracted voxel-wise BOLD contrast values (Deviant > Standard) strictly from the Yeo-defined DMN mask. No statistical filtering or voxel ranking was applied; instead, all voxels within the DMN mask (~8,337 voxels) were retained. We then applied PCA to reduce the dimensionality of these features and used the resulting components to train a logistic regression classifier. Pipeline B: Whole-Brain Voxel Selection. This pipeline started with the full-brain voxel matrix. Constant features (voxels with zero variance across samples) were removed, yielding approximately 78,000 valid voxel features. PCA was then applied to this high-dimensional space, and the resulting principal components were used in the same logistic regression framework.

Table 2. Classification Accuracy Comparison Between Feature Selection Strategies

Pipeline	Feature Set	80–20 Accuracy	5-Fold Cross-Validated Accuracy	F1-Score
DMN-Only + PCA	8,337 DMN voxels	0.4	0.5	0.38
Whole Brain + PCA	~78,000 voxels	0.8	0.675	0.8

The classification results from these two pipelines were notably different. As shown in Table 2, the DMN-constrained approach had poor classification performance, while the whole-brain model demonstrated much higher accuracy. This highlights the distributed nature of signals related to disease. Figure 1 compares classification accuracy between the DMN-only model and whole-brain models. Apart from the 80–20 hold out approach, we have also implemented 5 fold cross validation. The whole-brain pipeline achieved a significantly higher test accuracy of 0.80 and a cross-validated accuracy of 0.68, showing it has better generalizability. In contrast, the DMN-only model performed close to chance levels, which highlights the limited ability of DMN-restricted features on their own to classify schizophrenia.

This finding indicates failure of discriminability and lack of significant signals in task-evoked DMN activity patterns alone. These findings indicate DMN-specific contrast values alone might be inadequate to classify schizophrenia and suggest the need for inputs from more than one network in task-directed studies.

B. Overall Model Accuracy and Robustness

Two separate classification pipelines were used to investigate how different voxel selection strategies can help in diagnosis. The whole-brain PCA and logistic regression model achieved 80% classification accuracy on the held-out test set. It also had a macro-average F1 score of 0.80 and showed balanced performance in both schizophrenia and control

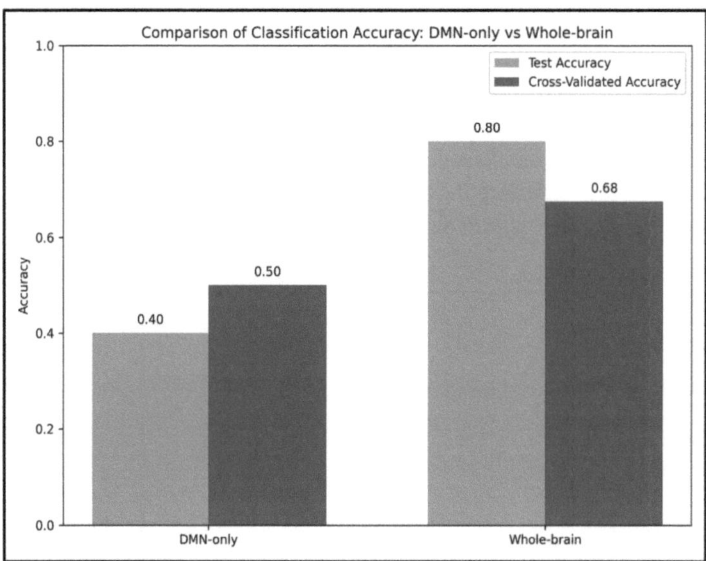

Fig. 1. Comparison of test and cross-validated accuracy between DMN-only and whole-brain models. The DMN-only model yielded 50% cross-validated accuracy as well as test accuracy. The whole-brain model yielded significantly improved 80% and 67.5% accuracy, respectively.

groups. Cross-validation on the training set gave an average classification accuracy of 67.5%, which shows moderate reliability. In contrast, the DMN-based model performed around chance level. This suggests that the task-evoked BOLD signal limited to the DMN does not offer enough difference for classification. These results highlight the importance of using broader, multi-network feature representations when creating machine learning classifiers for psychiatric diagnosis.

3.2 Important DMN Features for Classification

A. Top PCA Components

To assess how individual features affected classification decisions, SHAP scores were calculated on the principal components (PCs) from both DMN-constrained and whole-brain voxel features. In the DMN-only pipeline, researchers selected the top 1,000 voxels within the Yeo Default Mode Network using an F-test. They then applied PCA for dimensionality reduction and kept ten PCs to train a logistic regression classifier. SHAP analysis showed that PCs 1, 2, and 3 had a moderate influence. However, the model achieved only 50% accuracy and 0.5 cross-validated accuracy, which is about chance level. This suggests limited ability to discriminate in DMN-restricted task-evoked activity.

In contrast, the whole-brain pipeline involved removing constant features while retaining around 78,000 active voxels. PCA reduced these to ten components that were used in the same logistic regression setup. This model achieved 80% accuracy on the test set and 67.5% in cross-validation. In this case, SHAP scores displayed a clearer importance curve, with PC1 and PC2 being the main contributors to the prediction.

As shown in Fig. 2, each dot represents a subject's SHAP value per component, with colors indicating the corresponding feature intensity. Positive SHAP values support classification for schizophrenia, while negative values suggest healthy controls. Figure 3a and 3b show the bar plots of mean SHAP values for DMN-only and whole-brain features, respectively. The whole-brain PCs demonstrate stronger and more focused importance, particularly PC1 and PC2, indicating higher predictive relevance compared to the weaker contributions in the DMN-only model.

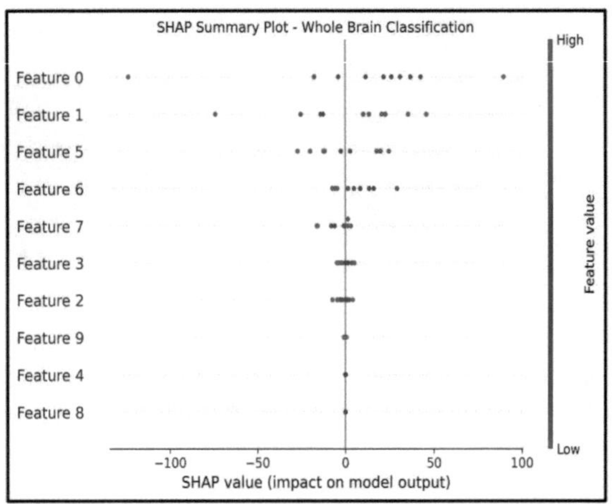

Fig. 2. SHAP Summary Plot for Whole-Brain Classification

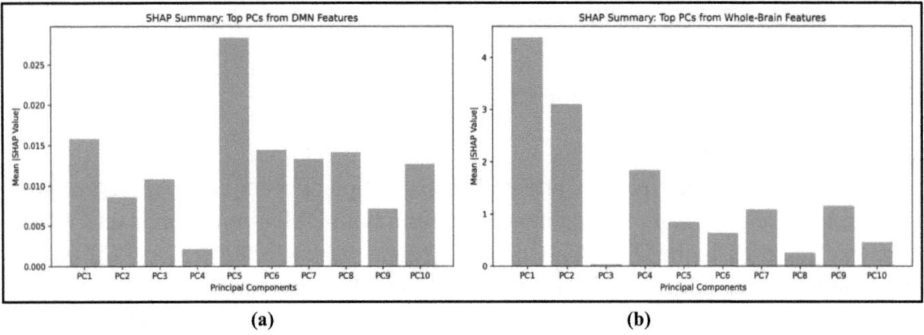

Fig. 3. (a) & (b) Illustrate the SHAP summary plots for the top principal components (PCs) derived from DMN-constrained voxel features and whole-brain voxel features, respectively.

To see how much of the variance was retained in dimensionality reduction, we plotted (see Fig. 4) the variance explained by the first 10 principal components of DMN-constrained and whole-brain feature sets. The scree plot shows the variance explained by the top 10 principal components for both DMN-only and whole-brain feature sets. The whole-brain data (red) captures significantly more variance in the first few components.

The first principal component alone explains over 45%. In contrast, the DMN-only features (orange) display a flatter trend, with each component contributing uniformly and modestly, around 2%. This suggests that whole-brain data contains richer, more varied information. It may offer stronger ability to differentiate in classification tasks. Meanwhile, DMN-only data is more uniform and less informative when reduced through PCA. The clear difference between the two plots supports the idea that whole-brain features maintain more meaningful variability. This variability is essential for tasks like classifying schizophrenia in fMRI analysis.

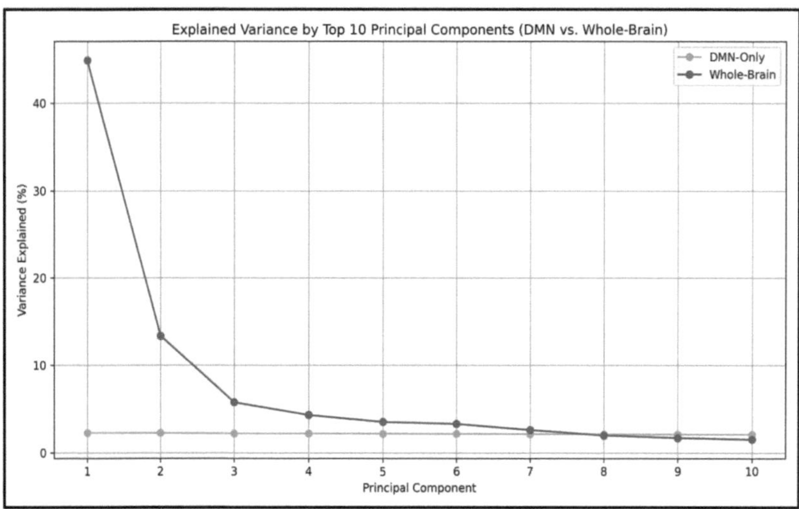

Fig. 4. Explained Variance by Top 10 Principal Components (DMN vs. Whole-Brain)

B. Identified DMN Voxels/Regions Contributing to Classification

SHAP analysis was run to identify the most influential voxel features under the DMN-constrained classification experiment. The top-ranked voxels, mapped with Harvard-Oxford and AAL anatomical atlases, turned out to be labeled as coordinates in "Unknown" or "Outside-Atlas" regions. That is also true for Yeo 7-network mapping which labeled most of these voxels as "Background." This means that they don't correspond to any well-defined anatomical subregion within the DMN. Thus, none of the SHAP-important voxels contributed to that DMN-based experiment located in its canonical hubs: PCC, mPFC, and IPL. Also, this lack of spatial overlap with already established DMN nodes may partially explain why poor classification performance was observed in this experiment. Contrary to the DMN-constrained setting, the unrestricted SHAP analysis at a whole-brain level revealed some very influential voxels mapping to quite meaningful anatomical areas. Most importantly, two voxels were found consistently within the Visual Network as per classification by Yeo's 7-network atlas. One voxel at MNI $[-27, -69, -12]$ mapped to the Occipital Fusiform Gyrus; the other at $[-30, -90, -21]$ corresponded to an area in the occipital lobe, both are involved in early visual processing. This spatial specificity is also corroborated by both Harvard-Oxford and AAL atlases. The finding indicates that regions involved in visual processing may carry more discriminative task-evoked information than DMN regions in this paradigm; hence they may serve as better biomarkers for schizophrenia identification through an auditory oddball task. These voxels, shown in Table 3, include contributions from the **visual cortex**, particularly the *occipital fusiform gyrus* and *occipital cortex*, as mapped via the Harvard-Oxford and AAL atlases.

Table 3. SHAP-mapped voxels from the whole-brain classification experiment

Voxel Index	MNI Coordinate	Yeo Network	Region (Harvard-Oxford/AAL)
1	[24, −48, 87]	Background	Unknown/Outside Atlas
2	[33, 84, 51]	Background	Unknown/Outside Atlas
3	[−24, −51, −21]	Background	Unknown/Outside Atlas
4	[−27, −69, −12]	Visual	Occipital Fusiform Gyrus
5	[27, −42, 30]	Background	Unknown/Outside Atlas
6	[−30, −90, −21]	Visual	Occipital Cortex
7	[−69, −15, 60]	Background	Unknown/Outside Atlas
8	[−12, 48, 90]	Background	Unknown/Outside Atlas
9	[−27, −72, −30]	Background	Unknown/Outside Atlas
10	[−27, −72, −27]	Background	Unknown/Outside Atlas

C. Visualization of Discriminative DMN Regions on Brain Maps

To visually describe the spatial distribution of the most discriminative voxels that we identified through a SHAP analysis, we superimposed the most discriminative voxels on the standard MNI152 brain template using Nilearn's glass brain visualization capabilities: The voxels we selected represented the highest SHAP values from the logistic regression classifier that was fit to PCA-reduced DMN and whole-brain features. Figure 5(a) shows a glass brain rendering where red markers indicate top 10 voxels contributing to classification decisions.

In the case of the DMN-constrained experiment, we found very few discriminative voxels of significance and not even one was in any of the canonical DMN hubs, such as the medial prefrontal cortex or posterior cingulate cortex. Therefore, the brain map derived from the DMN-only category yields sparse, spatially distributed voxel importance with no meaningful anatomical convergence. Figure 5b overlays these voxel coordinates on a sagittal anatomical template, providing spatial context relative to known brain landmarks. In contrast, for the whole-brain classification experiment, we discovered several clustered sites of high-SHAP voxels that are outside the DMN. Notable examples included parts of the occipital fusiform gyrus and visual association areas near this region, as well as regions of the inferior cerebellum, highlighting that it seems that the feature set for classification for schizophrenia when considering the auditory oddball task may more likely localize to sites outside of canonical DMN structures. The resultant brain map,

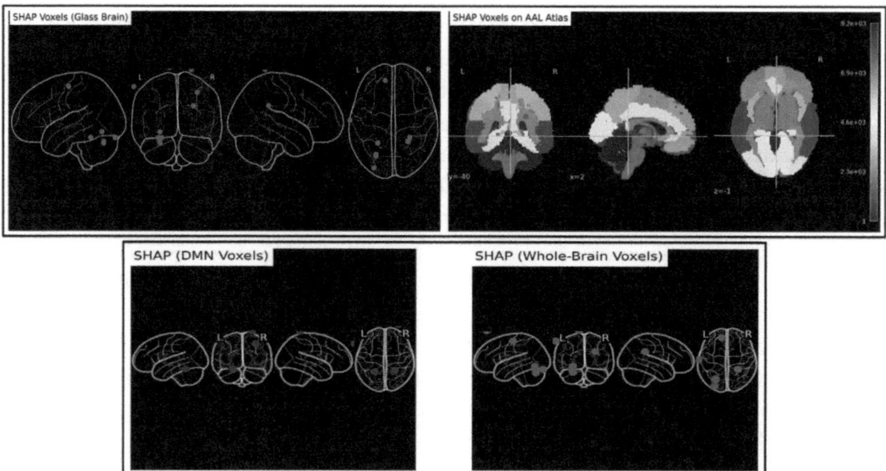

Fig. 5. Top 10 Discriminative Voxels: (a) Over Glass Brain; (b) Over Anatomical Overlay; (c) Discriminative Regions Overlay on MNI152 Template on DMN voxels; (d) Discriminative Regions Overlay on MNI152 Template on Whole-Brain voxels

shown in figures, serves to visually underscore that whole-brain activation patterns have more capability to govern classification than DMN-only features. Additionally, Fig. 5c & 5d presents an overlay of discriminative regions for DMN and Whole-Brain voxels, respectively on an MNI152 background using a heatmap-like visualization, allowing for better appreciation of spatial clusters. These visualizations highlight that the most informative voxels predominantly lie outside canonical DMN boundaries, especially in visual and cerebellar regions, underscoring the importance of whole-brain modeling.

DMN is often connected to schizophrenia due to reduced task-induced deactivation in key areas. However, our analysis of task-evoked BOLD contrasts (deviant > standard) within DMN voxels using PCA and classification showed chance-level accuracy, around 50%. SHAP interpretability did not reveal any consistent subregional DMN features. These results indicate that spatial DMN patterns alone do not have the ability to differentiate conditions, supporting the idea that schizophrenia is a result of widespread network dysfunction rather than just isolated DMN issues.

4 Discussion

This study looked at whether the spatial patterns of task-evoked BOLD contrast within the DMN could be used to classify schizophrenia with machine learning. We used FBIRN Phase 2 auditory oddball data to compare two approaches: one focusing only on DMN voxels and the other on whole-brain data. Both methods used PCA and logistic regression, followed by SHAP for interpretability. The DMN-only model performed at chance, indicating it had poor spatial discriminative power. In contrast, the whole-brain analysis reached 80% accuracy. The most significant features were found in visual and cerebellar areas. These results show that task-evoked DMN activity by itself does not provide useful diagnostic information.

In our study, using only DMN-related brain activity to classify patients from healthy controls did not yield better-than-chance accuracy. In contrast, whole-brain analysis led to significantly improved classification, highlighting features in visual and cerebellar regions. This suggests that schizophrenia-related brain dysfunctions extend beyond DMN. A study used explainable deep learning and dynamic functional network connectivity. It found that interactions in subcortical, sensory (including visual), and cerebellar networks were the main differences between schizophrenia patients and controls (Ellis et al., 2023).

We examined BOLD contrast (deviant > standard) in DMN voxels during the auditory oddball task, but the classification accuracy was almost at chance. Our SHAP-based analysis revealed that important features for discrimination are mainly outside the DMN, especially in visual and occipital areas. Similar findings appeared in a meta-analysis of task-based fMRI studies that used machine learning. It showed that attention-related tasks had higher classification accuracy in schizophrenia than in other cognitive areas (Wang X., et al., 2024). Another Brain Research Bulletin study using multi-feature fusion networks confirmed this, reporting that abnormalities in DMN and visual networks were key biomarkers, with occipital regions contributing strongly to classification accuracy (~91.7%) (Wang, C., et al., 2024).

Our findings highlight challenges in developing reliable neuroimaging biomarkers for schizophrenia. While DMN abnormalities are well-documented, task-evoked spatial patterns within the DMN alone were insufficient for classification. Improved performance with whole-brain features suggests broader network involvement. SHAP analyses emphasize visual and occipital areas, pointing to overlooked sensory disruptions. Future models should include improved functional connectivity features from large-scale datasets. A study showed that full connectome-based models, particularly those emphasizing primary sensory areas, outperform low-dimensional representations in distinguishing schizophrenia (Shevchenko, V., et al., 2025). A large-scale ENIGMA study found that changes in the cortex related to schizophrenia are linked to high-connectivity network hubs, especially in the occipital and temporoparietal regions. This highlights the importance of sensory and perceptual systems in the disorder's structural profile (Georgiadis, F., et al. 2024).

This study has several limitations that should be considered. First, the sample size was small, with only 50 subjects evenly divided between the schizophrenia and healthy control groups. This may limit how widely the findings apply. Second, the study focused solely on one task, the auditory oddball paradigm. While this task is useful for exploring attention, it might not show the full range of DMN dysfunction in different cognitive states. Third, only one contrast map (deviant > standard) was used, which may miss important information from other contrasts or conditions. Additionally, the analysis used static views of the DMN and did not account for possible changes in connectivity over time. Finally, while machine learning techniques like PCA and SHAP were used, more complex models or combined approaches might provide better classification results. Addressing these limitations in future research could help improve both the accuracy and understanding of DMN-based biomarkers for schizophrenia.

Future research should move beyond static contrast-based analyses to examine dynamic functional connectivity within the DMN. Temporal fluctuations may reveal more subtle abnormalities in schizophrenia. Using multimodal imaging data, such as diffusion tensor imaging (DTI) or structural MRI, could improve the understanding and strength of classification models by connecting functional issues to structural changes. Additionally, combining clinical and cognitive scores with imaging features may assist in creating useful biomarkers. We also need larger and more varied datasets to confirm current findings and make machine learning models more applicable. Repeating studies across different groups and imaging centers is crucial for establishing the reliability of the patterns found. Ultimately, these integrated and scalable approaches will be vital for turning neuroimaging insights into practical diagnostic tools for schizophrenia and other neuropsychiatric disorders.

5 Conclusion

This study looked at whether task-evoked BOLD contrast in DMN regions could effectively classify people with schizophrenia using machine learning. While features from the DMN alone performed poorly, whole-brain voxel features greatly improved accuracy. This revealed patterns that were mostly outside the DMN. SHAP analysis showed that areas like the occipital cortex and cerebellum had a bigger role than previously thought. These findings suggest that focusing only on DMN activity might miss wider network problems related to schizophrenia. We conclude that using multi-network, whole-brain methods along with explainable AI is more effective for capturing the complex neural signatures of schizophrenia during task engagement.

References

Chatterjee, I., Kumar, V., Rana, B., Agarwal, M., Kumar, N.: Impact of ageing on the brain regions of the schizophrenia patients: an fMRI study using evolutionary approach. Multimedia Tools Appl. **79**, 24757–24779 (2020)

Coluzzi, D., Baselli, G.: Diffuse and localized functional dysconnectivity in schizophrenia: a bootstrapped top-down approach. Fundamenta Informaticae, 189 (2023)

Dong, D., Wang, Y., Chang, X., Luo, C., Yao, D.: Dysfunction of large-scale brain networks in schizophrenia: a meta-analysis of resting-state functional connectivity. Schizophr. Bull. **44**(1), 168–181 (2018)

Marino, M., et al.: Default mode network alterations underlie auditory verbal hallucinations in schizophrenia. J. Psychiatr. Res. **155**, 24–32 (2022)

Menon, V.: 20 years of the default mode network: a review and synthesis. Neuron **111**(16), 2469–2487 (2023)

Sasabayashi, D., et al.: Resting state hyperconnectivity of the default mode network in schizophrenia and clinical high-risk state for psychosis. Cereb. Cortex **33**(13), 8456–8464 (2023)

Sendi, M.S., et al.: Aberrant dynamic functional connectivity of default mode network in schizophrenia and links to symptom severity. Front. Neural Circ. **15**, 649417 (2021)

Krakowski, M., Hoptman, M.J., Czobor, P.: Dysfunctional activation of the default mode network in response inhibition in schizophrenia. J. Psychiatr. Res. **180**, 411–417 (2024)

Hamilton, H.K., Mathalon, D.H., Ford, J.M.: P300 in schizophrenia: then and now. Biol. Psychol. **187**, 108757 (2024)

Nakahara, S., et al.: Auditory oddball hypoactivation in schizophrenia. Psychiatry Res. Neuroimaging **335**, 111710 (2023)

Schnack, H.G., Kahn, R.S.: Detecting neuroimaging biomarkers for psychiatric disorders: sample size matters. Front. Psych. **7**, 50 (2016)

Durstewitz, D., Koppe, G., Meyer-Lindenberg, A.: Deep neural networks in psychiatry. Mol. Psychiatry **24**(11), 1583–1598 (2019)

Munroe, L., et al.: Applications of interpretable deep learning in neuroimaging: a comprehensive review. Imaging Neurosci. **2**, 1–37 (2024)

Chatterjee, I., Baumgartner, L., Cho, M.: Detection of brain regions responsible for chronic pain in osteoarthritis: an fMRI-based neuroimaging study using deep learning. Front. Neurol. **14**, 1195923 (2023)

Guha, A., et al.: Task-based default mode network connectivity predicts cognitive impairment and negative symptoms in first-episode schizophrenia. Psychophysiology **61**(10), e14627 (2024)

Chen, X., Lu, B., Yan, C.G.: Reproducibility of R-fMRI metrics on the impact of different strategies for multiple comparison correction and sample sizes. Hum. Brain Mapp. **39**(1), 300–318 (2018)

Doshi-Velez, F., Kim, B.: Towards a rigorous science of interpretable machine learning. arXiv preprint arXiv:1702.08608 (2017)

Alves, C.L., et al.: Analysis of functional connectivity using machine learning and deep learning in different data modalities from individuals with schizophrenia. J. Neural Eng. **20**(5), 056025 (2023)

Chatterjee, I.: Machine learning and its application: a quick guide for beginners. Bentham Science Publishers (2021)

Ellis, C.A., Miller, R.L., Calhoun, V.D.: Pairing explainable deep learning classification with clustering to uncover effects of schizophrenia upon whole brain functional network connectivity dynamics. Neuroimage Rep. **3**(4), 100186 (2023)

Wang, X., et al.: Unveiling the potential of machine learning in schizophrenia diagnosis: a meta-analytic study of task-based neuroimaging data. Psychiatry Clin. Neurosci. **78**(3), 157–168 (2024)

Wang, C., et al.: Multi feature fusion network for schizophrenia classification and abnormal brain network recognition. Brain Res. Bull. **206**, 110848 (2024)

Shevchenko, V., et al.: A comparative machine learning study of schizophrenia biomarkers derived from functional connectivity. Sci. Rep. **15**(1), 2849 (2025)

Georgiadis, F., et al.: Connectome architecture shapes large-scale cortical alterations in schizophrenia: a worldwide ENIGMA study. Mol. Psychiatry **29**(6), 1869–1881 (2024)

Edge-Aware Lightweight Network for Medical Image Segmentation

Zhecheng Wu[1] [iD] and Lu Leng[2]([✉]) [iD]

[1] Jiangxi Provincial Key Laboratory of Image Processing and Pattern Recognition, Nanchang Hangkong University, Nanchang 330063, China
[2] School of Software, Nanchang Hangkong University, Nanchang 330063, China
leng@nchu.edu.cn

Abstract. In the field of medicine, image segmentation is highly important in automatic disease diagnosis from medical image and subsequent treatment. However, in deployment environments with limited computing and storage resources, it is necessary to balance the accuracy and complexity of the model. This paper presents a lightweight medical image segmentation network, dubbed ELU-Net, which includes two effective modules: Attention Edge Aware Module (AEAM) and Depthwise-Pointwise Convolution Group (DPG). AEAM combines low-level and high-level features with an attention mechanism to enhance and extract edge features in the image. This mechanism automatically focuses on the regions with significant boundary information, and can correctly segment the regions with ambiguous boundaries with edge detection. DPG uses a combination of depthwise and pointwise convolutions with different kernel sizes in each layer, remarkably reducing the number of model parameters while expanding the receptive field. With only 39KB of parameter amount, ELU-Net was tested on a self-built OCT dataset and the public ISIC 2018 dataset. Compared with the baseline, the mIoU scores increase by 0.1205 and 0.0321, respectively.

Keywords: Lightweight Network · Medical Image Segmentation · Edge-aware Attention

1 Introduction

We proposed a novel edge-aware lightweight medical image segmentation model, dubbed (Edge-Aware Lightweight U-Net) ELU-Net, on OCT images and dermatoscope images, which employs two effective modules: Attention Edge Aware Module (AEAM) and Depthwise-Pointwise Convolution Group (DPG). The contributions are summarized as follows.

(1) DPG encoder-decoder replaces the original standard convolutions with multiple depthwise and pointwise convolutions, reducing the number of model parameters. Additionally, it uses different kernel sizes to capture the features at various levels within the network.

© The Author(s) 2026
B.-G. Kim et al. (Eds.): MITA 2025, CCIS 2675, pp. 79–85, 2026.
https://doi.org/10.1007/978-981-95-3141-7_7

(2) AEAM combines low-level and high-level features with an attention mechanism to enhance and extract edge features in the image. This mechanism automatically focuses on the regions with significant boundary information, and can correctly segment the regions with ambiguous boundaries with edge detection.

(3) ELU-Net has a small number of parameters (only 39 KB) and low computational complexity. It was tested on the ISIC2018 dataset and our own OCT dataset. The extensive results show that the ELU-Net model strikes a balance among the parameter amount, computational complexity, and segmentation performance.

2 Related Works

Deep learning methods, such as convolutional neural networks (CNNs), are widely used in medical image segmentation. Ronneberger et al. developed popular U-Net [1] model, utilizing skip connections to integrate low-level and high-level features, enabling combination of local and global information. This U-shaped architecture has become a standard paradigm in medical segmentation due to its robust performance, and has several notable variants including: U-Net++ [2] proposed by Zhou et al., who improved skip connections, and Attention U-Net [3] proposed by Schlemper et al., who integrated the attention gates.

With the emergence of vision transformers (ViT) [4], the Transformers architecture stands out prominently. Wang et al. developed UCtransNet [5], which addresses potential semantic gaps in standard skip connections by introducing Channel Transformer modules. Cao et al. developed Swin-UNet [6], which utilized shifted windows for efficient computation, and employed patch expansion layers in the decoder for upsampling. Maaz et al. developed EdgeNeXt [7] which incorporated Spatially-Temporally Decoupled Attention encoders to achieve high efficiency, while maintaining performance on vision tasks.

Addressing computational constraints, lightweight architectures have gained prominence. Singh et al. developed MISegNet [8], which enhanced efficiency and feature representation by integrating discrete wavelet transform (DWT) for multi-resolution analysis alongside a novel attention module. Shi et al. developed LMFFNet [9] for efficient real-time segmentation. Ruan et al. developed MALUNet [10] reducing parameters while incorporating attention.

Compared with the existing methods, this paper solves three issues. Firstly, it is satisfactory to simultaneously meet the two requirements, accuracy and complexity. Secondly, it improves the accuracy by edge-aware mechanism, especially for ambiguous boundaries. Thirdly, it is suitable for different modalities of medical image, including OCT images and dermatoscope images.

3 Methodology

The U-shaped architecture is commonly used for image segmentation, so it is also used in our method, ELU-Net, which extracts features through the encoder, and then generates predicted images through the decoder. We proposed two effective modules, namely AEAM and DPG, which are embedded in ELU-Net, as show in Fig. 1.

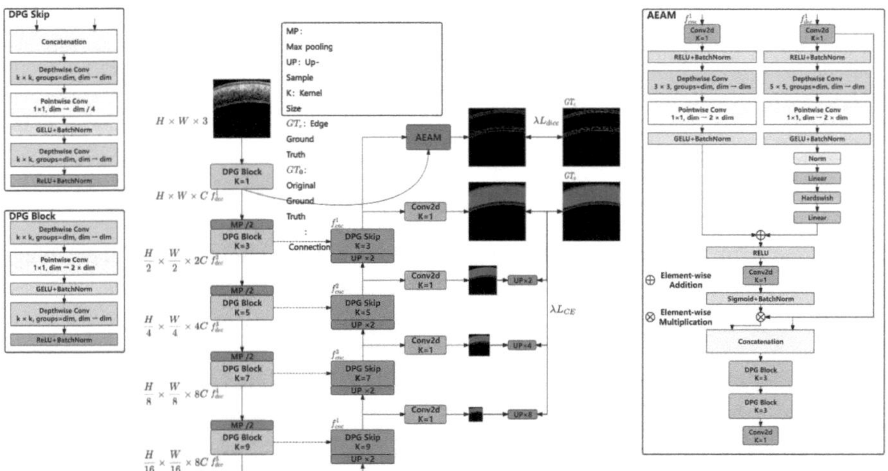

Fig. 1. ELU-Net architecture.

3.1 DPG

DPG replaces the original two ordinary convolutions with a combination of depth convolution, point convolution, and depth convolution. This combination significantly reduces the model's floating-point operation (FLOP) with little degradation of model accuracy. The main difference between the DPG in decoder module and the one in encoder is the additional Concat. The encoder formula is:

$$f_{dsc} = PConv(DConv_k(x_{in})) \tag{1}$$

where $PConv$ means pointwise convolution, $DConv_k$ means depth convolution of $k \times k$ size convolution kernel, pointwise convolution and depth convolution are combined to form a depth separable convolution $f_{dsc}(\cdot)$. Then a feature encoding is completed by a depth convolution of $k \times k$ size convolution kernel.

$$f_{dec}^l = BN(Relu\{DConv_k(BN(Gelu\{f_{dsc}\}))\}) \tag{2}$$

The decoder up-samples the features from the previous layer of decoding, and concatenates them with the features from the corresponding depth encoder through a single depth-separable convolution f_{dsc} and a depth convolution of $k \times k$ size convolution kernel.

$$f_{enc}^l = BN(Relu\{DConv_k(BN(Gelu\{f_{dsc}\}))\}) \tag{3}$$

3.2 AEAM

The high-level semantic information f_{enc}^1 and low-level semantic information f_{dec}^1 are abstracted into matrices k, q, respectively, as shown in Eqs. (4) and (5). The features are passed through two DPG encoders and a 1×1 convolution, followed by a Sigmoid function mapping the features into the range of (0, 1), in order to generate the final edge image. AEAM is a simple yet effective module.

$$f_{att}(q, k) = \left(q^T(q + k); q \right) \tag{4}$$

$$f_{AEAM} = Conv_1(f_{dec}(f_{dec}(f_{att}(q, k)))) \tag{5}$$

Multi-scale multi-shape predicted images help the model better understand the image information, and consider the targets or features from multiple perspectives. The loss function is:

$$L_{total} = \sum_{i=2}^{5} \left(\lambda_i CE(y_i, \widehat{y_i}) \right) + \lambda Bce(y_1, \widehat{y_1}) \tag{6}$$

This loss function incorporates multi-scale and multi-shape predictions. By predicting boundary shapes and addressing multi-scale features, it enables the model to achieve favorable prediction performance across feature representations at different hierarchical levels.

4 Experiments

All models were trained for 50 epochs with a batch size of 4. The experiments were conducted on ISIC2018 dataset, and a self-built OCT dataset, with more than 5000, 100 images, respectively. ELU-Net randomly splits the dataset into training and testing sets at a ratio of 7:3.

The results are shown in Table 1. The parameter amounts of some large models, such as U-Net, are 1709 times that of ELU-Net, while ELU-Net still has satisfactory accuracy. Compared with other lightweight models, ELU-Net surpasses MALUNet by 0.0626 in terms of mIoU on OCT dataset.

Table 1. Comparison of experimental results.

Dataset	Model	Params(M)↓	mIoU↑	DSC↑
OCT	UNet [1]	7.77	0.6875	0.7843
	U-Net++ [2]	9.16	0.7856	0.8650
	RESU-Net [11]	13.04	0.8012	0.8782
	ATTU-Net [3]	26.20	0.7952	0.8694
	uctransnetU-Net [5]	67.23	0.7923	0.8685
	MALUNet [10]	0.177	0.7454	0.8334
	transnetU-Net [12]	105.91	0.8059	**0.8820**

(continued)

Table 1. (*continued*)

Dataset	Model	Params(M)↓	mIoU↑	DSC↑
	ELU-Net	**0.039**	**0.8080**	0.8795
ISIC 2018	UNet [1]	7.77	0.8378	0.9061
	U-Net++ [2]	9.16	0.8398	0.9193
	ATTU-Net [3]	8.73	0.8351	0.9039
	EGE-UNet [13]	0.053	0.8498	0.9156
	ELU-Net	**0.039**	**0.8578**	**0.9220**

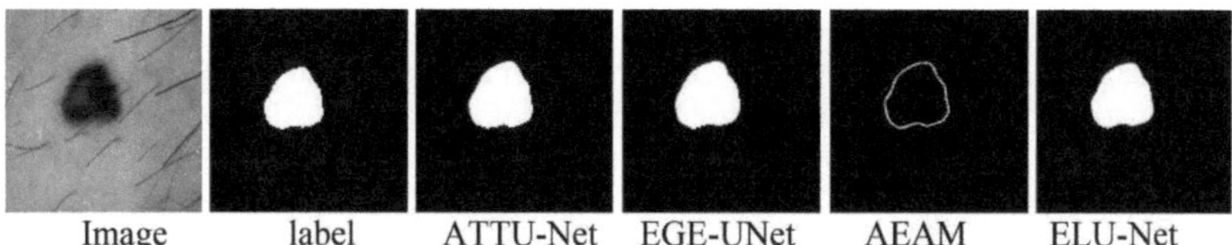

Fig. 2. Segmentation visualization results on ISIC2018 dataset.

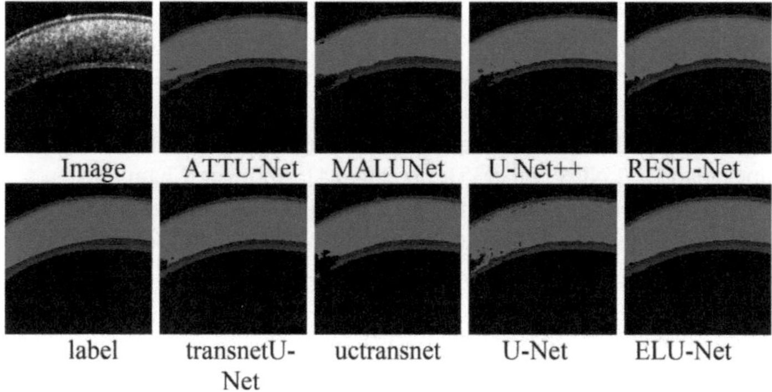

Fig. 3. Segmentation visualization results on OCT dataset.

Segmentation visualization result are shown in Figs. 2 and 3. ELU-Net has more accurate boundary than the other methods.

Table 2 shows ablation experiments. The integrating DPG and AEAM into the baseline model show distinct performance improvements. DPG increases the mIoU and DSC by 0.0976 and 0.0789, respectively, on OCT dataset, while AEAM improves the mIoU and DSC by 0.0769 and 0.0738, respectively, on the same dataset. These findings fully demonstrate the effectiveness of each module in enhancing segmentation accuracy.

Table 2. Ablation experiments.

Model	mIoU↑	DSC↑
U-Net (Baseline)	0.6875	0.7843
U-Net + DPG	0.7851	0.8632
U-Net + AEAM	0.7644	0.8581
U-Net + DPG + AEAM (ELU-Net)	0.8080	0.8795

Acknowledgments. This study was funded by National Natural Science Foundation of China (62466038), Jiangxi Provincial Key Laboratory of Image Processing and Pattern Recognition (2024SSY03111), Technology Innovation Guidance Program Project (Special Project of Technology Cooperation, Science and Technology Department of Jiangxi Province) (20212BDH81003), Open Foundation of Jiangxi Provincial Key Laboratory of Image Processing and Pattern Recognition (ET202404437), and Innovation Foundation for Post-graduate Students of Nanchang Hangkong University (YC2023-S746).

Disclosure of Interests. The authors declare no competing interests.

References

1. Ronneberger, O., Fischer, P., Brox, T.: U-net: convolutional networks for biomedical image segmentation. In: Medical Image Computing and Computer-Assisted Intervention, Proceedings, Part III. LNCS, vol. 9351, pp. 234–241. Springer, Cham (2015)
2. Zhou, Z., Siddiquee, M.M.R., Tajbakhsh, N., Liang, J.: UNet++: redesigning skip connections to exploit multiscale features in image segmentation. IEEE Trans. Med. Imaging **39**(6), 1856–1867 (2019)
3. Schlemper, J., et al.: Attention gated networks: learning to leverage salient regions in medical images. Med. Image Anal. **53**, 197–207 (2019)
4. Dosovitskiy, A., et al.: An Image Is Worth 16×16 Words: Transformers for Image Recognition at Scale. arXiv Preprint arXiv:2010.11929 (2020)
5. Wang, H., Cao, P., Wang, J., Zaiane, O.R.: UCTransNet: rethinking the skip connections in U-Net from a channel-wise perspective with transformer. In: Proceedings of the AAAI Conference on Artificial Intelligence, Vol. 36, No. 3, pp. 2441–2449, June (2022)
6. Cao, H., et al.: Swin-UNet: UNet-like pure transformer for medical image segmentation. In: European Conference on Computer Vision, pp. 205–218. Springer Nature Switzerland (2022)
7. Maaz, M., et al.: EdgeNeXt: efficiently amalgamated CNN-transformer architecture for mobile vision applications. In: European Conference on Computer Vision, pp. 3–20. Springer, Cham (2022)
8. Singh, V.K., et al.: Prior wavelet knowledge for multi-modal medical image segmentation using a lightweight neural network with attention guided features. Expert Syst. Appl. **209**, 118166 (2022)
9. Shi, M., et al.: LMFFNet: A well-balanced lightweight network for fast and accurate semantic segmentation. IEEE Trans. Neural Netw. Learn. Syst. **34**(6), 3205–3219 (2022)

10. Ruan, J., Xiang, S., Le, M., Liu, T., Fu, Y.: MALUNet: a multi-attention and light-weight UNet for skin lesion segmentation. In: IEEE International Conference on Bioinformatics and Biomedicine, pp. 1150–1156. IEEE (2022)
11. Zhang, Z., Liu, Q., Wang, Y.: Road extraction by deep residual U-Net. IEEE Geosci. Remote Sens. Lett. **15**(5), 749–753 (2018)
12. Chen, J., Lu, Y., Yu, Q., Luo, X., Adeli, E., Wang, Y., et al.: TransUNet: Transformers make strong encoders for medical image segmentation. arXiv preprint arXiv:2102.04306 (2021)
13. Ruan, J., Le, M., Gao, J., Liu, T., Fu, Y.: EGE-UNet: an efficient group enhanced UNet for skin lesion segmentation. In: International conference on medical image computing and computer-assisted intervention, pp. 481–490. Springer Nature Switzerland, Cham (2023)

Evaluating the Impact of Backbone Networks and Input Resolution on Forearm Acupoint Localization

V. P. Prathiksha[1] , H. M. K. K. M. B. Herath[1] , Hi-Joon Park[2] ,
Chang-Soo Na[3] , Myunggi Yi[4] , and Byeong-il Lee[5]($\boxtimes$)

[1] Industry 4.0 Convergence Bionics Engineering, Pukyong National University, Busan, Republic of Korea
[2] College of Korean Medicine, Kyung Hee University, Seoul, Republic of Korea
[3] College of Korean Medicine, Dongshin University, Jeonnam, Republic of Korea
[4] Major of Biomedical Engineering, Pukyong National University, Busan, Republic of Korea
[5] Major of HumanBio Convergence, Pukyong National University, Busan, Republic of Korea
bilee@pknu.ac.kr

Abstract. Accurate localization of anatomical keypoints is fundamental to a variety of clinical and research applications, including acupoint therapy, physical rehabilitation, and biomechanical motion analysis. In this study, we investigate the impact of different deep learning backbone architectures and input image resolutions on the localization accuracy of five clinically important forearm acupoints (LI11, LI10, TE5, LI4, and TE3) using a top-down pose estimation framework. Six backbone models, High-Resolution Network (HRNet), Lite High-Resolution Network (Lite-HRNet), Residual Network (ResNet), Swin Transformer, Visual Geometry Group (VGG) network, and Vision Transformer (ViT), are benchmarked across three input resolutions: 256×256, 384×384, and 512×512 pixels. Localization performance is evaluated using normalized Euclidean distance and its standard deviation, providing a resolution-independent measure of both accuracy and consistency. Among the tested models, HRNet consistently yields the most precise and stable predictions, achieving the lowest average error of 0.009 at the 512×512 resolution. Lite-HRNet and ResNet also demonstrate strong performance, particularly at higher resolutions, offering a compelling balance between accuracy and computational efficiency. While ViT exhibits higher error rates at lower resolutions, it significantly improves at 512×512, closing the performance gap with CNN-based models. Swin Transformer, however, records the highest average error across all resolutions, indicating its limited suitability for fine-grained localization tasks without additional architectural adaptation. Overall, our findings highlight the importance of backbone selection and resolution scaling in medical keypoint detection tasks. HRNet delivers over 50% lower normalized error compared to the weakest-performing model. These insights provide practical guidance for developing robust, high-precision AI systems for clinical and digital health applications, where anatomical accuracy is essential.

Keywords: Forearm Acupoints · Pose Estimation · HRNet · Vision Transformer · Keypoint Localization · Euclidean Distance

© The Author(s) 2026
B.-G. Kim et al. (Eds.): MITA 2025, CCIS 2675, pp. 86–97, 2026.
https://doi.org/10.1007/978-981-95-3141-7_8

1   Introduction

Accurate localization of anatomical keypoints is essential across a wide range of healthcare applications, including acupoint therapy, physical rehabilitation, and biomechanical analysis. In traditional Korean medicine, forearm acupoints such as LI11, LI10, TE5, LI4, and TE3 play a critical role in diagnosis and therapeutic procedures. Precise detection of these acupoints is important not only for clinical accuracy but also for assessing the consistency and effectiveness of treatments [1–3]. As digital health technologies continue to evolve, there is an increasing demand for automated, high-resolution keypoint localization systems that can support clinical decision-making and research [4].

Recent advances in deep learning, especially in the domain of human pose estimation, have significantly enhanced our ability to detect anatomical landmarks. Top-down pose estimation methods, which begin with bounding box detection followed by keypoint localization, have demonstrated strong performance in general vision tasks. However, much of the existing work has concentrated on full-body joint localization using general-purpose datasets such as COCO and MPII [5, 6]. These datasets, while useful for standard pose estimation, are not optimized for the fine-grained precision required in medical applications.

The backbone architecture of a pose estimation model plays a central role in determining its accuracy and efficiency. Convolutional Neural Network (CNN) backbones such as ResNet, HRNet, and Lite-HRNet are widely used for their ability to extract detailed spatial features. HRNet is particularly effective because it preserves high-resolution features throughout the network, making it ideal for tasks that require precise spatial detail. Lite-HRNet provides a lightweight alternative that balances accuracy with computational efficiency. On the other hand, transformer-based models like Swin Transformer and Vision Transformer (ViT) use self-attention mechanisms to capture global context and long-range dependencies. Although successful in various vision tasks, their performance in medical keypoint localization, especially for small, closely spaced points like acupoints, remains less explored.

Input image resolution is another important factor influencing localization performance. Higher resolutions tend to enhance spatial detail, improving model accuracy. However, they also increase computational costs, potentially limiting their use in real-time or mobile deployments. Despite this trade-off, little research has systematically studied the combined effects of resolution and backbone architecture in medical localization tasks.

To address these gaps, this study evaluates six backbone networks (HRNet, Lite-HRNet, ResNet, Swin Transformer, VGG, and ViT) for forearm acupoint localization using a top-down framework. We use a clinically annotated dataset with expert guidance and assess performance using normalized Euclidean distance and standard deviation across three input sizes (256×256, 384×384, and 512×512 pixels). The results highlight HRNet's superior accuracy and Lite-HRNet's efficiency, while revealing limitations in current transformer-based approaches.

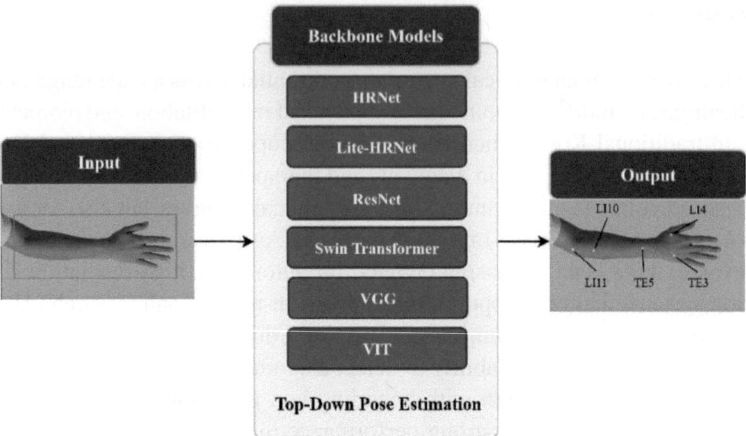

Fig. 1. Pipeline of top-down pose estimation using various backbone models for forearm keypoint detection.

2 Related Work

Keypoint localization is a fundamental task in computer vision and human pose estimation, supporting applications ranging from activity recognition and biomechanics to clinical diagnostics [7, 8]. In recent years, deep learning, particularly Convolutional Neural Networks (CNNs) and, more recently, transformer-based architectures, have driven significant progress in this field [6].

Early methods like DeepPose addressed keypoint localization through direct coordinate regression. While innovative, these models often struggled with spatial precision and robustness in complex or occluded environments. This led to the adoption of heatmap-based approaches, which represent keypoints as probability distributions across the image. This transition improved accuracy and interpretability, especially under challenging visual conditions.

CNN-based models like ResNet [9] and VGG [10] gained popularity for their strong feature extraction. However, extensive downsampling in these architectures compromises spatial resolution, which is critical for fine-grained localization tasks such as anatomical keypoint detection. HRNet addressed this limitation with a high-resolution design that preserves spatial detail across network stages, achieving state-of-the-art results on datasets like COCO and MPII. Its lightweight counterpart, Lite-HRNet [11], offers a balance between accuracy and efficiency, making it suitable for real-time and edge deployments.

Transformer-based models have recently emerged as a powerful alternative for pose estimation. These architectures employ self-attention to model global context and long-range spatial relationships capabilities that standard CNNs often lack. The Swin Transformer [12] introduces a hierarchical structure with shifted windows to support scalable and efficient learning. ViTPose [13], derived from the Vision Transformer (ViT) [14], uses global attention and positional embeddings for end-to-end keypoint regression, showing promising results on general-purpose benchmarks.

Despite these advances, most prior work focuses on full-body pose estimation using generic datasets. Clinical applications requiring high precision and domain-specific annotations remain underexplored. Tasks like forearm acupoint localization pose additional challenges due to the proximity of keypoints and anatomical variability.

To address this, our study systematically evaluates six leading backbone architectures, HRNet [15], Lite-HRNet, ResNet, Swin Transformer, VGG, and ViT across three input resolutions for the task of forearm acupoint detection. Using normalized Euclidean distance and standard deviation as evaluation metrics, we benchmark each model's accuracy and consistency. A comparative summary of their architectural features and trade-offs is presented in Table 1 to aid future research in medical keypoint localization.

Table 1. Comparison of the model architectures from the previous studies.

Backbone	Year	Type	Maintains Resolution	Lightweight	Pros	Cons
HRNet [15]	2019	CNN	✔	✗	High accuracy	High computation
Lite-HRNet [11]	2021	CNN	✔	✔	Compact, fast	Slight drop in accuracy
ResNet [9]	2016	CNN	✗	✗	Deep learning baseline	Spatial loss
Swin Transformer [12]	2021	Transformer	✔	✔	Hierarchical attention	Resolution sensitive
ViT [14]	2020	Transformer	✗	✗	Global reasoning	Needs high resolution
VGG [10]	2020	CNN	✗	✗	Simplicity	Outdated performance

3 Methodology

This study employs a top-down pose estimation framework to evaluate the effect of various backbone architectures on the accuracy of acupoint localization in forearm images.

3.1 Pipeline Overview

As shown in Fig. 1, the pipeline starts with cropped forearm images resized to three fixed resolutions (256×256, 384×384, and 512×512 pixels) to assess the impact of input size on localization accuracy. These images are processed using a top-down pose estimation framework with one of six backbone models: HRNet, Lite-HRNet, ResNet, Swin Transformer, VGG, or ViT. Each model predicts 2D keypoints for five clinically important acupoints: LI11, LI10, TE5, LI4, and TE3. While Fig. 2 illustrates the full workflow, including data collection, annotation, preprocessing, model training, evaluation, and the anatomical locations of the labeled forearm acupoints.

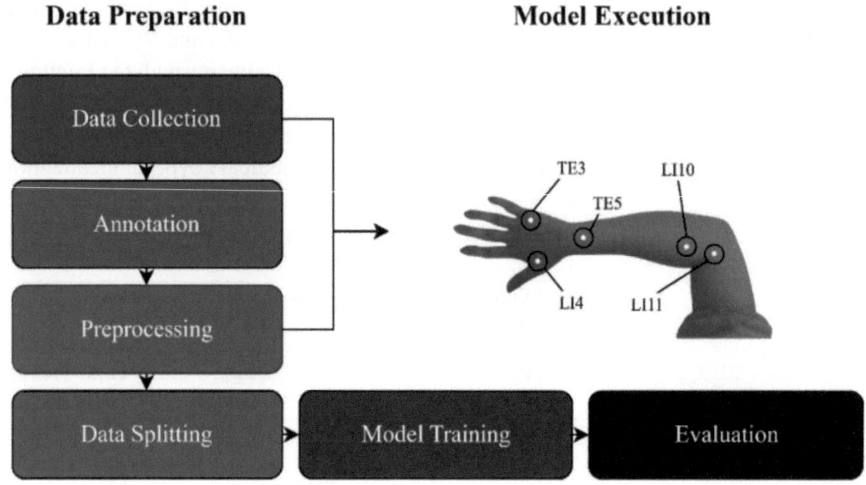

Fig. 2. Overview of the dataset preparation and model training workflow.

3.2   Dataset Annotation and Evaluation Metrics

Figure 3 presents sample forearm images from the training and testing datasets, annotated manually under expert supervision to serve as ground truth. Model accuracy is assessed using the Euclidean distance between predicted and actual keypoints, normalized by image resolution for consistent comparison across varying input sizes.

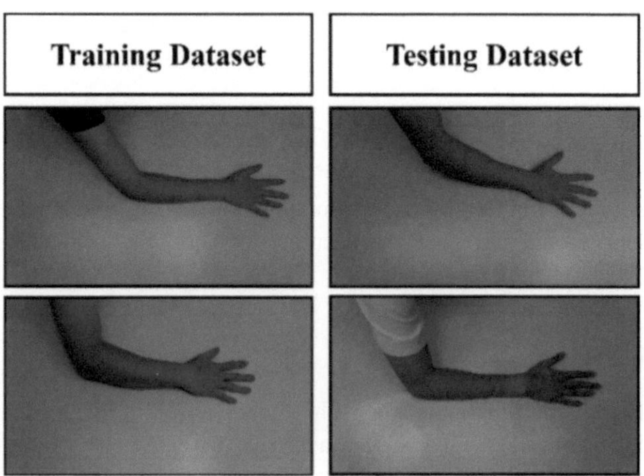

Fig. 3. Example images from the training and testing datasets used for forearm acupoint annotation.

In Eq. (1), x_{pred}, y_{pred} are the coordinates predicted by the model, and x_{true}, y_{true} are the annotated ground truth coordinates. The equation is applied to each keypoint, and the resulting errors are averaged to compute the model's overall localization error.

$$\text{Error} = \sqrt{\left(x_{pred} - x_{true}\right)^2 + \left(y_{pred} - y_{true}\right)^2} \tag{1}$$

To make the error scale-invariant, we normalize it as shown in Eq. 2.

$$\text{Normalized Error} = \frac{\text{Error}}{\text{Input Image Size}} \tag{2}$$

Here, in Eq. (2), the input image size denotes the width or height of the square image (e.g., 256, 384, or 512 pixels). Normalizing the localization error by this dimension allows fair comparisons across models trained at different resolutions. This normalized error is calculated per keypoint and averaged to determine overall model performance. Standard deviation is also computed to capture the variability in the predictions across the dataset.

4   Results and Analysis

To assess the localization performance across models and input resolutions, we analyzed the mean Euclidean distance and standard deviation for five forearm acupoints (LI11, LI10, TE5, LI4, and TE3). Results are summarized in the Tables 2, 3 and 4 and visualized in Figs. 4, 5, 6 and 7.

4.1   Performance Across Resolutions

Tables 2 and 3 present the normalized localization error across input resolutions of 256 × 256, 384 × 384, and 512 × 512 pixels. HRNet consistently achieves the lowest average error at each resolution, dropping from 0.018 to 0.009, which highlights its robustness and scale invariance. ViT exhibits relatively high error at 256 × 256 px (0.026) but improves at 512 × 512 px (0.017), although it still lags behind Lite-HRNet and VGG (both at 0.011). This indicates that higher resolution benefits ViT, but it remains less effective than CNN-based models. Swin Transformer records the highest error overall, peaking at 0.028 at 256 × 256 px and underperforming across all scales.

Table 2. Normalized Localization Error At 256 × 256 Px Input Resolution (Mean ± Standard Deviation in Pixels)

Input Size (px)	Backbone	LI11	LI10	TE5	LI4	TE3	Total Avg.(px)
	HRNet	0.019 ± 0.011	0.025 ± 0.015	0.021 ± 0.014	0.013 ± 0.007	0.014 ± 0.007	0.018
	Lite-HRNet	0.030 ± 0.017	0.029 ± 0.017	0.029 ± 0.018	0.020 ± 0.011	0.021 ± 0.010	0.026
256 × 256	ResNet	0.023 ± 0.013	0.028 ± 0.016	0.030 ± 0.018	0.018 ± 0.010	0.021 ± 0.010	0.024

(continued)

Table 2. (continued)

Input Size (px)	Backbone	LI11	LI10	TE5	LI4	TE3	Total Avg.(px)
	Swin Transformer	0.031 ± 0.019	0.032 ± 0.019	0.032 ± 0.020	0.021 ± 0.012	0.023 ± 0.012	0.028
	VGG	0.029 ± 0.017	0.031 ± 0.020	0.032 ± 0.019	0.017 ± 0.009	0.021 ± 0.011	0.026
	ViT	0.031 ± 0.020	0.035 ± 0.023	0.031 ± 0.021	0.016 ± 0.008	0.020 ± 0.011	0.026

Table 3. Normalized Localization Error At 384 × 384 Px Input Resolution (Mean ± Standard Deviation in Pixels)

Input Size (px)	Backbone	LI11	LI10	TE5	LI4	TE3	Total Avg.(px)
	HRNet	0.010 ± 0.005	0.013 ± 0.007	0.013 ± 0.007	0.009 ± 0.004	0.007 ± 0.004	0.012
	Lite-HRNet	0.015 ± 0.008	0.016 ± 0.009	0.016 ± 0.009	0.012 ± 0.006	0.012 ± 0.007	0.014
384 × 384	ResNet	0.012 ± 0.006	0.015 ± 0.008	0.016 ± 0.009	0.011 ± 0.005	0.012 ± 0.006	0.013
	Swin Transformer	0.018 ± 0.010	0.017 ± 0.009	0.018 ± 0.010	0.013 ± 0.007	0.012 ± 0.007	0.017
	VGG	0.015 ± 0.008	0.017 ± 0.010	0.017 ± 0.010	0.011 ± 0.006	0.013 ± 0.007	0.015
	ViT	0.015 ± 0.009	0.019 ± 0.010	0.016 ± 0.010	0.010 ± 0.005	0.013 ± 0.007	0.021

Table 4. Normalized Localization Error At 512 × 512 Px Input Resolution (Mean ± Standard Deviation in Pixels)

Input Size (px)	Backbone	LI11	LI10	TE5	LI4	TE3	Total Avg.(px)
	HRNet	0.005 ± 0.003	0.008 ± 0.005	0.007 ± 0.005	0.005 ± 0.002	0.005 ± 0.003	0.009
	Lite-HRNet	0.010 ± 0.005	0.010 ± 0.006	0.010 ± 0.006	0.008 ± 0.004	0.008 ± 0.004	0.011
512 × 512	ResNet	0.007 ± 0.004	0.010 ± 0.005	0.010 ± 0.006	0.006 ± 0.003	0.008 ± 0.003	0.010
	Swin Transformer	0.011 ± 0.006	0.011 ± 0.006	0.011 ± 0.007	0.008 ± 0.004	0.009 ± 0.005	0.013
	VGG	0.010 ± 0.005	0.011 ± 0.006	0.011 ± 0.006	0.006 ± 0.003	0.008 ± 0.005	0.011
	ViT	0.009 ± 0.005	0.012 ± 0.007	0.010 ± 0.007	0.006 ± 0.003	0.008 ± 0.005	0.017

Figure 4(A) shows a heatmap of model performance, with lighter areas indicating lower localization errors. HRNet consistently appears brightest, reflecting its high accuracy and stability. Swin Transformer and ViT show higher errors, especially at lower resolutions. Lite-HRNet and ResNet perform reliably, often surpassing VGG. Overall, higher resolution improves accuracy, though benefits vary by model architecture.

4.2 Accuracy for Each Keypoint

Figure 4(B) shows per-keypoint localization error at 512×512 resolution, with each line representing a model's average normalized error across five acupoints. HRNet displays the most compact and consistent profile, indicating uniformly low error. In contrast, Swin Transformer and ViT show higher errors, particularly for LI10 and TE5, likely due to anatomical variability. This underscores HRNet's robustness and other models' sensitivity to specific keypoint challenges.

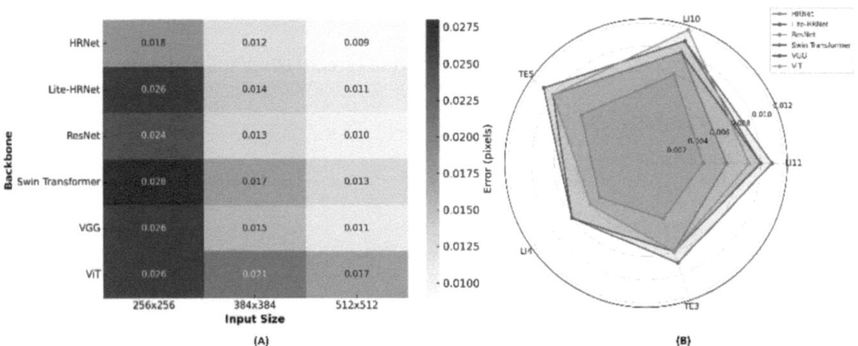

Fig. 4. (A) Heatmap of Total Average Localization Error Across Models and Resolutions. (B) Per-Keypoint Localization Error at 512×512 px Resolution

4.3 Trends Across Models and Resolutions

Figure 6 further illustrates how each model responds to changes in input resolution. HRNet remains stable and shows improvement as resolution increases. Lite-HRNet and ResNet also benefit from higher resolutions, especially at 384×384 and 512×512 px. On the other hand, Swin Transformer consistently exhibits higher error, and although ViT starts with relatively high error at lower resolutions, its performance improves notably at 512×512 px, eventually matching Lite-HRNet and VGG.

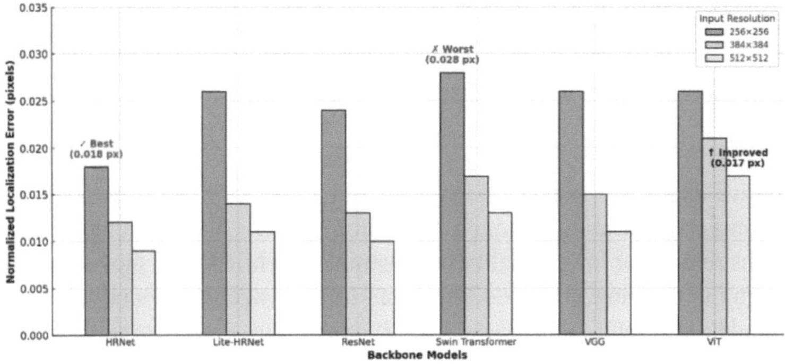

Fig. 5. Model-Wise Comparison of Mean Localization Error Across Input Sizes

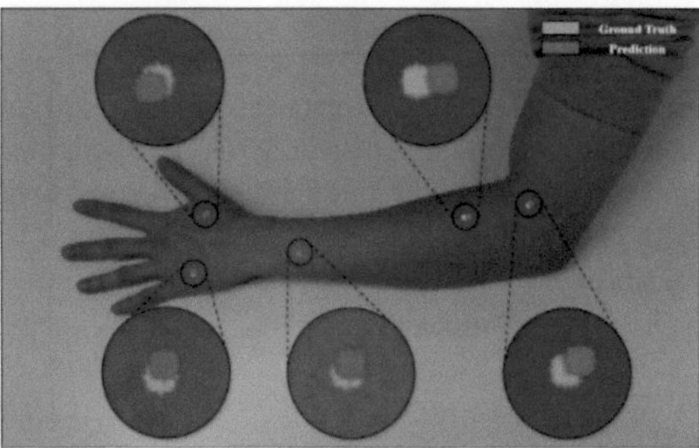

Fig. 6. Comparison of predicted (red) and ground truth (green) acupoint positions on the forearm.

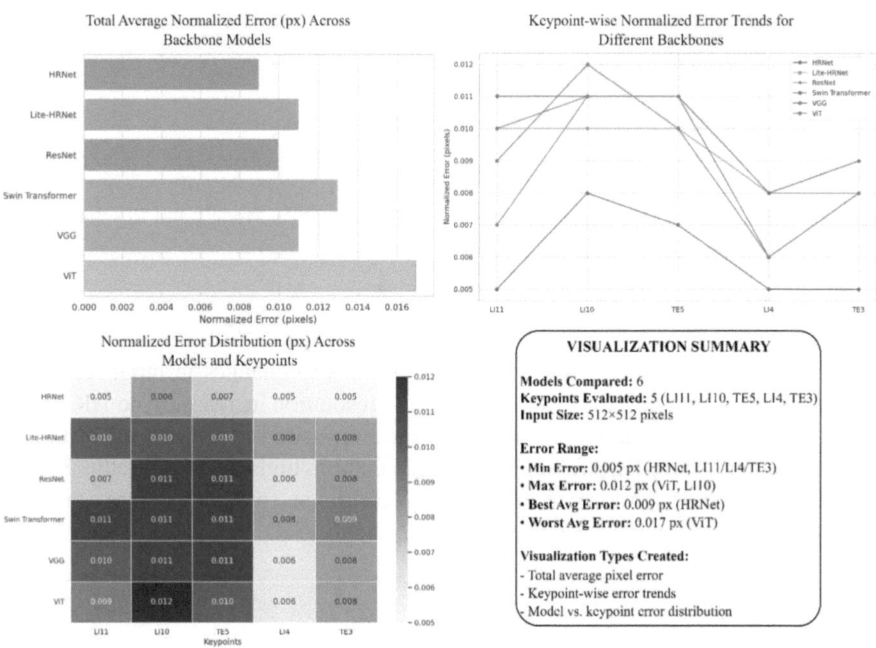

Fig. 7. Comparative Visualization of Acupoint Localization Errors at 512×512 Px Input Resolution

Qualitative analysis is presented in Fig. 6 and 7. Figure 6 provides additional side-by-side examples illustrating common prediction patterns and challenges, particularly in ambiguous regions or lower-quality input samples. While Fig. 7 shows representative predictions by overlaying predicted keypoints (in red) against ground truth (in green) for each model. HRNet demonstrates visually consistent alignment with ground truth, while Swin Transformer often displays noticeable deviations.

Overall, HRNet and Lite-HRNet demonstrate the best balance of accuracy and consistency, making them well-suited for detailed acupoint localization. While transformer-based models like ViT have succeeded in other vision tasks, they may require further architectural tuning or hybrid designs to perform effectively in fine-grained localization scenarios.

5 Discussion and Conclusion

This study presents a comprehensive evaluation of six widely used deep learning backbones, HRNet, Lite-HRNet, ResNet, Swin Transformer, VGG, and ViT for forearm acupoint localization using a top-down pose estimation framework. We focused on five clinically relevant acupoints (LI11, LI10, TE5, LI4, and TE3) and assessed model performance across three input resolutions (256×256, 384×384, and 512×512 px), using normalized Euclidean distance and standard deviation to measure accuracy and consistency.

Among all models, HRNet consistently achieved the best localization accuracy and stability across keypoints and resolutions. Its high spatial fidelity makes it particularly suitable for fine-grained anatomical tasks. Lite-HRNet and ResNet also performed well, especially at higher resolutions, positioning them as efficient candidates for real-time or edge-based medical applications, such as wearable or mobile health systems.

In contrast, transformer-based models, Swin Transformer and ViT, exhibited higher localization errors. While ViT showed improvements at higher resolutions, it did not surpass convolutional models. These results indicate that transformer architectures may require further refinement, such as hybrid CNN-transformer designs or better multi-scale feature extraction, to meet the precision demands of clinical localization.

Despite promising outcomes, our study has limitations. The dataset was collected in a controlled environment, which may not capture real-world variations in lighting, occlusions, or anatomical differences. Furthermore, our focus was limited to forearm acupoints, leaving generalizability to other body regions unaddressed.

Future directions include incorporating 3D keypoint estimation to improve spatial understanding and support applications like robotic acupuncture and motion rehabilitation. As AI systems move toward clinical use, privacy-preserving methods such as federated learning and on-device inference will be crucial for secure deployment.

In summary, this work establishes a benchmark for acupoint localization and highlights the significance of backbone architecture and resolution. HRNet emerges as a strong baseline for building AI-assisted acutherapy systems. With continued advancements, deep learning-based localization holds transformative potential for personalized and intelligent digital healthcare.

Acknowledgment. This research was supported by the National Research Foundation of Korea (NRF), funded by the Ministry of Science and ICT (No. 2022M3A9B6082791).

References

1. Du, H., Zhang, P., Lei, L., Qi, X., He, Y., Zhao, B.: Deep learning-based intelligent localization of acupoints. In: Proceedings - 2024 5th International Conference on Computer, Big Data and Artificial Intelligence, ICCBD+AI 2024, Institute of Electrical and Electronics Engineers Inc., pp. 99–103 (2024). https://doi.org/10.1109/ICCBD-AI65562.2024.00024
2. Wang, H., Liu, L., Wang, Y., Du, S.: Hand acupuncture point localization method based on a dual-attention mechanism and cascade network model. Biomed. Opt. Express **14**, 5965–5978 (2023). https://doi.org/10.1364/BOE.501663
3. Yang, S., et al.: Exploring an innovative deep learning solution for acupuncture point localization on the weak feature body surface of the human back. IEEE J. Biomed. Health Inform. (2024). https://doi.org/10.1109/JBHI.2024.3511128
4. Sun, Q., Ma, J., Craig, P., Dai, L., Lim, E.G.: AcuSim: a synthetic dataset for cer-vicocranial acupuncture points localisation. Sci. Data **12** (2025). https://doi.org/10.1038/s41597-025-04934-9
5. Lin, T.Y., et al.: Microsoft COCO: common objects in context. In: LNCS (including subseries Lecture Notes in Artificial Intelligence and Lecture Notes in Bioinformatics), Springer Verlag, pp. 740–755 (2014). https://doi.org/10.1007/978-3-319-10602-1_48
6. Andriluka, M., Pishchulin, L., Gehler, P., Schiele, B.: 2D human pose estimation: new benchmark and state of the art analysis. In: Proceedings of the IEEE Computer Society Conference on Computer Vision and Pattern Recognition, IEEE Computer Society, pp. 3686–3693 (2014). https://doi.org/10.1109/CVPR.2014.471
7. Toshev, A., Szegedy, C.: DeepPose: human pose estimation via deep neural networks. In: Proceedings of the IEEE Computer Society Conference on Computer Vision and Pattern Recognition, IEEE Computer Society, pp. 1653–1660 (2014). https://doi.org/10.1109/CVPR.2014.214
8. Zhao, J., Mathieu, M., Goroshin, R., LeCun, Y.: Stacked what-where auto-encoders (2015). https://doi.org/10.1007/978-3-319-46484-8_29
9. He, K., Zhang, X., Ren, S., Sun, J.: Deep residual learning for image recognition. In: Proceedings of the IEEE Computer Society Conference on Computer Vision and Pattern Recognition, IEEE Computer Society, pp. 770–778 (2016). https://doi.org/10.1109/CVPR.2016.90
10. Simonyan, K., Zisserman, A.: Very deep convolutional networks for large-scale image recognition. In: 3rd International Conference on Learning Representations, ICLR 2015 - Conference Track Proceedings, International Conference on Learning Representations, ICLR (2015). https://doi.org/10.48550/arXiv.1409.1556
11. Yu, C., et al.: Lite-HRNet: a lightweight high-resolution network. In: Proceedings of the IEEE Computer Society Conference on Computer Vision and Pattern Recognition, IEEE Computer Society, pp. 10435–10445 (2021). https://doi.org/10.1109/CVPR46437.2021.01030
12. Liu, Z., et al.: Swin transformer: hierarchical vision transformer using shifted windows. In: Proceedings of the IEEE International Conference on Computer Vision, Institute of Electrical and Electronics Engineers Inc., pp. 9992–10002 (2021). https://doi.org/10.1109/ICCV48922.2021.00986
13. Xu, Y., Zhang, J., Zhang, Q., Tao, D.: ViTPose: simple vision transformer base-lines for human pose estimation. In: Advances in Neural Information Processing Systems, Neural Information Processing Systems Foundation (2022). https://doi.org/10.48550/arXiv.2204.12484
14. Dosovitskiy, A., et al.: An image is worth 16x16 words: transformers for image recognition at scale. In: ICLR 2021 - 9th International Conference on Learning Representations, International Conference on Learning Representations, ICLR. arXiv:2010.11929v2 (2021)
15. Sun, K., Xiao, B., Liu, D., Wang, J.: Deep high-resolution representation learning for human pose estimation (2019). https://doi.org/10.48550/arXiv.1902.09212

Pronoun Matters: A Benchmark for Diagnosing Gender Bias in Emotion Classification

Qurat Ul Ain Aisha, Yu-Jin Cho, and Byung Gyu Kim[✉]

Department of IT Engineering, Sookmyung Women's University, Seoul, South Korea
{aishanazar65,yj2431101,bg.kim}@sookmyung.ac.kr

Abstract. Emotion recognition systems are increasingly embedded in socially sensitive applications, ranging from mental health support to education and human-computer interaction, where biased predictions can lead to real-world harm. This study investigates whether SOTA (state-of-the-art) emotion classifiers introduces systematic bias by altering predictions when only the pronoun in a sentence is changed ("he", "she", "they"). We construct and release a novel benchmark of 1,000 emotionally neutral sentence triplets, each systematically varied only by subject pronoun ('he', 'she', 'they'), to serve as a controlled testbed for diagnosing shifts induced by pronouns in emotion classification. Our results reveal non-trivial mismatch rates in predicted emotions, with some models showing up to a 7.7% shift when substituting gendered pronouns with plural forms. For example, phrases labeled as *anger* or *disapproval* for "she" often shift to *confusion* or *neutral* for "they", indicating potential loss of emotional specificity. While the degree of drift varies across model architectures, all models exhibit asymmetric behavior in emotion prediction. These findings highlight the need for robust evaluation protocols in affective AI and motivate deeper analysis of pronoun-sensitivity in pretrained emotion models.

Keywords: Emotion Recognition · Gender Bias · Fairness in NLP · Affective Computing · Ethical AI

1 Introduction

1.1 Motivation: Why Gender Bias in Emotion AI Matters

Emotion AI is increasingly deployed in sensitive, human-facing applications such as virtual therapy, education platforms, social robots, and mental health support tools. These systems do not only classify emotions but they actively shape how individuals are perceived, supported, or judged. Misclassifications in emotional inference can therefore have far-reaching personal and social consequences. For example, a virtual counselor interpreting "she looked away after the meeting" as "anger" rather than "embarrassment" or "anxiety" could lead to misguided interventions that do more harm than good. Crucially, most emotion recognition

© The Author(s) 2026
B.-G. Kim et al. (Eds.): MITA 2025, CCIS 2675, pp. 98–110, 2026.
https://doi.org/10.1007/978-981-95-3141-7_9

systems rely on large pretrained language models that inherit and perpetuate historical biases from their training corpora. While gender bias in tasks like coreference resolution or occupation prediction has been widely studied, affective reasoning like how models assign emotional labels to gendered language remains a largely unexamined area. Yet, emotions are more subjective and socially constructed than factual tasks, making them especially vulnerable to subtle biases. This work investigates a simple but powerful question: if only the pronoun in a sentence is changed (e.g., from "he" to "she" or "they"), does the predicted emotion change too? Such a minimal change should not alter the emotional meaning, and yet, we find that it often does. This phenomenon suggests that emotion classifiers may be encoding and acting upon implicit gender associations, which can systematically distort emotional understanding. Given the growing reliance on emotion AI in socially impactful contexts, diagnosing and addressing such biases is not just a technical challenge but it is a matter of fairness, trustworthiness, and ethical responsibility. Our work introduces a focused and interpretable benchmark to expose these biases and spark a broader re-evaluation of how affective AI systems are trained, evaluated, and deployed.

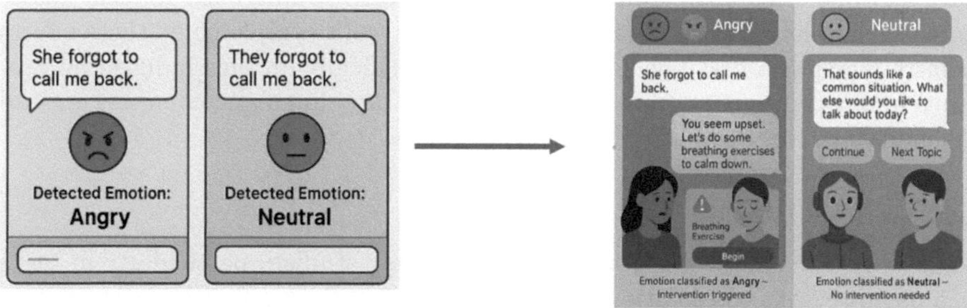

Fig. 1. Impact of Emotion variation induced by pronouns in Real-World Applications. Changing the pronoun from "she" to "they" shifts the model's predicted emotion from *angry* to *neutral*, which in turn affects downstream actions in a therapeutic AI assistant. This highlights how subtle linguistic changes can lead to different interventions that potentially overlook the distress signals due to gender-related bias in emotion inference.

This paper makes the following key contributions to the emerging field of fairness and bias analysis in affective AI:

– **Introduced a Pronoun-Sensitive Evaluation Benchmark:** We construct and release *PronounBiasEval-1K*, a diagnostic dataset of 1,000 sentence triplets with controlled pronoun substitutions ("he", "she", "they") designed to isolate gender and plurality effects on emotion classification.
– **Revealed Model-Wide Sensitivity through Cross-Architecture Analysis:** We systematically evaluate five diverse, pretrained emotion classification models, revealing consistent and architecture-agnostic drift in predictions caused solely by pronoun variation.

- **Developed Diagnostic Tools for Bias Attribution:** We propose an interpretable evaluation framework comprising label mismatch rates and an emotion shift matrix that exposes asymmetric patterns of pronoun-induced bias across emotion categories.
- **Uncovered Systematic Bias from Plural Pronouns:** Our analysis highlights that the singular "they" a commonly used gender-neutral pronoun, elicits distinct prediction patterns compared to "he" or "she", exposing a previously overlooked dimension of pronoun bias in affective models. [1]

Section 2 summarizes prior work on gender bias and fairness in affective computing. Section 3 introduces the dataset construction, and evaluation strategy. Section 4 presents detailed mismatch analysis with heatmaps and case studies. Section 6 concludes with insights and future work for mitigating bias in emotion-aware AI.

2   Background and Related Work

Several benchmarks have been proposed to observe bias in NLP models. For example, the WinoBias dataset [15] evaluates gender bias in coreference resolution, while StereoSet [16] quantifies social bias in language models across sentence completions and entailment tasks. Our work complements these efforts by introducing the first benchmark focused specifically on bias induced by pronouns in emotion recognition, a domain where small linguistic changes can lead to significantly different affective interpretations.

2.1   Gender Bias in NLP

Gender bias in NLP systems has been extensively studied, particularly in tasks such as co-reference resolution, word embeddings, and occupational stereotyping. For example, Kotek et al. [1] demonstrated that large language models (LLMs) often reinforce gendered occupational associations (e.g., linking "nurse" to women), reflecting historical biases in training corpora. Nemani et al. [2] further critiqued the methodological inconsistencies in bias evaluation, highlighting the need for more reliable and standardized diagnostic tools. In response, recent metrics such as StereoSet++ [29] and BiasBERTScore [30] have emerged to provide model-agnostic bias evaluation frameworks.

However, most prior work has focused on factual or syntactic tasks such as sentence completion, analogy resolution, or co-reference while overlooking emotion classification, a domain where gender bias may have more subjective and socially consequential effects. In contrast, our study investigates how minimal linguistic changes, such as altering a subject pronoun ("he," "she," "they"), can shift a model's emotional inference. This affective bias remains underexplored despite its potential to impact high-stakes applications like mental health assessment, hiring tools, and conversational agents.

---

[1] Dataset and evaluation toolkit available at: https://github.com/smu-ivpl/Diagno sing-Emotion-Classification-Drift-from-Pronoun-Substitution. Licensed under CC BY 4.0.

2.2   Fairness in Emotion Recognition

Fairness in emotion recognition remains a relatively underexplored yet critical concern, particularly as emotion AI systems are increasingly deployed in high-stakes domains like mental health, education, and hiring. Recent studies have begun to expose fairness issues in both speech and facial modalities. For example, Upadhyay et al. [3] found that speech emotion recognition (SER) models often fail to generalize gender-consistently across datasets, while Rizvi et al. [4] proposed latent alignment techniques to mitigate bias in facial emotion classification.

However, much of this work focuses on modality-specific or dataset-level bias and largely overlooks how subtle linguistic variations such as changing a subject's pronoun can systematically affect emotion predictions. Our work addresses this gap by introducing a fine-grained, pronoun-controlled benchmark that isolates and quantifies such sensitivity, enabling a more precise and interpretable analysis of fairness in affective NLP.

2.3   Limitations of Prior Studies

Despite growing attention to gender bias in NLP and emotion recognition, existing studies exhibit several key limitations. First, most analyses are confined to binary pronouns ("he" vs. "she"), neglecting plural references like "they" even when "they" is used unambiguously to denote multiple individuals. This narrow focus restricts the ecological validity of bias evaluations and fails to capture the full range of pronoun-driven model behaviors in real-world language.

Second, prior work lacks standardized, fine-grained benchmarks that systematically isolate and measure the effect of subtle linguistic perturbations such as pronoun substitution on emotion predictions. In the absence of such tools, it remains difficult to assess model robustness, compare bias across architectures, or track progress over time.

To address these gaps, we introduce a controlled, sentence-level benchmark explicitly designed to quantify prediction drift caused by pronoun variation. Our framework enables interpretable, reproducible evaluations of gender and plurality sensitivity in emotion classification models.

2.4   Sociolinguistic Perspective on Gender and Emotion Language

Human perception of emotion is shaped by sociolinguistic factors, notably the encoding of gender stereotypes within language [18,19]. Women are often associated with sadness or empathy, whereas men are linked to anger or assertiveness. These implicit biases influence linguistic choices and interpretation of emotional expressions [20]. Even minimal cues, such as pronouns, activate gender-based schemas affecting emotional inference. Sentences like "She confronted the manager" may be perceived as more emotionally charged than their masculine counterparts. Emotion recognition models trained on biased corpora risk internalizing such associations, potentially reinforcing harmful stereotypes. Our analysis reveals that minor linguistic variations, such as pronoun substitutions, systematically shift model-predicted emotions, indicating sensitivity to embedded social signals. Recognizing the interplay between linguistic form and social meaning is critical for developing fair and socially responsible affective AI. Our benchmark explicitly evaluates gendered linguistic cues, exposing subtle sociolinguistic biases in computational emotion recognition.

3   Methodology

3.1   Benchmark Construction

To assess bias caused by pronoun changes in emotion recognition, we created **PronounBiasEval-1K**, a dataset of 1,000 syntactically neutral English sentence templates reflecting everyday contexts (e.g., workplace, social settings). Each template is instantiated into three versions using subject pronouns: "he", "she", and "they", yielding 3,000 total inputs (triplets). Verbs and objects were carefully selected to avoid emotionally charged content (e.g., "_ stayed behind after the meeting"). Figure 2 illustrates this process.

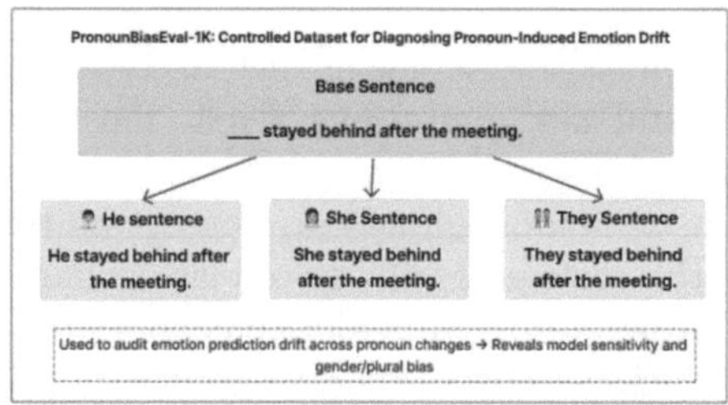

Fig. 2. From each base sentence, three variants are generated by substituting only the subject pronoun ("he", "she", "they"), enabling controlled analysis of emotion drift.

We note that "they" is used strictly as a plural form, though models may interpret it as singular and gender-neutral, potentially contributing to prediction variance.

3.2   Evaluation Metrics

Label Consistency Rate. To measure stability, we computed the mismatch rate across all sentence triplets. Table 1 shows results of evaluation of three pairwise comparisons: HeShe, HeThey, and SheThey.

Emotion Shift Matrices. We constructed directional confusion-style heatmaps for each pronoun pair, where rows represent predicted emotions for the first pronoun and columns denote shifts when the pronoun is changed. Figures 3a–3c are the heatmaps that reveal asymmetric drift trends, for example, *anger* for "she" frequently changing to *joy* for "they", showing the subtle impact of gendered or plural references on affective interpretation.

4   Experimental Results

4.1   Emotion Drift Analysis and Significance

We evaluated five emotion recognition models on 1,000 sentence triplets, each varying only in subject pronoun ("he", "she", "they"). For each model, we computed the proportion of mismatched top-1 emotion predictions between pronoun variants. Table 1 summarizes mismatch rates across pronoun pairs.

Table 1. Mismatch Rates (%) Across Models for Pronoun Pairs.

Model	He–She	He–They	She–They
BERT-base (GoEmotions)	3.6	6.4	6.5
BERT-alt (Nateraw)	2.9	5.5	5.8
RoBERTa-base	1.5	2.9	3.8
DistilBERT	2.0	4.1	4.3
DistilBART	4.1	7.5	7.7

DistilBART was most sensitive to pronoun variation, while RoBERTa was most stable. Across models, "they" substitutions showed higher drift, indicating that plural or non-specific references introduce more prediction variance. Generative models (e.g., DistilBART) exhibited greater instability than classification-based models (e.g., RoBERTa, BERT).

Statistical Validation. To assess whether these shifts were statistically significant, we conducted McNemar's tests, suitable for paired nominal data. The chi-square statistic is:

$$\chi^2 = \frac{(|b - c| - 1)^2}{b + c}, \tag{1}$$

Table 2. McNemar's Test Results for Pronoun Variants.

Pair	b	c	p-value
he-she	72	98	0.0147
he-they	115	164	0.0011
she-they	109	158	0.0020

where b and c represent the asymmetric prediction disagreements across variants. Results (Table 2) show that all shifts were significant ($p < 0.05$), confirming that pronoun changes meaningfully affect predictions.

Observed Drift Patterns. "She" variants frequently triggered intense emotions (*anger, fear, sadness*), while "he" produces neutral or confused. "They" often shifted predictions to softer emotions like *joy, curiosity,* or *neutral.* Notably, transitions were asymmetric: "she" → "they" yielded more change than the "they" → "she" . These trends reveal latent gender-associated biases in model behavior despite identical semantics.

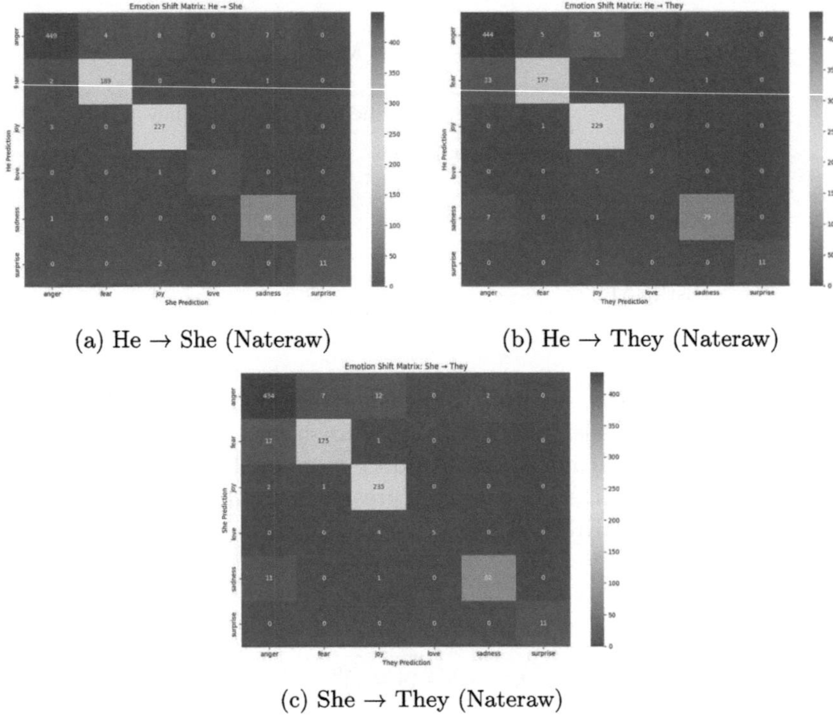

(a) He → She (Nateraw)   (b) He → They (Nateraw)

(c) She → They (Nateraw)

Fig. 3. Emotion shift matrices for pronoun substitutions.

4.2 Discussion and Analysis

Even modest mismatch rates (2–7%) have serious implications for emotionally sensitive applications such as mental health support, education platforms, sentiment analysis, and conversational agents. A subtle misclassification, for instance labeling a sentence as *neutral* rather than *disapproval* solely due to a pronoun change, can obscure critical emotional cues and degrade user trust. Our analysis reveals these mismatches are systematic rather than random, disproportionately affecting emotions like *anger, fear,* and *sadness,* and highlighting the influence of gendered and plural linguistic markers. Such biases may inadvertently reinforce harmful stereotypes, associating anger predominantly with males or sadness with females, thus negatively impacting downstream tasks like chatbot responses or content moderation. The proposed benchmark uncovers these subtle yet consequential biases, providing an interpretable, lightweight diagnostic for pre-deployment audits. Early detection of these vulnerabilities is crucial for developing fair and trustworthy affective AI systems.

4.3   Toward Enhanced Metrics for Affective Bias Evaluation

To build on this work, future fairness assessments in emotion recognition should go beyond binary accuracy and incorporate nuanced metrics that reflect pronoun sensitivity and interpretive stability. We suggest the development of additional diagnostic measures such as:

- **Drift Stability Score (DSS):** Quantifies the proportion of predictions that remain unchanged across all pronoun variants.
- **Asymmetric Emotion Shift Index (AESI):** Captures directional drift patterns (e.g., from negative to neutral) across gendered vs. plural substitutions.
- **Pronoun Fairness Gap (PFG):** Measures the variance in emotion prediction confidence across different pronoun forms for the same base sentence.
- **Latent Attribution Discrepancy (LAD):** Compares internal attention or feature attributions between pronoun variants to detect deeper representational biases.

Table 3. Fairness Metric Evaluation Across Emotion Classification Models. Higher DSS and AESI indicate robustness and directional bias detection, respectively. Lower PFG and LAD imply less confidence drift and internal bias.

Model	DSS ↑	AESI (She→They) ↑	PFG ↓	LAD ↓
BERT-base (GoEmotions)	0.921	0.043	0.087	0.132
BERT-alt (Nateraw)	0.905	0.051	0.091	0.148
RoBERTa-base	**0.953**	**0.018**	**0.066**	**0.108**
DistilBERT	0.931	0.035	0.072	0.120
DistilBART	0.872	0.072	0.102	0.165

Table 3 tells that incorporating such metrics will enable more comprehensive and model-agnostic evaluation of fairness in affective NLP. Moreover, these tools can guide debiasing efforts by identifying where and how models internalize gendered affect associations, ultimately contributing to the development of more inclusive and robust emotion-aware systems.

4.4   Case Studies: Real-World Risks of Pronoun-Sensitive Emotion Misclassification

To highlight the practical risks of pronoun-induced emotion drift, we present hypothetical case studies across three key applications of emotion AI. These examples demonstrate how minor inconsistencies in model predictions can lead to tangible harm or bias.

Mental Health Chatbots. A sentence like "She didn't respond after the interview" may trigger *anger*, while the same sentence with "he" or "they" elicits *sadness* or *neutral*. Such inconsistencies can result in inappropriate responses-e.g., unnecessary de-escalation or missed signs of distress-undermining trust and effectiveness in therapeutic or crisis-support settings.

AI-Assisted Hiring. Emotion classification in candidate evaluations may skew decisions if, for instance, "He discussed the project setback" is labeled *confident*, while "She discussed the project setback" is tagged *nervous* or *regretful*. Such bias silently reinforces gender stereotypes and may lead to unfair assessments over time.

Social Media Monitoring. Emotion AI used for moderation or sentiment analysis may over-attribute *anger* to masculine pronouns or under-detect *fear* in non-binary expressions. This distorts the emotional landscape, potentially misallocating moderation efforts and failing to flag harmful content accurately.

5   Benchmark Toolkit and Extensibility

To promote reproducibility and adoption, we release the **PronounBiasEval-1K** benchmark and a modular evaluation toolkit.[2] The toolkit enables consistency checks across sentence triplets, with visualizations such as drift matrices and confidence histograms.

Designed for flexibility, it supports diverse model types (e.g., transformers, RNNs), both zero-shot and fine-tuned evaluations, and can be extended with custom fairness metrics. The schema also supports future expansion across:

- **Linguistic variation**: informal styles, alternative sentence templates, and conversational discourse;
- **Multilingual adaptation**: localization with attention to grammatical gender and cultural context;
- **Intersectional attributes**: analysis of drift induced by race, age, or dialect;
- **Multimodal inputs**: integration with speech or vision encoders for broader emotion consistency checks.

This open, extensible platform enables fine-grained bias diagnostics and fosters transparency in emotion AI.

---

[2] https://github.com/smu-ivpl/Diagnosing-Emotion-Classification-Drift-from-Pronoun-Substitution.

6 Conclusion and Future Work

6.1 Summary and Analysis

We introduced *PronounBiasEval-1K*, a controlled benchmark for diagnosing bias caused by pronoun changes in emotion recognition. Using 1,000 sentence triplets differing only in subject pronoun ("he", "she", "they"), we evaluated five diverse NLP models. Results reveal that even minimal pronoun shifts can induce significant changes in predicted emotions, up to 7.7% mismatch, particularly in classes like *anger*, *fear*, and *sadness*. These findings indicate that affective models may encode subtle gender-linked biases despite identical semantic content.

Such misclassifications are not just technical artifacts but ethical risks: in domains like therapy bots or educational feedback, emotion misjudgment may reinforce stereotypes or invalidate user experiences. Our benchmark highlights the need for fairness-sensitive evaluations in affective AI pipelines.

6.2 Limitations and Future Work

While *PronounBiasEval-1K* offers a systematic and reproducible framework for evaluating pronoun-induced drift in emotion classification, it also presents several limitations that warrant further investigation. Recognizing these limitations is essential for guiding the next phase of research on fairness in affective NLP.

Template-Based and Text-Only Design: Our benchmark uses controlled, template-based sentences to isolate pronoun effects, abstracting away complexities such as sarcasm, idioms, code-switching, and informal cues.

Absence of Multimodal and Contextual Signals: Emotion perception is inherently multimodal, incorporating vocal, visual, and dialogic context. Our text-only, sentence-level design may underestimate drift effects that real-world contextual signals could resolve. Extending this approach to dialogue systems and multimodal models is necessary for evaluating pronoun sensitivity under richer conditions.

Ambiguity in Singular vs. Plural "They": Despite attempts at clarity, the inherent ambiguity of "they" poses challenges. Its reference may vary between singular gender-neutral, plural, or unknown entities. Without explicit disambiguation cues, it remains unclear if observed prediction drift arises from gender neutrality, plurality, or ambiguity itself. Incorporating explicit semantic or syntactic disambiguation is a critical future direction.

Evaluation in Zero-Shot Settings: We evaluate publicly available pretrained models without fine-tuning, thus capturing only initial biases. This does not reveal how biases might shift during adaptation. Additionally, our English-only scope omits potential multilingual variations. Cultural differences in pronoun use and emotion interpretation should be explored in future multilingual studies.

To address these limitations, we propose several research directions:

- **Bias-Aware Fine-Tuning:** Creating datasets explicitly balanced for pronoun use and fine-tuning models accordingly may reduce pronoun-induced bias without compromising accuracy.
- **Contrastive Data Augmentation:** Training models with minimally different pronoun pairs using contrastive or adversarial strategies can enforce prediction consistency.
- **Cross-Lingual Extensions:** Extending benchmarks to languages with gendered grammar (e.g., Spanish, Arabic) or diverse pronoun norms can clarify whether pronoun sensitivity is universal or language-specific.
- **Context-Aware Modeling:** Incorporating broader context and explicit coreference resolution might mitigate models' overreliance on isolated pronouns, improving robustness in realistic settings.
- **Multimodal Integration:** Expanding the benchmark to multimodal data, such as speech and facial expressions, would reveal interactions between textual pronoun bias and non-verbal emotional signals.

Disclosure of Interests. The authors have no competing interests to declare that are relevant to the content of this article.

References

1. Kotek, H., Dockum, R., Sun, D.Q.: Gender bias and stereotypes in large language models. arXiv preprint arXiv:2308.14921 (2023)
2. Nemani, P., Joel, Y.D., Vijay, P., Liza, F.F.: Gender bias in transformer models: A comprehensive survey. arXiv preprint arXiv:2306.10530 (2023)
3. Upadhyay, S.G., Chien, W.-S., Lee, C.-C.: Is it still fair? Investigating gender fairness in cross-corpus speech emotion recognition. arXiv preprint arXiv:2501.00995 (2025)
4. Rizvi, S.S.A., Seth, A., Narang, P.: Balancing the scales: enhancing fairness in facial emotion recognition with latent alignment. In: International Conference on Pattern Recognition, pp. 113–128 (2025)
5. Stanczak, K., Augenstein, I.: A survey on gender bias in natural language processing. arXiv preprint arXiv:2112.14168 (2021)
6. Plaza-del-Arco, F.M., Cercas Curry, A., Curry, A., Abercrombie, G., Hovy, D.: Angry men, sad women: Large language models reflect gendered stereotypes in emotion attribution. arXiv preprint arXiv:2403.03121 (2024)
7. Bhardwaj, R., Majumder, N., Poria, S.: Investigating gender bias in BERT. arXiv preprint arXiv:2009.05021 (2020)
8. Zhao, J., et al.: Gender bias in contextualized word embeddings. arXiv preprint arXiv:1904.03310 (2019)
9. Park, J.H., Shin, J., Fung, P.: Reducing gender bias in abusive language detection. arXiv preprint arXiv:1808.07231 (2018)
10. Sobhani, N., Delany, S.: Towards fairer NLP models: handling gender bias in classification tasks. In: Proceedings of 5th Workshop on Gender Bias in NLP (GeBNLP) (2024)
11. Anonymous: Examining and mitigating gender bias in text emotion detection task. Neurocomputing **489**, 1–10 (2022)

12. Anonymous: Responsible AI: Gender bias assessment in emotion recognition. arXiv preprint arXiv:2103.11436 (2021)
13. Anonymous: Gender bias in transformers: a comprehensive review of detection and mitigation techniques. J. Artif. Intell. Res. **76**, 1–30 (2023)
14. Anonymous: Less can be more: representational vs. stereotypical gender bias in facial emotion recognition. Int. J. Intell. Syst. **39**(2), 1–15 (2024)
15. Zhao, J., Wang, T., Yatskar, M., Ordonez, V., Chang, K.: Gender bias in coreference resolution: evaluation and debiasing methods. In: Proceedings of NAACL-HLT, pp. 15–20 (2018)
16. Nadeem, M., Bethke, A., Reddy, S.: StereoSet: measuring stereotypical bias in pretrained language models. In: Proceedings of ACL, pp. 5356–5371 (2021)
17. Anonymous: Facial trustworthiness dampens own-gender bias in emotion recognition. Psychol. Res. **87**(4), 1–10 (2023)
18. Plant, E.A., Hyde, J.S., Keltner, D., Devine, P.G.: The gender stereotyping of emotions. Psychol. Women Q. **24**(1), 81–92 (2000)
19. Brody, L.R., Hall, J.A.: Gender, emotion, and expression. In: Handbook of Emotions, pp. 325–414. Guilford Press (1999)
20. Lakoff, R.: Language and Woman's Place. Harper and Row (1975)
21. Kusner, M.J., Loftus, J., Russell, C., Silva, R.: Counterfactual fairness. In: Advances in Neural Information Processing Systems (NeurIPS), pp. 4066–4076 (2017)
22. Saravia, E., Liu, H., Huang, Y., Wu, J., Cambria, E.: Examining gender and race bias in sentiment analysis systems. In: Proceedings of the 27th International Conference on Computational Linguistics (COLING), pp. 629–634 (2018)
23. Mitchell, M., et al.: Model cards for model reporting. In: Proceedings of the Conference on Fairness, Accountability, and Transparency (FAccT), pp. 220–229 (2019)
24. McNemar, Q.: Note on the sampling error of the difference between correlated proportions or percentages. Psychometrika **12**(2), 153–157 (1947)
25. Anonymous: Age and gender differences in emotion recognition. Front. Psychol. **10**, 2371 (2019)
26. Saravia, E., et al.: Examining gender and race bias in sentiment analysis systems. In: Proceedings of EMNLP, pp. 1–10 (2018)
27. Anonymous: Theories of 'gender' in NLP bias research. In: Proceedings of Conference on Fairness, Accountability, and Transparency (FAccT), pp. 1–10 (2023)
28. Anonymous: A large scale evaluation of social bias on speech emotion recognition models. arXiv preprint arXiv:2406.05065 (2024)
29. Luo, Y., Yin, J., Mihalcea, R.: StereoSet++: measuring robustness and calibration of social bias in language models. In: Proceedings of ACL, pp. 2334–2346 (2024)
30. Ramachandran, A.J., Zhou, E.: BiasBERTScore: a reference-free metric for evaluating gender bias in text classification. In: Proceedings of EACL, pp. 551–563 (2025)

Analyzing Hyperparameter Optimization Methods for Federated Learning Systems

Sa Jim Soe Moe[1], Qazi Waqas Khan[1,2], Nguyen Anh Tuan[1], Misbah Bibi[1], and Dohyeun Kim[1,2(✉)]

[1] Jeju National University, Jeju 63243, Republic of Korea
kimdh@jejunu.ac.kr
[2] Bigdata Research Center, Jeju National University,
Jeju 63243, Republic of Korea

Abstract. The growing interest in federated learning (FL) has led to increased attention on hyperparameter optimization (HPO) within distributed settings. However, effectively applying HPO in practical FL scenarios presents unique challenges owing to the decentralized characteristics of data and computation. This study provides a comprehensive examination of various HPO strategies tailored for FL, addressing the limitations of earlier analyses that primarily focused on centralized environments with unrestricted data access and consolidated processing resources. In contrast, FL imposes constraints where individual participants operate on isolated local datasets without sharing raw data. As a result, conventional HPO techniques must be adapted to accommodate these decentralized conditions. We explore these adaptations and highlight promising directions for future work. Furthermore, we evaluate the performance of Random Search, a robust yet straightforward HPO approach, through empirical testing in a realistic federated setup using the MNIST dataset in a non-IID setting.

Keywords: Hyperparameter Optimization · Federated Learning · Decentralized Optimization · Distributed Machine Learning

1   Introduction

The growing adoption of deep neural networks (DNNs) across diverse application domains stems from their ability to automate complex tasks with minimal human intervention. In centralized machine learning, tuning hyperparameters, such as learning rate, momentum, and batch size, remains a nontrivial and time-intensive process, often relying on expert intuition and iterative experimentation. This challenge becomes significantly more complex in decentralized settings, such as federated learning (FL), where limited communication, heterogeneous client environments, and varying data distributions constrain hyperparameter optimization (HPO).

Federated learning enables collaborative model training across distributed clients, each retaining its local dataset to preserve privacy and confidentiality.

B.-G. Kim et al. (Eds.): MITA 2025, CCIS 2675, pp. 111–117, 2026.
https://doi.org/10.1007/978-981-95-3141-7_10

However, the absence of a centralized data repository complicates the direct application of conventional HPO techniques. In response, automated HPO methods have been developed to help practitioners efficiently fine-tune model parameters in FL scenarios. These approaches aim to optimize performance while accounting for the inherent challenges of FL, including communication costs, system heterogeneity, and strict privacy requirements.

2   Federated Hyperparameter Optimization

2.1   Problem Definition

In a centralized system for machine learning, we have a model class $\mathcal{M}$ paired with a learning algorithm $\mathcal{A}$, which is governed by a set of hyperparameters (HPs) h from the space $\mathcal{H}$. Given a training dataset d, the model is derived as:

$$\mathcal{A}(\mathcal{M}, h, d) \rightarrow m \in \mathcal{M}.$$

The model's performance on a separate holdout dataset d' is assessed using a loss function $L(m, d')$. The centralized hyperparameter optimization (HPO) problem is then formulated as:

$$\min_{h \in \mathcal{H}} L\big(\mathcal{A}(\mathcal{M}, h, d), d'\big) \tag{1}$$

During federation, assume there are c clients, each with its private dataset d_i, where $i \in \{1, 2, \ldots, c\}$. The union of these datasets forms the overall training set:

$$d = \bigcup_{i=1}^{c} d_i.$$

Similarly, $d' = \{d'_i\}_{i=1}^{c}$ represents the collection of validation datasets for all clients. Each model class, along with its learning algorithm, is governed by local hyperparameters h_i specific to each client, resulting in the overall HP set:

$$h = \{h_i\}_{i=1}^{c}.$$

Federated Learning (FL) frameworks typically include an aggregation mechanism introducing additional HPs, denoted by ϕ. The FL learning algorithm $\mathcal{F}$ uses these inputs to generate a model. Depending on the objective, the FL-HPO problem can be formulated as:

$$\min_{\phi, h} L\big(\mathcal{F}(\mathcal{M}, \phi, h, d), d'\big) \tag{2}$$

On the other hand, the issue arises when the assessment is carried out utilizing individual client validation datasets d'_i. In such a case, the problem becomes:

$$\min_{\phi, h_i} \mathrm{Agg} \{L\left(\mathcal{F}(\mathcal{M}, \phi, h = \{h_i\}_{i=1}^{c}, d), d'\right)\} \tag{3}$$

where the aggregation function $\mathrm{Agg} : \mathbb{R}^c \rightarrow \mathbb{R}$ aggregates the losses for each client into a single number.

It is evident that HPO in FL (FL-HPO) adds complexity when contrasting the FL-HPO formulations 2 and 3 with the centralized HPO problem 1.

2.2   Hyperparameter Tuning in Federated Learning

Conventional hyperparameter optimization methods typically assume centralized access to data and computational resources. These assumptions break down in FL, where data remains decentralized across clients and communication is constrained. As a result, specialized HPO strategies for FL have been developed to address issues such as client heterogeneity, limited observability, and resource trade-offs. Existing FL-HPO approaches can be broadly categorized based on their search strategies, including generic black-box optimization, swarm intelligence, reinforcement learning, gradient-based methods, and Population-based methods. Table 1 summarizes representative methods from each category, outlining their key contributions, target hyperparameters, and experimental settings.

These methods address various aspects of FL-HPO:

1. *Black-box Optimization*: Methods like FloRA [1] and FedEx [2] treat the optimization problem without assuming any specific structure, making them versatile but potentially less efficient.
2. *Swarm Intelligence*: HPO-PSO [3] and Genetic-CFL [4] leverage collective behavior principles to explore the hyperparameter space, offering robustness against local minima.
3. *Reinforcement Learning*: Auto-FedRL [5] dynamically adapts hyperparameters based on feedback, making it suitable for non-stationary environments.
4. *Gradient-based Methods*: FATHOM [6] introduces hypergradient descent, enabling efficient online tuning by leveraging gradient information.
5. *Population-based Methods*: FedPop [7] employs evolutionary strategies to explore a diverse set of hyperparameters, striking a balance between exploration and exploitation.

3   Experiment and Results

Selecting appropriate hyperparameters is crucial to the success of FL systems, yet effective optimization remains challenging due to data heterogeneity and limited coordination across clients.

In this section, we experimentally evaluate Random Search [8] as a baseline method for HPO in FL. Random Search operates by randomly sampling configurations from the defined search space, offering a straightforward and easily parallelizable approach. We chose to investigate Random Search due to its simplicity, computational efficiency, and widespread use as a baseline in the HPO literature. Assessing its performance in a real federated setting provides insight into both the achievable gains from automated HPO and the practical limitations of this non-adaptive method. This evaluation serves as a reference point for future comparisons with more advanced HPO strategies.

3.1   Experimental Setup

We implemented our FL-HPO system using six Raspberry Pi devices as clients and a PC as the central server to reflect a practical distributed computing environment. Table 2 summarizes the hardware and software configurations used

Table 1. Summary of notable FL-HPO methods and their characteristics

Method (Year)	Category	Key Idea	Optimized HPs	Experimental Data
FLoRA (2021) [1]	Black-box Optimization	Aggregates local HP trials asynchronously to build a global loss surface.	LR, BS, optimizer	Seven OpenML datasets
FedEx (2021) [2]	Black-box Optimization	Applies weight-sharing from NAS to simplify HPO in FL.	General HPs	Shakespeare, FEMNIST, CIFAR-10
HPO-PSO (2021) [3]	Swarm Intelligence	Uses particle swarm optimization to iteratively tune $[n, \eta, m, c, e]$.	Network config, LR, momentum, etc.	MNIST
Genetic-CFL (2021) [4]	Swarm Intelligence	Evolves client clusters' HPs using a genetic algorithm.	LR, batch size	CIFAR-10, MNIST
Auto-FedRL (2022) [5]	Reinforcement Learning	Trains RL agents to adjust HPs during training dynamically.	LR, epochs, batch size	CIFAR-10, COVID-19 CT, pancreas CT
FATHOM (2022) [6]	Gradient-based Method	One-shot HPO via hypergradient descent in decentralized settings.	LR, local steps, batch size	FEMNIST, Stack Overflow
FedPop (2025) [7]	Population-based Method	Evolves HPs across clients and server jointly using evolutionary strategies.	Various HPs	ImageNet-1K, CIFAR-10, FEMNIST

in our testbed. The MNIST dataset was partitioned among clients in a non-IID fashion using a Dirichlet distribution ($\alpha = 0.5$) to mimic real-world data heterogeneity. For hyperparameter optimization, Random Search was employed to explore the configuration space, and the resulting performance is compared to that achieved with standard default hyperparameters. A lightweight convolutional neural network (CNN) with two convolutional layers (10 and 20 filters, kernel size 5), each followed by max pooling, and a fully connected layer with 50 units, finalized by a softmax output for classification.

Table 2. Experimental Testbed Environment

Entity	Hardware	Software
Server	PC, Windows 10 Pro (i9-11900F 2.5GHz, 64GB RAM, 1TB SSD)	Python 3.9, TensorFlow 2.6, Keras 2.6, Flask 2.2.2
Client	Raspberry Pi 4B, Ubuntu 20.04, 1.5GHz, 4GB RAM, 32GB SD	Python 3.8, TensorFlow 2.6, Keras 2.6, Flask 2.2.2

3.2   Results and Analysis

The following Table 3 presents the best hyperparameters (HPs) found by the Random Search-based HPO for the main FL task. For the search, the learning rate was sampled continuously from [0.0001, 0.01], batch size was chosen from 32, 48, 64, activation function from relu, sigmoid, and optimizer from adam, sgd. Local best HP sets are aggregated to generate the global HP that reflects the overall distribution of data.

Table 3. Random Search HPO: Best Hyperparameters

HP	Clients 1–6 (local)	Global
Lr	$(32, 48, 87, 87, 32, 32) \times 10^{-4}$	53×10^{-4}
BS	(32, 48, 64, 64, 32, 32)	45
Activation	relu, relu, sigmoid, sigmoid, relu, relu	relu
Optimizer	adam, adam, sgd, sgd, adam, adam	adam

Table 4 presents the average global test accuracy across all clients over 30 communication rounds. The final accuracy achieved using Random Search-based HPO was 0.96, compared to 0.90 with default hyperparameters (without HPO). While both configurations demonstrated stable convergence, the HPO-assisted training consistently outperformed the approach without HPO. These results suggest that even simple hyperparameter tuning strategies, such as Random Search, can yield meaningful improvements in federated learning performance.

Table 4. Performance comparison with and without HPO

Metric	Without HPO	With HPO
Initial Accuracy (Round 1)	0.35	0.65
Best Validation Accuracy	0.89	0.94
Final Accuracy (Round 30)	0.90	0.96

4   Conclusion

This paper investigated the effectiveness of Random Search-based hyperparameter optimization (HPO) within a practical federated learning (FL) framework. Through experiments using six real devices and a non-IID partitioned MNIST dataset, we demonstrated that even a simple and easily deployable HPO method, such as Random Search, can yield notable improvements in global test accuracy and training convergence compared to default hyperparameter settings. The results highlight the value of automated HPO for FL, especially when computational resources or communication budgets are limited. Future work will explore more advanced and adaptive HPO strategies, as well as their integration with privacy-preserving and resource-aware FL environments.

Disclosure of Interests.   The author declares no conflict of interest.

References

1. Zhou, Y., Ram, P., Salonidis, T., Baracaldo, N., Samulowitz, H., Ludwig, H.: Flora: single-shot hyper-parameter optimization for federated learning. arXiv preprint (2021)
2. Khodak, M., et al.: Federated hyperparameter tuning: challenges, baselines, and connections to weight-sharing. Adv. Neural. Inf. Process. Syst. **34**, 19184–97 (2021)
3. Li, Z., Li, H., Zhang, M.: Hyper-parameter tuning of federated learning based on particle swarm optimization. In: Proceedings of the 2021 IEEE 7th International Conference on Cloud Computing and Intelligent Systems (CCIS), pp. 99–103 (2021)
4. Agrawal, S., et al.: Genetic CFL: hyperparameter optimization in clustered federated learning. Comput. Intell. Neurosci. **2021**, 7156420 (2021). https://doi.org/10.1155/2021/7156420
5. Guo, P.: Auto-FedRL: federated hyperparameter optimization for multi-institutional medical image segmentation. In: Computer Vision–ECCV 2022: 17th European Conference, Tel Aviv, Israel, October 23–27, 2022, Proceedings. Part XXI, pp. 437–55 (2022)
6. Kan, A.K.: Federated hypergradient descent. arXiv preprint arXiv:2211.02106 (2022)
7. Chen, H., et al.: FedPop: federated population-based hyperparameter tuning. In: Proceedings of the AAAI Conference on Artificial Intelligence. Vol. 39. No. 15 (2025)
8. Bergstra, J., Bengio, Y.: Random search for hyper-parameter optimization. J. Mach. Learn. Res. **13**(1), 281–305 (2012)

Recognition of Radicals of Guqin Music Notation by YOLOs

Meguru Hayami[1], Shun Kuremoto[2], Mamiko Koshiba[3], Takashi Kuremoto[1 (✉)], and Shingo Mabu[2]

[1] Nippon Institute of Technology, 4-1, Gakuendai, Miyashiro, Saitama, Japan
kuremoto.takashi@nit.ac.jp
[2] Yamaguchi University, 2-16-1 Tokiwadai, Ube, Yamaguchi, Japan
[3] Arts and Sciences, University of Human, 1288 Magome, Iwatsuki-Ku, Saitama, Japan

Abstract. The music notation of Guqin (古琴), a traditional Chinese instrument with a history of over 3,000 years, are difficult to be understood by people today. In this study, the radicals of Jian-Zi-Pu ((減字譜)), the traditional Guqin music notation, are recognized by YOLOv8 and YOLO11. A dataset including 2,352 images of radicals was created at first, which had 20 classes for 26 single characters of Jian-Zi-Pu, collected from 6 kinds of versions of Guqin music "Chun Xiao Yin" ((春暁吟)). Then the learning performances of YOLOv8 and YOLO11 were verified by the experiments. It was found that YOLO11 achieved 99.3% mAP50, meanwhile, YOLOv8's accuracy was 99.2% for a 20-class recognition problem of radicals of Jian-Zi-Pu of Chun Xiao Yin.

Keywords: YOLOv8 · YOLO11 · Guqin · Jian-Zi-Pu · Chun Xiao Yin · radicals

1 Introduction

Guqin (see Figs. 1 and 2) (古琴) is a seven-stringed zither that existed in ancient China with a history of over 3,000 years. It is considered one of the most representative Chinese classical instruments. It also had a deep connection with Japanese history. By the Nara period, it had been introduced to Japan, and during the Heian period, it was primarily favored by the aristocracy. In The Tale of Genji, the protagonist, Hikaru Genji, is depicted playing Guqin. Furthermore, during the Edo period, it was cherished by literati and tea masters. In 2003, it was inscribed on UNESCO's "Representative List of the Intangible Cultural Heritage of Humanity," reflecting its rich historical and cultural significance [1, 2].

Guqin notation is a type of musical score that represents the performance techniques and structure of Guqin music. It is written using "Jian-Zi-Pu ((減字譜))" (abbreviated character notation) (see Fig. 3), which employs Chinese-like characters as symbols, making it difficult to decipher in modern times. Today, more than 2,000 pieces of Guqin notation still exist, but most of them are no longer performed because it is hard to understand Jian-Zi-Pu by modern people. Understanding the preserved scores and lyrics

B.-G. Kim et al. (Eds.): MITA 2025, CCIS 2675, pp. 118–124, 2026.
https://doi.org/10.1007/978-981-95-3141-7_11

of Guqin pieces provides insight into past cultures, as well as the tastes and education of historical figures. By studying Guqin music, one can gain a new perspective on history.

Fig. 1. A sample of Guqin.

Fig. 2. Playing Guqin (Player: Kuremoto, S.).

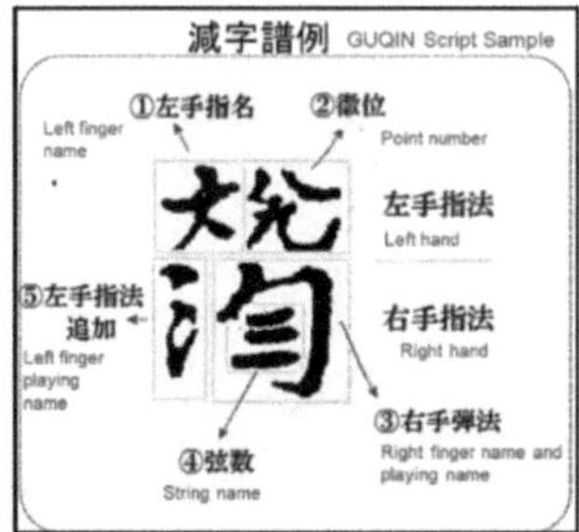

Fig. 3. A sample of a single character of Jian-Zi-Pu with descriptions of 5 radicals.

In this study, we focus on the recognition of the radicals of Jian-Zi-Pu (See Fig. 3) to inspire the study of restoration of Guqin music. As the problem of Jian-Zi-Pu recognition can be dealt with methods of hand-written character recognition, there have been some prior research using machine learning methods [3–5]. In our previous studies, deep learning methods, such as VGG16, VGG19, and YOLOv5 were adopted to recognize the Guqin music "Sen-O-So" written in Jian-Zi-Pu format [6–8]. However, all these studies are limited to recognize single characters of Jian-Zi-Pu to realize the restoration of Guqin music, without the essential part of Guqin performance given in the radicals (See Fig. 3).

As the first challenge of radical recognition of Jian-Zi-Pu, we chose a Guqin music "Chun Xiao Yin (《春晓吟》)" to create a dataset of radicals of single characters in its first paragraph (Fig. 4). Six kinds of Chun Xiao Yin images were used as shown in Fig. 4. Details of the dataset and recognition methods are described in Sect. 2.

2 Methods

2.1 Datasets

Creating a Dataset from "Chun Xiao Yin" Guqin Score Image Data. The steps are as follows:

(1) Collect image data.
(2) Perform image data augmentation (apply smoothing, noise processing, resizing, and rotation).
(3) Conduct annotation and save the results in a label file.
(4) Separate the data into folders for training and evaluation.
(5) Summarize the dataset structure in a YAML file.

A dataset was created using data containing 20 radical classes from 26 types of characters. The dataset consists of 1,176 images, with 943 images for training and 233

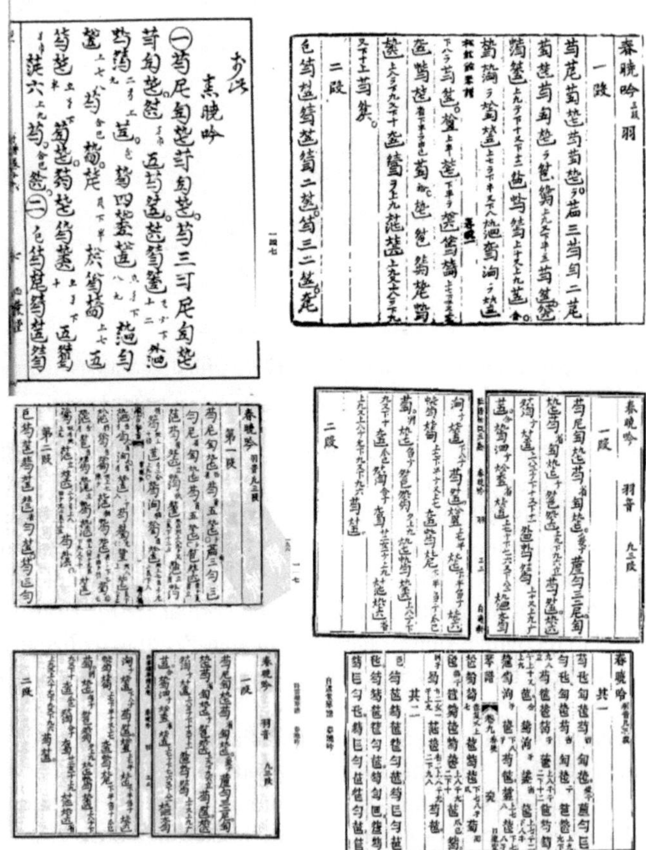

Fig. 4. Samples of Guqin music "Chun Xiao Yin" in different versions (provided by Mr. Hieda, H.).

images for evaluation as shown in Table 1. Samples of single characters obtained from Chun Xiao Yin images (see Fig. 4) are shown in Fig. 5, and the 20 radicals of these single characters are shown in Fig. 6.

Table 1. Radical dataset.

Characters	Radicals	Training images	Validation images	Total images
26	20	943	233	1,176

2.2 YOLOs

In our previous studies, VGG16, VGG19, ResNet50 and hybrid models composed by these deep neural networks with support vector machine (SVM) were utilized as classifiers of single characters [6–8]. YOLOv5 and YOLOv8 [9] were also verified with high recognition accuracies. In this study, YOLOv8n and YOLO11 [10] are adopted as classifiers for the radical recognition. The fine-tuning setup utilizes early stopping which means when the mean-average accuracy (mAP) converged during training.

Fig. 5. Samples of single characters in "Chun Xiao Yin".

Fig. 6. Samples of radicals in single characters in "Chun Xiao Yin".

Table 2. Experiment results.

Model	Precision	Recall	mAP50	mAP50–90	Time (hour)
YOLO11n	0.970	0.991	0.993	0.769	32.815
YOLOv8n	0.970	0.991	0.992	0.789	31.291

3 Experiments and Results

The limitation of training epochs in the fine-tuning process of YOLOs was 2,000. The computer used in the experiment had a CPU 12th Gen Intel ® Core ™) i7-12700F, 2.10 GHz, 32.0 GB RAM and Windows 11 64bit OS.

3.1 Recognition Rates

The experiment results were shown in Table 2. It can be confirmed that the performance of YOLO11n was better than YOLOv8n slightly with the metric mAP50 99.3% and 99.2% respectively, but mAP50–90 which was 76.9% and 78.9% respectively. The training time of YOLO11n consumed longer than YOLOv8, i.e., 32.815 h vs 31.291 h.

3.2 Fine-Tuning of YOLOs

To confirm the performance of fine-tuning of YOLO11n and YOLOv8n, learning curves till 100 epochs were plotted as shown in Figs. 7 and 8 which were the changes of training/validation loss (left 3 pictures) and accuracies (right 2 pictures), respectively. As the early stopping function was used to avoid the overfitting of the models, the training iteration stopped at 945 epochs for a limitation of training times 2,000 epochs in both cases.

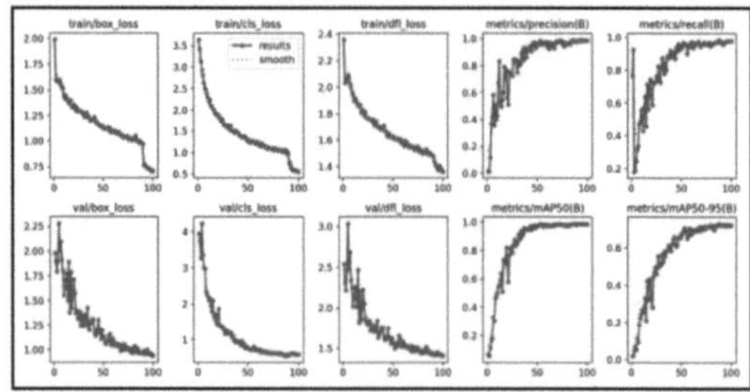

Fig. 7. Learning curves of YOLO11n in fine-tuning.

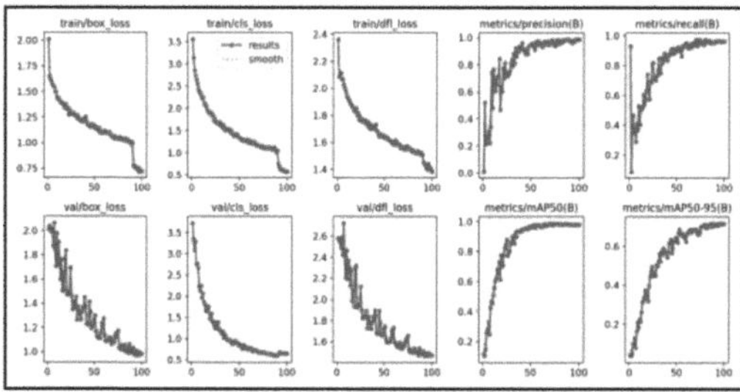

Fig. 8. Learning curves of YOLOv8n in fine-tuning.

Fig. 9. Radical recognition results by YOLO11n (left) and YOLOv8n (right).

3.3 Radical Recognition Results

For single characters of Jian-Zi-Pu, YOLOs recognized their radicals as same as object recognition process. Samples of radical recognition results by YOLO11n and YOLOv8n are shown in Fig. 9. Meanwhile, it was also confirmed that the fine-tuned YOLOs detected radicals in Chun Xiao Yin images.

4 Conclusions

Recognition of radicals of Jian-Zi-Pu, which is a music notation of traditional Chinese instrument Guqin (seven-stringed zither), was approached by deep learning models YOLO11n and YOLOv8n in this study. A dataset of radicals in single characters of six kinds of Chun Xiao Yin Jian-Zi-Pu was created which included the original images and data augmentation (noise, smoothing, resize, rotations). As a 20-class recognition problem, the dataset was utilized to train YOLO11n and YOLOv8n, and the recognition rates achieved 99.3% and 99.2% respectively to single characters of Chun Xio Yin. Meanwhile, the fine-tuned YOLOs detected few radicals when the input was an image of a full notation of Jian-Zi-Pu, and this problem needs to be tackled in the future.

Acknowledgments. Our thanks to Mr. Hiroo HIEDA (1945-2024) for his extremely valuable contribution to this study over the past four years. This work was supported by JSPS KAKENHI Grant (No. 22H03709, No.22K12152).

References

1. Japan society for promotion of Guqin. https://www.guqin.jp/about. (in Japanese)
2. Kuremoto, T.: Guqing music recognition by machine learning methods. Impact **2024**(1), 40–42 (2024). https://doi.org/10.21820/23987073.2024.1.40
3. Pan, Z.X., Zhou, C.L.: Text segmentation and extraction from images of Guqin Jianzi Pu. Mind Comput. **1**(2), 286–295 (2007). (in Chinese)
4. Shi, C.: Guqin notation and music style recognition. Comput. Sci. (2016). Corpus ID: 31634157
5. Wang, L., Sun, Y., Luo, Z. L., Zhang, H.: AI automatic translation of Jianzi Pu a case study of "LIOUSHUI" and "BURAN". In: Art Education, vol. 3 (2019). (in Chinese)
6. Yang, Y., et al.: Recognition of Guqin music by deep learning methods. In: Proceedings of the Electronics, Information and Systems Conference Electronics, Information and Systems Society, I.E.E. of Japan, pp. 512–515 (2022). (in Japanese)
7. Yang, B., Kuremoto, S., Koshiba, M., Mabu, S., Hieda, H., Kuremoto, T.: Recognition of Guqin notation using deep learning. In: Proceedings of Innovative Application Research and Education (ICIARE2022), pp. 61–64 (2022)
8. Kuremoto, T., et al.: Restoration of Guqin music by deep learning methods. In: Proceedings of the International Conference on Artificial Alife and Robotics (ICAROB2024), pp. 320–324 (2024)
9. Redmon, J., Divvala, S., Girshick, R., Farhadi, A.: You Only Look Once: unified, real-time object detection. arXiv:1506.02640 (2016)
10. YOLO11 (2024). https://github.com/ultralytics/ultralytics

RMSF-ViT: Randomized Multi-scale Fusion Vision Transformer

Yu-Jin Cho[1], Ah-Hyeon Lee[1], Byung-Gyu Kim[1(✉)], and Jan Platoš[2]

[1] Department of IT Engineering, Sookmyung Women's University, Seoul, Republic of Korea
{yjcho,ahlee}@ivpl.sm.ac.kr, bg.kim@sookmyung.ac.kr
[2] VSB – Technical University of Ostrava, Ostrava, Czech Republic
jan.platos@vsb.cz

Abstract. The Vision Transformer (ViT) has demonstrated remarkable performance in a wide range of computer vision tasks, such as image classification, object detection, and image generation. Unlike convolutional neural networks (CNNs), ViT benefits from a global receptive field, which enables more effective modeling of relationships between image patches. However, the lack of inductive biases makes ViT models difficult to train stably, especially on limited datasets. Without access to large-scale pretrained weights, performance often degrades significantly. To address this issue, we propose a novel architecture called RMSF-ViT. It employs a progressive fusion strategy that incorporates fine-grained patch information beyond the fixed single patch size used in conventional ViT architectures. In addition, RMSF-ViT reduces the number of attention heads by half compared to vanilla ViT models. This design improves both performance and computational efficiency, as demonstrated on the CIFAR-10, CIFAR-100, Flowers, and Pets datasets.

Keywords: Vision Transformer · Multi-Scale Patch Embedding · Multi-Scale Fusion · Image Classification · Deep Learning

1 Introduction

The Vision Transformer (ViT) [1] has emerged as a strong alternative to convolutional neural networks (CNNs). It has demonstrated impressive performance across a wide range of computer vision tasks, such as image classification, object detection, and image generation. ViT-based architectures have also been successfully applied to object detection [2] and video super-resolution [3], highlighting their versatility beyond traditional classification tasks. Unlike CNNs, ViT utilizes a self-attention mechanism to effectively capture global dependencies across the entire image, resulting in a broader receptive field.

Despite these strengths, practitioners often face practical challenges when applying ViT models. Pre-trained ViT models provided by libraries such as Hugging Face, Timm, and Torchvision deliver high performance, but they are typi-

B.-G. Kim et al. (Eds.): MITA 2025, CCIS 2675, pp. 125–137, 2026.
https://doi.org/10.1007/978-981-95-3141-7_12

cally large and difficult to adapt to task-specific needs. On the other hand, training ViT from scratch offers architectural flexibility but often results in unsatisfactory performance. This performance degradation stems from the absence of inductive biases-such as locality and translation invariance-inherent in CNNs. Consequently, ViT models require large-scale datasets and extensive computational resources, making training unstable and prone to overfitting, especially with small- or medium-sized datasets. Without leveraging structural priors embedded in visual data, ViT must learn all spatial relationships directly from data, limiting generalization from small samples. Figure 1 visually compares the training behaviors on medium-sized datasets. As shown in Fig. 1 (a), a ViT baseline model trained from scratch exhibits training instability and performance degradation. In contrast, our proposed model demonstrates stable convergence and effective learning, as shown in Fig. 1 (b).

For example, the ViT-B/16 model divides input images into fixed-size patches (16×16), which structurally limits its ability to capture multi-scale information and reduces its sensitivity to small objects or fine-grained visual details [4]. Reducing the patch size can help alleviate these issues, but it significantly increases the number of tokens, leading to excessive memory usage and high computational cost. While several multi-scale ViT variants have been proposed to address this, many either discard the fixed patch structure entirely or fail to utilize it effectively, thereby limiting the model's potential.

In this paper, we propose a novel architecture that combines the powerful feature extraction capabilities of CNNs with the global representation power of Transformers.

The main contributions of this work are as follows:

1) We propose a residual fusion mechanism that progressively integrates semantic information across stages, enhancing feature richness and robustness.
2) We bridge local feature representation and global modeling by integrating CNN-based architectures with transformers through the MSPE module.
3) We empirically demonstrate that our proposed model achieves significantly better performance than publicly available ViT models on several image classification benchmarks.

2   Related Works

2.1   Hybrid Vision Architectures

To address the limitations of Vision Transformers (ViTs), many studies have explored hybrid architectures that combine CNNs with Transformers. Models such as CvT [6] and CoaT [7] introduce convolutional layers in the early stages to improve training stability. MobileViT [8] shows that incorporating CNN-based locality, even in lightweight settings, can enhance both efficiency and representational power. Recent models like Super Vision Transformer [9] further adopt pyramid structures to integrate multi-scale features. Other works, such as MambaVision [10], explore new backbones by combining Mamba and Transformers

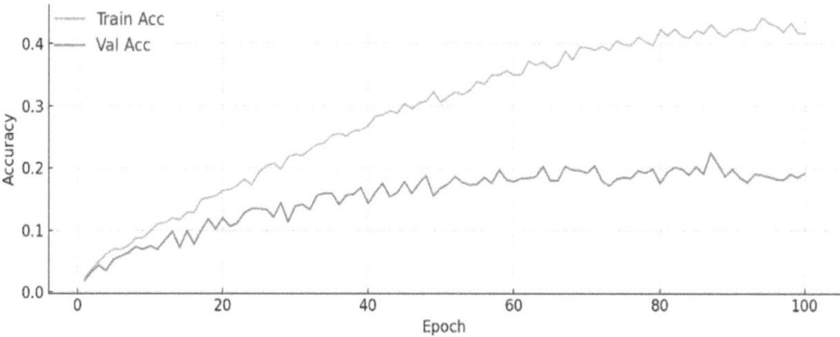

(a) Training curve of a ViT baseline trained from scratch on CIFAR-10. The model shows unstable training and poor generalization.

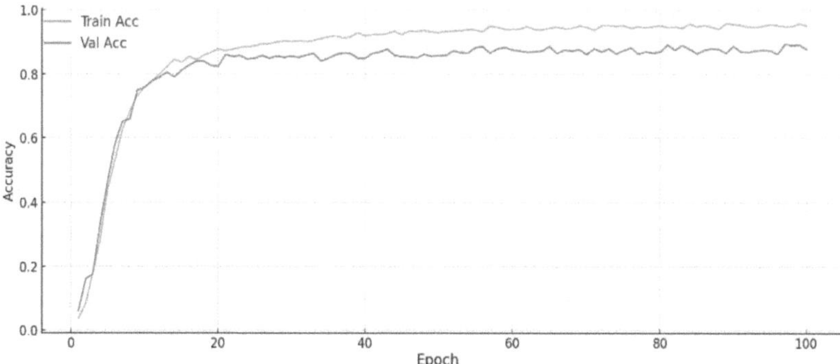

(b) Training curve of the proposed RMSF-ViT on CIFAR-10. The model shows stable convergence and high accuracy.

Fig. 1. Comparison of training behaviors on the CIFAR-10 dataset. (a) The ViT baseline trained from scratch exhibits unstable training. (b) The proposed RMSF-ViT achieves significantly more stable and effective learning.

for improved efficiency. ViT-CoMer [11] introduces bidirectional fusion tailored for dense prediction tasks. Our model also adopts a CNN–Transformer hybrid approach but with key differences. It fully merges multi-scale features at the backbone stage using a Feature Pyramid Network (FPN) to produce a single high-resolution feature map. Then, it simplifies complex token interactions through a dedicated module that adaptively selects and fuses informative tokens.

2.2   Multi-scale and Resolution Adaptation

The fixed patch size in ViT baseline architectures limits their ability to process information at multiple resolutions. To overcome this, models like CrossViT, DaViT [12], and Pyramid ViT [13] adopt parallel branches or hierarchical structures to capture multi-scale features. More recent works have expanded this direction. FlexiViT [14] introduces a flexible training scheme that supports varying input resolutions, improving generalization. Other approaches, such as Rotary Position Embedding (RoPE) [15], enhance robustness to resolution changes by refining positional encodings. For generative tasks, FiT [16] makes the tokenization process itself resolution-aware. Our work applies this principle of resolution flexibility to classification tasks. Rather than modifying positional encodings or tokenization grids, we propose a novel mechanism that dynamically selects and prunes input tokens after standard patch embedding. This enables adaptive processing of multi-scale information with minimal architectural overhead.

2.3   Dynamic Token Selection and Fusion

Most existing multi-scale ViT models rely on predefined fixed scales or parallel branch structures. Some studies attempt to increase diversity by randomly varying patch sizes during training. For example, Patch Slimming [17] reduces computational cost by removing redundant tokens. Inspired by this idea, our model randomly selects a subset of scales at each training iteration and performs *importance-based token pruning*.

Throughout this process, the *standard* 16×16 *patch size* is maintained as a structural anchor. The most informative tokens are fused with fixed-patch tokens and residual signals from earlier stages through an iterative mechanism. This approach minimizes representational loss while enhancing expressiveness, resulting in clear performance improvements over prior methods.

3   The Proposed Method

This section presents the architecture of RMSF-ViT (Randomized Multi-Scale Fusion Vision Transformer), designed to address two major limitations of ViT-based models: weak inductive bias and poor multi-scale information processing. RMSF-ViT adopts a three-stage pipeline that combines the strengths of CNNs and Transformers.

3.1   Previous Studies

The Vision Transformer (ViT) operates by splitting an input image into fixed-size patches, converting them into a token sequence, and feeding them into a Transformer encoder. Given an input image $\mathbf{X} \in \mathbb{R}^{H \times W \times C}$, it is divided into non-overlapping patches of size $P \times P$, resulting in a total of $N = \frac{HW}{P^2}$ patches. Each patch is flattened and linearly projected into a D-dimensional embedding vector:

$$\mathbf{z}_0 = [\mathbf{x}_{\text{cls}}; \mathbf{x}_p^1 \mathbf{E}; \mathbf{x}_p^2 \mathbf{E}; \dots; \mathbf{x}_p^N \mathbf{E}] + \mathbf{E}_{\text{pos}}. \tag{1}$$

Here, $\mathbf{x}_{\text{cls}}$ is a learnable class token, $\mathbf{x}_p^i$ denotes the i-th image patch, $\mathbf{E} \in \mathbb{R}^{(P^2 C) \times D}$ is a trainable patch embedding matrix, and $\mathbf{E}_{\text{pos}} \in \mathbb{R}^{(N+1) \times D}$ is the positional embedding.

The token sequence $\mathbf{z}_0$ is then passed through the transformer encoder blocks L, each consisting of a multi-head self-attention layer (MHSA) followed by a Feed-Forward Network (FFN):

$$\mathbf{z}_\ell = \mathrm{FFN}(\mathrm{MHSA}(\mathbf{z}_{\ell-1})), \quad \ell = 1, \ldots, L. \tag{2}$$

Unlike CNNs, ViTs lack inductive biases such as locality and translation invariance, which makes them difficult to train on small datasets without large-scale pretraining. This often leads to unstable training or overfitting. However, given sufficient data and computational resources, ViTs can effectively learn global dependencies and achieve strong performance.

To address these structural limitations of ViT, this paper proposes a new architecture that incorporates multi-scale patch information at the input level and progressively merges residual information across stages.

3.2 Overall Architecture

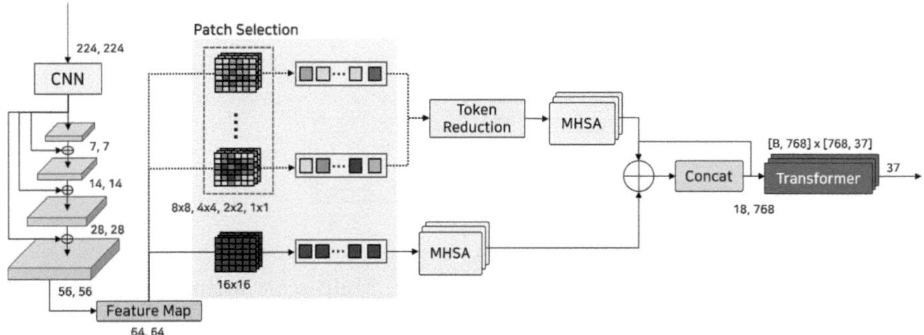

Fig. 2. Overall architecture of the proposed RMSF-ViT. The model consists of a pyramidal feature extractor and a Transformer encoder with convolutional modulation.

The proposed RMSF-ViT follows a three-stage pipeline-a pyramidal feature extractor, an adaptive multi-scale token embedding module, and a feature-enhanced Transformer encoder-as illustrated in Fig. 2.

In the first stage, a ResNet-50 backbone with FPN is used to generate a high-resolution feature map rich in local patterns and multi-scale contextual information. This provides more meaningful input to the attention-based modules.

The second stage, the MSPE (Iterative Multi-Scale Patch Embedding) module, constructs a token sequence by combining information from multiple scales. It preserves the global structure using anchor tokens derived from fixed-size patches, while dynamically generating summary tokens from smaller patches via attention-based pooling. This approach effectively captures fine-grained visual details without the computational overhead of processing all small patches. The detailed structure of the MSPE module is shown in Fig. 3, which highlights its multi-scale processing and iterative residual fusion mechanism.

In the final stage, the resulting token sequence is passed to the Transformer encoder. Each encoder block applies a lightweight 1D convolution to the Value vectors within the self-attention mechanism, enabling the model to learn both global dependencies and local spatial features. The final prediction is made using the output [CLS] token.

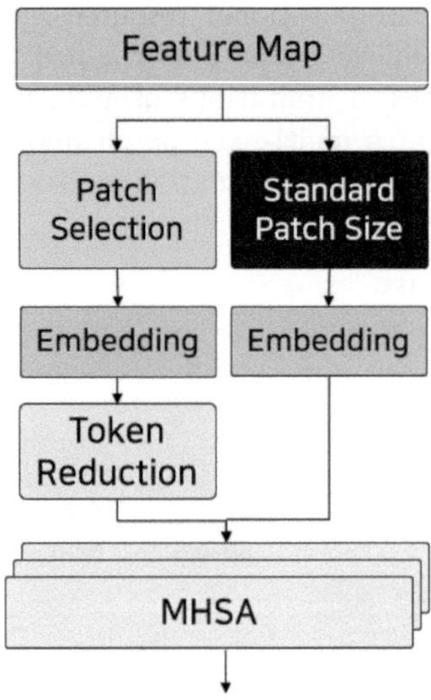

Fig. 3. Structure of the proposed MSPE module. Multi-scale features are processed through attention-based pooling.

Backbone: Pyramidal Feature Extraction. The backbone of our model is a convolutional neural network (CNN) based on the ResNet-50 architecture [18], pretrained on the ImageNet-1k dataset. To address the lack of inductive bias in pure Vision Transformers, we first apply this CNN backbone to extract robust local representations before global modeling by the Transformer encoder.

The hierarchical feature maps $\{C_2, C_3, C_4, C_5\}$ extracted from different stages of ResNet-50 carry varying levels of semantic information and are fused using a Feature Pyramid Network (FPN). Through a top-down pathway with lateral connections, semantic features from higher levels (starting from C_5) are progressively upsampled and merged with spatially finer features. The fusion is performed via element-wise addition, followed by a 3×3 convolution to refine the output. The fusion at each level is defined as:

$$P_i = \mathrm{Conv}_{3\times3}\left(\mathrm{Conv}_{1\times1}(C_i) + \mathcal{U}(P_{i+1})\right) \tag{3}$$

From the resulting feature pyramid $\{P_2, P_3, P_4, P_5\}$, we select only the P_2, as the output of the backbone. This map retains fine spatial detail while being enriched with semantic information from deeper layers.

To ensure consistency in the tokenization stage, P_2 is interpolated to a fixed spatial resolution of $H' \times W'$ (set to 64×64 in our implementation). The final feature map used as input to the next stage is:

$$F_{\text{in}} \in \mathbb{R}^{H' \times W' \times D_{\text{in}}} \tag{4}$$

Multi-scale Patch Embedding (MSPE). The MSPE module is the core technical contribution of our architecture. It is designed to transform the single, high-resolution feature map F_{in} provided by the backbone into a compact yet highly informative token sequence for the Transformer encoder. This is achieved through a novel process that combines stable anchor tokens with dynamically summarized fine-grained features via an iterative fusion mechanism.

Dual-Path Token Generation. The module begins by processing the input feature map F_{in} through two parallel conceptual paths to capture information at different levels of granularity.

- **Fixed-Scale Anchor Path:** A token sequence T_{fix} is generated from a reference fixed-scale ($s = 16$) patch. These anchor tokens provide a stable, low-frequency representation of the overall image structure and serve as the backbone of the final token sequence.

$$T_{\text{fix}} = E_{16}(\text{Patchify}(F_{\text{in}}, 16)) \tag{5}$$

Here, $\text{Patchify}(\cdot, s)$ is a patching operation with kernel and stride size s, and $E_s(\cdot)$ is an embedding function via linear projection.
- **Dynamic Small-Scale Path:** To capture fine-grained details, patch token sets are also generated for smaller scales $s \in \mathbb{S} = \{8, 4, 2, 1\}$.

Attention-Based Token Summarization. Smaller-scale patches lead to an exponential increase in the number of tokens ($N_s \propto 1/s^2$), making full attention computation prohibitively expensive. To address this, we introduce an attention-based summarization function $\mathcal{A}(\cdot)$, which condenses a set of small-scale tokens T_s into a single summary token t_s.

We first apply self-attention to T_s, obtaining both the attention outputs O_s and weights W_s. Then, we compute a weighted sum of O_s using the normalized average of W_s as weights:

$$t_s = \mathcal{A}(T_s) = \text{WeightedSum}(O_s, \text{Normalize}(\text{Avg}(W_s))) \tag{6}$$

This method summarizes the most salient information, producing an efficient representation while retaining fine-grained visual details.

Iterative Residual Fusion. The final token sequence is constructed via a two-stage (`repeat=2`) iterative process that progressively refines the feature representation. The detailed process is illustrated in Fig. 4.

- **Stage 1 (Initial Fusion):** Two summary tokens (t_a, t_b) from two randomly chosen small scales are concatenated with the anchor tokens T_{fix}. The last summary token, t_b, is saved as the residual r_1 for the next stage.

$$T_{\text{stage1}} = \text{Concat}(T_{\text{fix}}, t_a, t_b), \quad r_1 = t_b \tag{7}$$

- **Stage 2 (Residual Refinement):** A new summary token (t_c) is generated and then fused with the previous residual via element-wise addition ($r_2 = r_1 + t_c$). This refined token r_2, which now contains integrated information from two different scales, is then concatenated with the anchor tokens.

$$T_{\text{stage2}} = \text{Concat}(T_{\text{fix}}, r_2) \tag{8}$$

This iterative process effectively combines multi-scale features, enriching the token representation passed to the encoder.

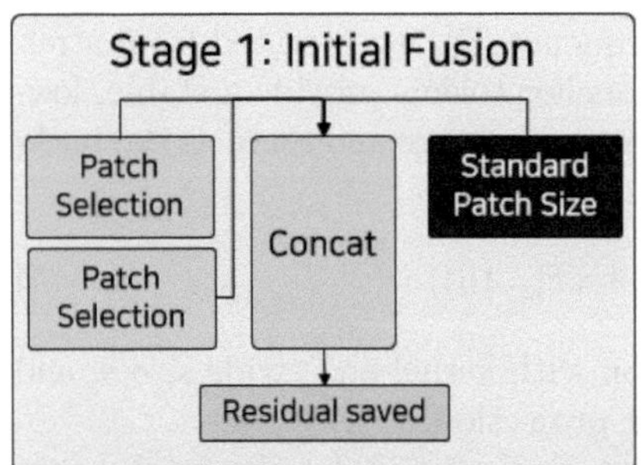

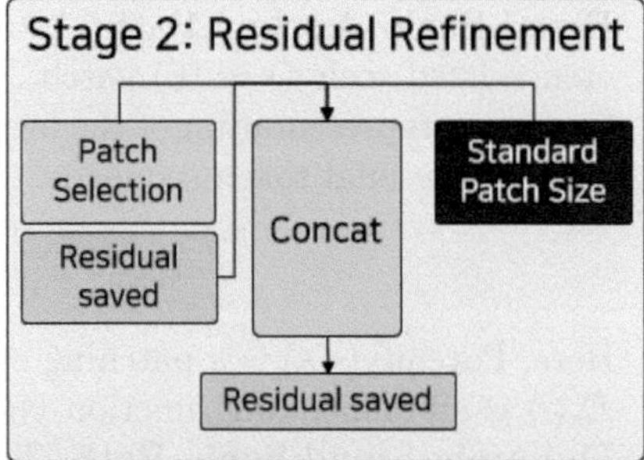

Fig. 4. Illustration of the iterative residual fusion process. Standard patch size(Anchor tokens) and dynamically generated summary tokens from smaller scales are combined via concatenation and additive residual fusion across two iterative stages.

We now evaluate the proposed architecture through experiments on standard benchmarks.

4   Experiments

To validate the effectiveness of our proposed architecture, we conducted a series of experiments on several benchmark datasets for image classification. We compare the performance of the proposed model against a standard baseline model to demonstrate its superiority.

4.1   Datasets

We evaluated our model on four widely used datasets to assess its performance in both general and fine-grained classification tasks.

- **CIFAR-10 & CIFAR-100:** These datasets consist of 32×32 pixel color images. CIFAR-10 contains 10 classes, while CIFAR-100 contains 100 classes. They are standard benchmarks used to evaluate models in low-resolution image classification tasks.
- **Oxford-IIIT Pet:** This dataset contains images of 37 different breeds of cats and dogs. It features significant variations in scale, pose, and lighting, making it a challenging fine-grained classification problem.
- **Oxford Flowers-102:** This is a fine-grained classification dataset containing 102 flower categories commonly found in the United Kingdom, which requires capturing subtle visual details.

4.2   Implementation Details

All input images were resized to 224×224 and augmented using `RandomResizedCrop`, `RandomHorizontalFlip`, and `RandAugment`. The model was trained for 100 epochs using SGD (momentum 0.9, learning rate 0.003) with cosine annealing and warmup. Batch size was set to 64. Experiments were conducted using PyTorch 2.4.1 with CUDA 12.1 on an RTX 3090 Ti GPU running Ubuntu 22.04.

4.3   Main Results and Comparison

To demonstrate the effectiveness of our proposed RMSF-ViT, we compare its performance against a ViT baseline baseline model across all four datasets. The quantitative results are summarized in Table 1.

Table 1. Comparison of classification accuracy (%) on benchmark datasets.

Dataset	ViT-baseline	RMSF-ViT	Δ Acc
CIFAR-10 [19]	63.48%	**96.0%**	+32.52%
CIFAR-100 [19]	36.60%	**82.0%**	+45.40%
Oxford-IIIT Pet [20]	12.10%	**92.0%**	+79.90%
Oxford Flowers [21]	27.79%	**80.0%**	+52.21%

As shown in the table, our model outperforms the baseline across all benchmarks. It achieves accuracy gains of +32.52% on CIFAR-10 and +45.40% on CIFAR-100, demonstrating strong performance on general classification tasks. On fine-grained datasets such as Oxford-IIIT Pet and Flowers, the model shows improvements of +79.90% and +52.21%, respectively, confirming the effectiveness of multi-scale fusion and adaptive token selection in capturing subtle visual differences.

4.4 Ablation Studies

To analyze the contribution of each component in our proposed RMSF-ViT, we conducted ablation studies on the Oxford-IIIT Pet dataset. Starting from a simple baseline, we incrementally incorporated our design modules to measure their individual impact on classification accuracy.

(a) **ViT with ResNet-50 backbone:** A standard ResNet-50 backbone followed by a linear classification head.
(b) **+ FPN:** Replaces the vanilla backbone with a ResNet-FPN to provide rich multi-scale features.
(c) **+ MSPE:** Adds our Multi-Scale Patch Embedding module on top of FPN, with a single-step fusion.
(d) **+ MSPE with Residual Fusion:** Extends (c) by enabling iterative residual fusion to refine token representation.

Table 2. Ablation study on the Oxford-IIIT Pet dataset.

Configuration	Accuracy (%)
(a) ViT with ResNet-50 backbone	91.09
(b) + FPN	91.22
(c) + MSPE	91.47
(d) + MSPE with Residual Fusion	**91.93**

The results in Table 2 clearly show the additive benefits of each module. Replacing the vanilla ResNet-50 with an FPN backbone yields a significant improvement, indicating the importance of enriched multi-scale features. Incorporating MSPE further enhances performance by efficiently summarizing fine-grained spatial details from multiple resolutions. Finally, enabling residual fusion provides the final performance boost, confirming the effectiveness of our iterative refinement mechanism for progressively fusing multi-scale information.

4.5 Results and Analysis

To validate the effectiveness of our proposed architecture, we conducted a comprehensive quantitative comparison against a ViT baseline on four diverse image classification benchmarks. The primary classification results are summarized in Table 3.

As shown in the table, the proposed model consistently and significantly outperforms the baseline across all evaluated datasets. On general image classification benchmarks, it achieves 96.0% on CIFAR-10 and 82.0% on CIFAR-100, demonstrating the effectiveness of the hybrid architecture. Notably, in fine-grained classification tasks such as Oxford-IIIT Pet and Oxford Flowers, the

Table 3. Comparison of accuracy (%) between the ViT-baseline and the proposed model.

Dataset	ViT-baseline	RMSF-ViT
CIFAR-10	63.5%	**96.0%**
CIFAR-100	36.6%	**82.0%**
Oxford-IIIT Pet	12.1%	**91.0%**
Oxford Flowers-102	27.8%	**80.0%**

model achieves 91.0% and 80.0% accuracy, respectively, significantly surpassing the baseline. This highlights its ability to capture subtle visual details necessary for distinguishing between similar subcategories.

These performance gains stem from the core architectural design of RMSF-ViT. The ResNet-FPN backbone compensates for the limitations of ViT by providing strong feature representations, while the MSPE module effectively summarizes and fuses fine-grained visual information-leading to outstanding performance, especially in fine-grained classification.

5 Conclusion

This paper proposes a novel Vision Transformer architecture for image recognition. The proposed model is based on the ViT structure but integrates a CNN backbone with an FPN to effectively extract robust multi-scale features. By modifying the input scheme, we introduce a new training methodology, aiming to balance computational efficiency and performance through the Multi-Scale Patch Embedding (MSPE) module.

To evaluate the model's effectiveness, we conducted experiments on the CIFAR-10, CIFAR-100, Oxford-IIIT Pet, and Flowers datasets. The results show that our model consistently outperforms the standard baseline in terms of accuracy across all datasets. In future work, we plan to apply the proposed architecture to various computer vision tasks to assess its scalability.

References

1. Dosovitskiy, A., et al.: An Image is Worth 16×16 Words: Transformers for Image Recognition at Scale. arXiv preprint arXiv:2010.11929 (2020)
2. Lee, Y.-W., Kim, B.-G.: Attention-based scale sequence network for small object detection. Heliyon **10**(12), e23678 (2024). https://doi.org/10.1016/j.heliyon.2024.e23678
3. Choi, Y.-J., Kim, B.-G.: HiRN: hierarchical recurrent neural network for video super-resolution (VSR) using two-stage feature evolution. Appl. Soft Comput. **143**, 110422 (2023). https://doi.org/10.1016/j.asoc.2023.110422
4. Chen, C.F.R., Fan, Q., Panda, R.: CrossViT: cross-attention multi-scale vision transformer for image classification. In: Proceedings of IEEE/CVF International Conference on Computer Vision (ICCV), pp. 357–366 (2021)

5. Lin, T.-Y., Doll'ar, P., Girshick, R., He, K., Hariharan, B., Belongie, S.: Feature pyramid networks for object detection. In: Proceedings of IEEE Conference on Computer Vision and Pattern Recognition (CVPR), pp. 2117–2125 (2017)
6. Wu, H., et al.: CvT: introducing convolutions to vision transformers. In: Proceedings of IEEE/CVF International Conference on Computer Vision (ICCV), pp. 22–31 (2021)
7. Xu, W., et al.: Co-scale conv-attentional image transformers. In: Proceedings of IEEE/CVF International Conference on Computer Vision (ICCV), pp. 9981–9990 (2021)
8. Mehta, S., Rastegari, M.: MobileViT: Light-Weight, General-Purpose, and Mobile-Friendly Vision Transformer. arXiv preprint arXiv:2110.02178 (2021)
9. Lin, M., Chen, K., He, Z., Wu, J., Zha, Z.: Super vision transformer. Int. J. Comput. Vis. **131**(12), 3136–3151 (2023)
10. Hatamizadeh, A., Kautz, J.: MambaVision: a hybrid mamba-transformer vision backbone. In: Proceedings of the Computer Vision and Pattern Recognition Conference, pp. 25261–25270 (2025)
11. Xia, C., Wang, X., Lv, F., Hao, X., Shi, Y.: ViT-CoMer: vision transformer with convolutional multi-scale feature interaction for dense predictions. In: Proceedings of the IEEE/CVF Conference on Computer Vision and Pattern Recognition, pp. 5493–5502 (2024)
12. Ding, M., Xiao, B., Codella, N., Luo, P., Wang, J., Yuan, L.: DaViT: dual attention vision transformers. In: Proceedings of European Conference on Computer Vision (ECCV), pp. 35–52. Springer, Cham (2022)
13. Wang, W., Xie, E., Yu, Z., Anandkumar, A., Alvarez, J.M., Luo, P.: Pyramid vision transformer: a versatile backbone for dense prediction without convolutions. In: Proceedings of IEEE/CVF International Conference on Computer Vision (ICCV), pp. 568–578 (2021)
14. Beyer, L., Kolesnikov, A., Zhai, X., Houlsby, N.: FlexiViT: one model for all patch sizes. In: Proceedings of IEEE/CVF Conference on Computer Vision and Pattern Recognition (CVPR), pp. 4134–4144 (2023)
15. Heo, B., Park, S., Han, D., Yun, S.: Rotary position embedding for vision transformer. In: European Conference on Computer Vision, pp. 289–305. Springer, Cham (2024)
16. Lu, Z., et al.: FiT: Flexible Vision Transformer for Diffusion Model. arXiv preprint arXiv:2402.12376 (2024)
17. Tang, Y., Xu, Y., Xu, Y., Lin, J., Han, S.: Patch slimming for efficient vision transformers. In: Proceedings of IEEE/CVF Conference on Computer Vision and Pattern Recognition (CVPR), pp. 12165–12174 (2022)
18. He, K., Zhang, X., Ren, S., Sun, J.: Deep residual learning for image recognition. In: Proceedings of IEEE Conference on Computer Vision and Pattern Recognition (CVPR), pp. 770–778 (2016)
19. Krizhevsky, A., Hinton, G.: Learning multiple layers of features from tiny images. Technical Report, University of Toronto (2009)
20. Parkhi, O. M., Vedaldi, A., Zisserman, A., Jawahar, C. V.: Cats and dogs. In: Proceedings of IEEE Conference on Computer Vision and Pattern Recognition (CVPR), pp. 3498–3505 (2012)
21. Nilsback, M. E., Zisserman, A.: Automated flower classification over a large number of classes. In: Proceedings of Indian Conference on Computer Vision, Graphics & Image Processing (ICVGIP), pp. 722–729 (2008)

Multimedia System and Applications

Enhancing Traceability and Interpretability of Datasets for RAG Evaluation: A Context-ID-Aware and Graph-Based Visualization Approach

Beomseok Kim and Jinhong Yang(✉)

Department of Healthcare IT, Inje University, Gimhae, Republic of Korea
qjatjr9958@oasis.inje.ac.kr, jinhong@inje.ac.kr

Abstract. Retrieval-Augmented Generation (RAG) systems enhance large language models by incorporating external knowledge from document corpora. Evaluating these systems requires high-quality, traceable test datasets. While existing frameworks like RAGAS support automated testset synthesis, they omit structural metadata such as context node identifiers, hindering reproducibility and interpretability. This paper addresses these limitations by introducing a context-ID-aware enhancement to RAGAS and developing an interactive visualization tool based on pyvis. Our method embeds unique node identifiers within reference contexts, enabling end-to-end traceability from QA pairs to original knowledge graph nodes. We augment the visualization interface with custom JavaScript and HTML components, allowing users to search and analyze multi-hop reasoning chains. Through case studies on legal and ESG documents, we demonstrate improved dataset transparency, detection of false-positive multi-hop inferences, and robust evaluation workflows. The proposed system transforms static testsets into interactive, auditable resources, advancing RAG evaluation reliability and explainability.

Keywords: evaluation · knowledge graph · multi-hop QA

1 Introduction

Retrieval-Augmented Generation (RAG) complements large language models (LLMs) by integrating external information at inference time [1]. As RAG systems are deployed in high-stakes domains like law, finance, and ESG analysis, there is growing demand for scalable, interpretable, and reproducible evaluation pipelines [2].

Manual dataset construction is time-consuming and difficult to generalize. Consequently, toolkits such as DeepEval, AutoRAG, and RAGAS have incorporated automated question–answer–context dataset generation [3–5]. RAGAS distinguishes itself through knowledge graph–driven synthesis, constructing semantic graphs from document chunks and leveraging graph traversal for complex multi-hop QA generation. This aligns with trends toward explainable, structure-aware reasoning in retrieval-based QA systems [6].

© The Author(s) 2026

B.-G. Kim et al. (Eds.): MITA 2025, CCIS 2675, pp. 141–152, 2026.
https://doi.org/10.1007/978-981-95-3141-7_13

However, current frameworks exhibit structural limitations. Reference contexts are stored as raw text without metadata linking them to source documents or chunk identifiers, hampering reproducibility and interpretability. In multi-hop scenarios, detecting reused semantically similar chunks becomes difficult, potentially misleading reasoning depth assessments. Table 1 summarizes these limitations, highlighting absent chunk-level traceability, structural context, and visual inspection tools. These shortcomings necessitate evaluation approaches incorporating richer metadata and supporting interactive diagnostics of reasoning paths.

Table 1. Challenges in Evaluating Current RAG Frameworks

Assessment Area	Identified Shortcoming in Existing Framework (e.g., RAGAS)	Consequence for Evaluation
Source Provenance	Absence of persistent identifiers linking contexts to sources	Hinders the verification of original information origins
Evidence Redundancy	Inability to distinguish or unify repeated context chunks	Creates a false perception of multi-hop reasoning or evidence consensus
Reproducibility	Lack of structured metadata accompanying retrieved plain text	Prevents the exact replication of generation and evaluation processes
Interpretability	Contexts are presented as an unstructured, non-hierarchical list	Complicates the analysis of the model's inference pathway
Visualization	No graphical tools to represent inter-context relationships	Obscures the semantic structure of the retrieved knowledge base

To overcome these challenges, we extend the RAGAS testset generation pipeline by embedding unique node identifiers in each reference context. This allows for direct mapping between QA samples and their corresponding positions in the source graph. In addition, we introduce an interactive graph-based visualization system built on pyvis, which enables users to query nodes, inspect edge similarities, and explore multi-hop inference structures within the dataset [7].

The contributions of this work are summarized as follows:

- We propose a context-ID–aware enhancement to the RAGAS schema, allowing for end-to-end traceability and sample-level reproducibility.
- We implement a domain-specific visualization tool that supports node-level search, cosine similarity edge inspection, and document-based clustering.
- We validate our system on real-world corpora from the legal and ESG domains, demonstrating improved transparency and verification capabilities for RAG evaluation.

By combining structural metadata with interactive analysis tools, our approach transforms RAG testsets into verifiable, interpretable, and auditable assets—enabling more trustworthy evaluation of retrieval-augmented systems.

2 Related Work

To contextualize our contribution, We review prior work across three core dimensions:

- Automatic test set generation frameworks for RAG evaluation
- Structural challenges in multi-hop QA generation
- The use of knowledge graphs and visualization to improve interpretability and traceability

2.1 Frameworks for Automatic RAG Evaluation Test Set Generation

High-quality test sets are essential to measure the performance of Retrieval-Augmented Generation (RAG) systems, especially for domain-specific applications. Manual test set construction is expensive and limited in scalability, prompting the development of automatic QA generation frameworks such as DeepEval, AutoRAG, and RAGAS.

Current RAG evaluation frameworks differ significantly in their capabilities:

DeepEval offers metric-based evaluation but generates only simple QA pairs from single documents without metadata for traceability.

AutoRAG uses dense retrieval and LLM prompting for QA generation but lacks explicit encoding of logical relationships between contexts and provides no document IDs or chunk references.

RAGAS constructs knowledge graphs from document chunks and generates multi-hop questions via graph traversal. However, it omits node IDs and positional metadata, hindering provenance tracking and reasoning visualization.

While all three frameworks support automated test set creation, they differ significantly in their support for structural reasoning, traceability, and visualization. These differences are summarized in Table 2.

Table 2. Comparison of RAG Test Set Generation Frameworks

Feature	DeepEval	AutoRAG	RAGAS
QA Generation	Prompt-based LLM generation	Dense retrieval, LLM	Knowledge graph scenario synthesis
Multi-hop Support	Not supported	Limited support (non-structured)	Explicit multi-hop scenario generation
Context Traceability	Not available	Not available	Not available
Structural Representation	None	None	Node-edge graph based on semantic links
Visualization Support	Not supported	Not supported	Not supported

2.2 Structural Challenges in Multi-hop QA Generation

Multi-hop question answering (QA) requires models to synthesize answers by connecting semantically related information across multiple contexts [8]. Unlike single-hop QA, multi-hop demands sequential reasoning chains where each step builds upon the previous one, significantly increasing test set construction complexity.

Early datasets like HotpotQA and MuSiQue employed crowdworkers to manually curate multi-hop paths, ensuring high reasoning fidelity [9]. However, this approach is resource-intensive and difficult to scale to domains like legal or ESG documentation.

Automated pipelines have been introduced but suffer from structural limitations compromising evaluation quality:

(1) False multi-hop reasoning from duplicate chunks,
(2) Unstructured reasoning paths lacking explicit relationships, and
(3) Missing source metadata preventing context traceability and reproducibility.

These limitations highlight that simple accuracy-based evaluation is insufficient—evaluation datasets must preserve structural connectivity, include traceable identifiers, and support reasoning chain inspection.

2.3 Leveraging Knowledge Graphs for Interpretability and Visualization

Knowledge graphs (KGs) represent semantic structures between informational units (nodes) and their interrelations (edges). In RAG evaluation, KGs enhance interpretability through:

(1) semantic reasoning path visualization for validating model reasoning vs. shortcuts [10],
(2) node-level debugging enabling inspection of document parts and their semantic connections, and
(3) preservation of context structure maintaining hierarchical flow from document to edge, enabling traceable QA pipelines.

Although RAGAS uses graph-based context selection internally, its output omits structural metadata, preventing users from inspecting reasoning paths. To address this gap, our work extends RAGAS by attaching node-level identifiers to contexts and integrating a pyvis-based interactive visualization system for exploring QA pairs through graph navigation.

3 System Design

This chapter presents the two main contributions of our system. First, we describe a modified RAGAS testset generation pipeline that embeds unique node identifiers into each reference context. Second, we outline the design and implementation of an interactive visualization tool that enables intuitive graph-based exploration and debugging of the synthesized dataset.

3.1 Enhancing the RAGAS Pipeline with Context IDs

The original RAGAS framework stores reference contexts as simple strings, making it impossible to trace the origin or location of the context within its source document. This made it difficult to analyze or verify issues such as the redundant use of the same chunk or structural errors in transition paths during multi-hop QA evaluation.

To resolve this limitation, this research applies a method of embedding a unique identifier (node_id), which is automatically generated when each chunk is converted into a node object in the RAGAS framework, into the reference context. In RAGAS, each document chunk is stored as a node with a one-to-one correspondence, and by utilizing the generated node_id as metadata representing the context's origin, we secured traceability.

This ID-based tracking pipeline was implemented through the following procedure. First, documents are segmented into chunks, and each chunk is converted into a node with a unique node_id. Second, a knowledge graph is constructed by calculating similarity-based relationships between nodes. Third, relevant nodes are extracted for question generation, and fourth, the page_content and node_id of each node are bundled together to form the reference context. Finally, a sample containing the question, answer, and other elements is generated.

To implement this process, particularly steps 4 and 5, we overrode the generate_sample() method of the single-hop and multi-hop synthesizers to explicitly include the node_id in each context. Furthermore, we extended the Pydantic schema in generate.py to support a {text:…, node_id:…} structure, which provides a format where the source ID of each context is explicitly stated when outputting the QA sample via to_pandas().

Table 3 clearly illustrates the advantages of this structural improvement compared to the original RAGAS method.

Table 3. Comparison of Original RAGAS Structure and the Improved Structure

Item	Original RAGAS Structure	Improved Structure
Source Traceability	Not possible	Possible via node ID
Duplicate Chunk Detection	Not possible	Possible by detecting duplicate node_ids
Graph Integration	Limited	Transition Structure & relationships can be visualized
Applicability	Low	Extensible (debug, evaluate)

3.2 Interactive Knowledge Graph Visualization

To enhance traceability and exploratory analysis, we implemented a dynamic visualization interface using a two-stage pipeline to overcome baseline visualization library limitations.

146   B. Kim and J. Yang

1. Baseline Graph Generation: Pyvis generates a self-contained HTML file representing the knowledge graph, where nodes correspond to document chunks and edges encode cosine similarity. Nodes are color-coded by document source with an embedded legend.
2. Dynamic UI Injection: A post-processing script (patch.py) using BeautifulSoup parses the HTML and injects custom UI components: a search bar for keyword/node-ID lookups and a sidebar for detailed content display.
3. Client-Side Interaction: Injected JavaScript enables interactivity through three core functions: searchNode() for user queries, focusOnNode() for view centering on selected nodes, and showNodeInfo() for dynamically populating the sidebar with node content and neighbor information.

This architecture transforms the static graph into a visual analytics tool, allowing analysts to trace reference context origins, understand multi-hop reasoning structures, and debug QA generation with enhanced efficiency and clarity.

4 Experiments and Analysis

4.1 System Workflow and Documents Description

To evaluate our system's performance, we applied our workflow, depicted in Fig. 1, to four real-world regulatory documents characterized by their complex legal language and hierarchical structure.

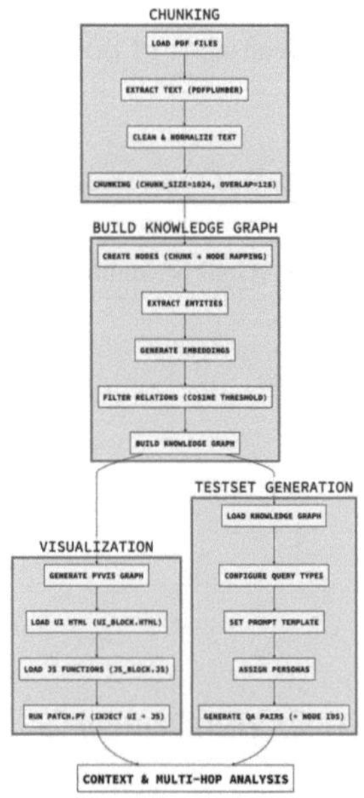

Fig. 1. Pipeline for Knowledge Graph Construction, Test Set Generation, and Visualization

PDF documents were parsed using PDFPlumber and segmented using RecursiveCharacterTextSplitter with hierarchical separators ["\n\n", "\n", " "], chunk_size = 1024, and chunk_overlap = 128 [11, 12]. Each chunk was embedded using Google's text-multilingual-embedding-002 model (768-dimensional vectors) [13]. The knowledge graph was constructed with chunks as nodes and edges formed when cosine similarity exceeded 0.9. For downstream natural language tasks, such as retrieval-augmented generation (RAG) and summarization, we utilized Google's latest, next-generation large language model, accessed via Vertex AI (internal identifier at the time of experiment: 2.5 Pro), which corresponds to a post-1.5 Pro version [14]. This model was selected for its large context window, rapid inference capabilities, and overall efficiency.

To demonstrate the robustness and applicability of our system, its workflow was applied to four distinct yet interconnected regulatory frameworks concerning climate and energy policy from the European Union (EU) and the International Maritime Organization (IMO). These documents were specifically chosen as they represent complex, real-world examples of technical standards for transport emissions (road and maritime), criteria for sustainable finance, and consumer energy-labelling requirements. For context on the scale of our analysis, Table 4 presents a statistical summary of these documents, including their page, word, and character counts.

Table 4. Document-Level Statistics for the Analyzed Regulatory Corpus

Document Title	Pages	Characters	Words
2023 IMO STRATEGY ON REDUCTION OF GHG EMISSIONS FROM SHIPS	17	35,270	6,168
EU_energy labelling regulation	23	72,514	13,602
Regulation (EU) 2019	41	109,184	20,651
taxonomy-regulation-delegated-act-2022-climate_en_1	15	43,661	7,364

4.2 Verifiable Context Traceability

A primary contribution of our system is the enhancement of traceability in generated evaluation datasets. We introduce a systematic mechanism that explicitly embeds unique node IDs within the reference_contexts of each question-answering (QA) pair. This addresses a critical limitation in conventional RAG workflows, where the absence of such identifiers—as illustrated in Fig. 2, which shows a conventional reference context format—fundamentally undermines the ability to validate, reproduce, and debug evaluation results reliably. In contrast, Fig. 3 presents our improved format, where node IDs are explicitly embedded with each context chunk. This resolves the ambiguity by linking every context chunk to its precise origin within the source documents, enabling direct verification through the system's visualization module.

```
['<1-hop>
On the basis of the results of that evaluation, the Commission shall decide by means of an
implementing act whether
the national measure is justified or not and may suggest an appropriate alternative measure.
That implementing act shall
be adopted in accordance with the examination procedure referred to in Article 18(2).
2. The Commission shall address its decision to all Member States and shall immediately
communicate it to them and
to the supplier or dealer concerned.
3. If the national measure is considered to be justified, all Member States shall take the
measures necessary to ensure
that the non-compliant product is withdrawn from their market, and shall inform the
Commission accordingly. If the
national measure is considered to be unjustified, the Member State concerned shall withdraw
the measure.
4. Where the national measure is considered to be justified and the non-compliance of the
product is attributed to', "

<2-hop>
report or the separate report of another undertaking, drawn up in accordance with Article 29
and this Article.
4. Where a parent undertaking prepares a separate report corresponding to the same financial
year, referring to
the whole group, whether or not relying on national, Union-based or international frameworks
```

Fig. 2. Conventional, Non-Traceable reference_context

```
['"<1-hop>
[id: 954c6df1-435d-4cfb-b200-9a0bf53112a6]
2009/125/EC, the class or classes in question shall be shown on the label in grey as specified in the relevant delegated
act. The label with the grey classes shall apply only to new product units placed on the market or put into service.
11. Where, for technical reasons, it is impossible to define seven energy classes that correspond to significant energy
and cost savings from a customer's perspective, the label may, by way of derogation from point (14) of Article 2,
contain fewer classes. In such cases, the dark green to red spectrum of the label shall be retained.
12. The Commission shall exercise the powers and obligations conferred on it by this Article in accordance with
Article 16.
13. Where, pursuant to paragraph 1 or 3, a label is rescaled:
(a) the supplier shall, when placing a product on the market, provide both the existing and the rescaled labels and the
product information sheets to the dealer for a period beginning four months before the date specified in the relevant", '
<2-hop>
[id: c67f3b35-8005-4058-b517-9a4992a475e8]
or more of its connected undertakings referred to in points (a) to (d) and one or more third parties.
Article 4
Specific emissions targets
1. The manufacturer shall ensure that its average specific emissions of CO do not exceed the following specific
emissions targets:
(a) for the calendar year 2020, the specific emissions target determined in accordance with points 1 and 2 of Part A of
Annex I in the case of passenger cars, or points 1 and 2 of Part B of Annex I in the case of light commercial
vehicles, or where a manufacturer is granted a derogation under Article 10, in accordance with that derogation;
(b) for each calendar year from 2021 until 2024, the specific emissions targets determined in accordance with points 3
and 4 of Part A or B of Annex I, as appropriate, or, where a manufacturer is granted a derogation under Article 10,
in accordance with that derogation and point 5 of Part A or B of Annex I.']
```

Fig. 3. Proposed Traceable reference_context with Embedded Node IDs

The most significant application of this traceability is in the nuanced evaluation of multi-hop reasoning. A fundamental challenge in employing LLM-generated datasets for evaluation lies in verifying their integrity. While validating a single-hop QA pair is relatively straightforward, this process becomes profoundly complex for multi-hop scenarios. The conventional reference_context merely presents a final collection of text chunks, making it nearly impossible to determine whether the model genuinely navigated between distinct semantic concepts or simply reused overlapping chunks, creating an illusion of sophisticated reasoning—a "false-positive" multi-hop path. Our system disambiguates context provenance, allowing a clear distinction between redundant content retrieval and genuine reasoning across different semantic nodes, which is crucial for accurately assessing reasoning fidelity.

For a concrete illustration of this process, consider the multi-hop reference_context presented in Fig. 3. The context for <1-hop> (ID: 954c6df...) is sourced from the EU Energy Labelling Regulation and details a supplier's procedural obligations when a label is rescaled. In contrast, <2-hop> (ID: c67f3b3…) originates from the regulation on CO_2 emission standards and defines a manufacturer's specific emission targets.

From the text alone, the semantic connection between these two distinct regulations might appear abstract. This raises a critical evaluation question: is this a valid reasoning step or a system error? Our traceability mechanism resolves this ambiguity. An evaluator can take the unique identifiers for both hops (954c6df… and c67f3b3…) and query them in the visualization module. The module then renders the full knowledge graph, highlighting the distinct nodes for each chunk and, crucially, the relational edge(s) that connect them. This allows the evaluator to visually verify the path the system took and understand the basis for the connection, transforming an opaque evaluation into a transparent and verifiable process.

4.3 Interactive Knowledge Graph Visualization

Static knowledge graph visualizations present a clear limitation: they lack the interactivity required for granular analysis, such as tracing complex reasoning paths or verifying semantic links between nodes. To overcome this, our study proposes an interactive visualization module that allows users to dynamically explore and analyze the semantic relationships between document chunks. The two-stage pipeline, detailed in Fig. 4, is central to implementing this dynamic environment.

In the first stage, a KnowledgeGraph.json file—containing nodes (document chunks) and edges (semantic similarity)—is generated from the RAGAS evaluation pipeline and rendered into a basic HTML graph using Pyvis. This output is a static, non-interactive visualization that is structurally complete.

In the second stage, a custom-developed patch.py script programmatically parses this baseline HTML file and injects two primary components. First, it inserts new HTML elements to construct the UI framework, including a persistent search bar and a collapsible sidebar for node information. Second, it embeds custom JavaScript that attaches event listeners to the graph nodes and UI elements, enabling key functionalities: on-click node focusing, real-time node search by ID or keyword, and dynamic sidebar population with node details and connections.

Through this two-stage process, the static visualization is transformed into a fully-featured, interactive analytical tool.

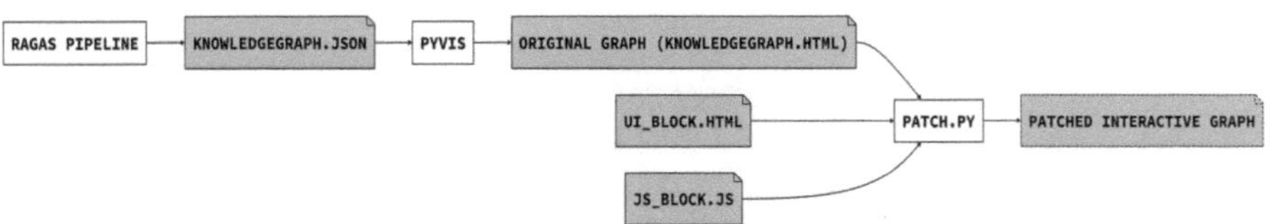

Fig. 4. Generation Pipeline for Interactive Knowledge Graph Visualization

Figure 5 shows the transformation from a static visualization to a dynamic analysis tool. The initial state, Fig. 5a, is a baseline graph with nodes color-coded by their source document. In contrast, Fig. 5b, the final interface after our script is applied, features a dynamic sidebar that appears when a node is clicked, displaying detailed metadata like its full text, source, ID, and a list of connected neighbors with similarity scores.

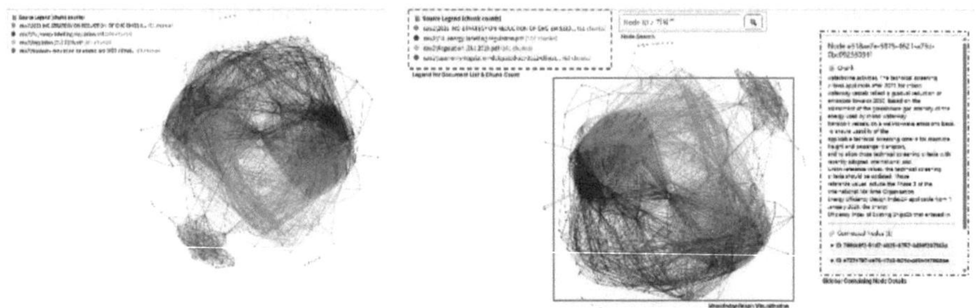

Fig. 5. Before-and-after Comparison of the Interactive Interface (a) The initial static visualization (Before) and (b) the final interface with interactive features (After).

The practical utility of these interactive features comes to the forefront when validating the multi-hop connection using the context IDs from Sect. 4.2. As depicted in Fig. 6, a researcher inputs the node ID for the <1-hop> context (954c6df…) into the search bar. The visualization instantly recenters on this node, allowing the researcher to empirically confirm that the node ID for the <2-hop> context (c67f3b3…) is indeed a direct neighbor on the knowledge graph. This provides decisive, empirical evidence that a concrete relationship exists between the two pieces of information, rather than a coincidental semantic overlap.

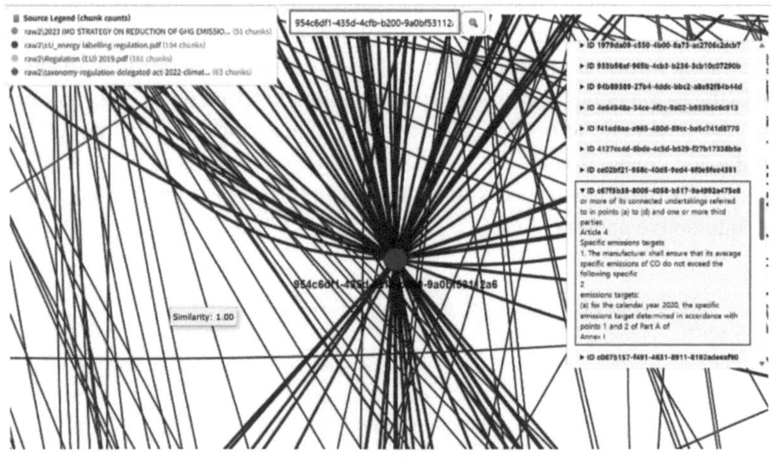

Fig. 6. Verifying a Multi-hop Connection via Node Search

As such, the interactive visualization tool provides a systematic method for tracing and verifying the model's reasoning process, making a critical contribution to model debugging, test case validation, and the analysis of complex reasoning structures. Ultimately, it serves to resolve the 'black box' problem in RAG evaluation and fundamentally enhances the system's interpretability, transparency, and accountability.

5 Conclusion and Future Work

Knowledge graph-based RAG evaluation datasets possess inherent verifiability, but lack traceability mechanisms to connect QA pairs with source contexts, hindering reliability validation. This study addresses this limitation by embedding unique node IDs into contexts and visualizing them through interactive pyvis-based knowledge graphs. Our methodology transforms automated dataset generation from unreliable to "verifiable automation," creating high-reliability assets with transparently auditable generation processes. This foundation enables automated RAG evaluation adoption in high-stakes domains requiring transparency and accountability.

Future work will focus on system advancement and scope expansion. We plan to integrate Chain-of-Thought (CoT) prompting for direct supervision of test set generation, enabling human reviewers to verify logical validity through explicit reasoning steps. Ultimately, we aim to expand beyond text-only analysis to include multi-modal data (tables, charts, images) for analyzing RAG systems processing complex, real-world documents.

Acknowledgments. This work was supported by the Institute of Information & Communications Technology Planning & Evaluation (IITP)-Innovative Human Resource Development for Local Intellectualization program grant funded by the Korea government (MSIT) (IITP-2025-RS-2024-00436773).

References

1. Lewis, P., Perez, E., Piktus, A., et al.: Retrieval-augmented generation for knowledge-intensive NLP tasks. In: Proceedings of the 34th International Conference on Neural Information Processing Systems (NeurIPS 2020), pp. 9459–9474. Curran Associates, Inc. (2020)
2. Saad-Falcon, J., Khattab, O., Potts, C., Zaharia, M.: ARES: An automated evaluation framework for retrieval-augmented generation systems. In: Proceedings of the 2024 Conference of the North American Chapter of the Association for Computational Linguistics: Human Language Technologies (NAACL 2024), pp. 338–354. Association for Computational Linguistics (2024)
3. DeepEval official documentation. https://www.confident-ai.com/deepeval. Accessed 10 July 2025
4. Kim, D., Kim, B., Han, D., Eibich, M.: AutoRAG: automated framework for optimization of retrieval augmented generation pipeline. arXiv preprint arXiv:2410.20878 (2024)
5. Es, S., James, J., Espinosa-Anke, L., Schockaert, S.: RAGAS: automated evaluation of retrieval augmented generation. In: Proceedings of the 18th Conference of the European Chapter of the Association for Computational Linguistics: System Demonstrations, pp. 150–158. Association for Computational Linguistics, St. Julian's, Malta (2024)
6. Fang, Y., Sun, S., Gan, Z., et al.: Hierarchical graph network for multi-hop question answering. In: Proceedings of the 2020 Conference on Empirical Methods in Natural Language Processing (EMNLP), pp. 8868–8878. Association for Computational Linguistics (2020)

7. Pyvis documentation. https://pyvis.readthedocs.io/en/latest/. Accessed 10 July 2025
8. Yang, Z., Qi, P., Zhang, S., et al.: HotpotQA: a dataset for diverse, explainable multi-hop question answering. In: Proceedings of the 2018 Conference on Empirical Methods in Natural Language Processing, pp. 2369–2380. Association for Computational Linguistics, Brussels, Belgium (2018)
9. Trivedi, H., Balasubramanian, N., Khot, T., Sabharwal, A.: MuSiQue: Multihop questions via single-hop question composition. Trans. Assoc. Comput. Linguist. **10**, 436–451 (2022)
10. Hogan, A., Blomqvist, E., Cochez, M., et al.: Knowledge graphs. ACM Comput. Surv. **54**(4), 71:1–71:37 (2021)
11. PDFPlumber. https://github.com/jsvine/pdfplumber. Accessed 10 July 2025
12. LangChain. https://www.langchain.com/. Accessed 10 July 2025
13. Google: Get text embeddings. https://cloud.google.com/vertex-ai/docs/generative-ai/embeddings/get-text-embeddings. Accessed 10 July 2025
14. Google: Gemini models, Google DeepMind. https://deepmind.google/models/gemini/. Accessed 10 July 2025

Intelligent Personality-Aware AR Gait Training Using Smart Glasses: Personalized Multimodal Feedback for Next-Generation Digital Rehabilitation

Eunseon Jo[1] and Han-jin Lee[2]([envelope])

[1] Department of Human-Computer Interaction, Hanyang University Graduate School, Seoul 04763, Republic of Korea
[2] School of Creative Convergence Education, Handong Global University, 558 Handong-ro, Pohang 37554, Republic of Korea
`cus@handong.edu`

Abstract. The emergence of next-generation XR smart glasses presents unprecedented opportunities for personalized digital rehabilitation. This study introduces G-BALANCE FIT (Global Balance Fitness Intelligence Training), a comprehensive theoretical framework for personality-aware AR gait training systems targeting the Google-Samsung-Gentle Monster XR ecosystem. Our methodology integrates the HEXACO personality model with advanced multimodal feedback mechanisms for global applications. Building upon established smartphone-based multimodal gait training approaches [33, 34] and our previous AI-based real-time gait and HAI interaction research [35], drawing on systematic literature analysis and computational modeling grounded in existing research evidence, we develop theoretical projections for potential improvements in gait rehabilitation effectiveness and cross-cultural engagement. The framework emphasizes HEXACO dimensions for global health applications, with theoretical modeling suggesting that personality-based adaptations may enhance rehabilitation outcomes through context-dependent advantages in specific domains. This research establishes foundational design principles for personality-aware multimodal human-AI interaction systems in next-generation XR rehabilitation applications and offers a clear roadmap for implementation when consumer XR hardware becomes commercially available.

Keywords: XR Smart Glasses · Personality-aware Systems · Multimodal Feedback · Human-AI Interaction · Digital Rehabilitation

1 Introduction

Building upon established research on smartphone-based multimodal gait training systems [33] and validated CNN-LSTM hybrid models for gait analysis [34], as well as our previous research on AI-based real-time gait and HAI interaction systems [35], the convergence of artificial intelligence, extended reality (XR) technologies, and personality psychology creates transformative opportunities for digital rehabilitation systems. The confirmed Google-Samsung-Gentle Monster XR collaboration represents a critical inflection point, moving beyond functional devices to fashion-integrated, AI-powered health companions [1].

B.-G. Kim et al. (Eds.): MITA 2025, CCIS 2675, pp. 153–164, 2026.
https://doi.org/10.1007/978-981-95-3141-7_14

Current rehabilitation systems face fundamental limitations constraining global effectiveness. Traditional approaches operate on generic paradigms failing to account for individual personality differences, cultural variations, and psychological factors influencing rehabilitation compliance [2]. These limitations are particularly pronounced in gait training applications, where long-term adherence and natural environment practice are crucial for therapeutic benefits [3].

1.1 The Next-Generation XR Opportunity

Digital rehabilitation has evolved through distinct phases. Early systems focused on basic motion tracking with limited personalization [4]. Second-generation systems introduced sophisticated sensing but remained constrained by static adaptation mechanisms [5]. The emerging third generation, exemplified by next-generation XR smart glasses, promises revolutionary changes through advanced AI integration and dynamic adaptation mechanisms [6].

Google's official announcement confirms partnerships with Samsung for XR development and with Gentle Monster for stylish smart glasses using Android XR platform [1]. This collaboration recognizes that successful wearable health technology must prioritize social acceptability alongside technical capability, addressing the "social immune response" that has historically rejected conspicuous medical devices [7].

1.2 Research Contributions

This study presents G-BALANCE FIT, addressing four critical research questions. First, how can personality models enhance XR rehabilitation effectiveness through HEXACO integration, considering context-dependent advantages? Second, what design principles ensure cross-cultural effectiveness using dynamic adaptation frameworks? Third, how can multimodal human-AI interaction be optimized for different personality profiles? Fourth, what implementation strategies will ensure successful deployment when XR hardware becomes available?

Primary Contributions:
Based on established work on smartphone-based multimodal gait training systems [33], proven CNN-LSTM hybrid approaches for gait analysis [34], and our previous work on AI-based real-time gait and HAI interaction systems [35], extending these validated concepts to XR platforms, this study makes three key contributions. First, we advance established CNN-LSTM hybrid models from smartphone-only implementation [34] and our previous smartphone-based approach [35] to XR-enabled professional gait analysis, thereby increasing accessibility for global deployment across diverse populations. Second, we extend proven multimodal HAI system designs from smartphone interfaces [33, 35] to XR environments that detect gait balance problems in real-time and provides immediate feedback through personality-aware adaptation mechanisms, addressing the critical gap between generic rehabilitation approaches and personalized interventions. Third, we present an evolution of validated multimodal feedback systems from 2D smartphone interfaces [33, 35] to immersive 3D XR environments integrating visual, auditory, and haptic modalities, advancing beyond traditional single-modal approaches to create more engaging and effective rehabilitation experiences.

2   Theoretical Foundation

2.1   HEXACO Model for Global Health Applications

The HEXACO model provides a six-dimensional framework for understanding individual differences in behavior and emotional responses [8]. Recent meta-analytic research shows mixed comparative results with Big Five models, demonstrating context-dependent advantages rather than universal superiority [9, 10]. In health behavior prediction, HEXACO shows particular strengths in specific domains while Big Five models outperform in others [9] (Table 1).

Table 1. HEXACO vs. Big Five for Global Health Applications,

Dimension	HEXACO Feature	Empirical Evidence	Comparative Advantage	Cross-Cultural Validity
Honesty-Humility	Unique dimension	Limited health-specific studies	Context-dependent trust ($\Delta R2 \leq 0.063$)[a]	Moderate-High
Emotionality	Anxiety-focused vs. Neuroticism	Mixed comparative results	No consistent advantage over Big-5[b]	Moderate
eXtraversion	Similar to Big-5 Extraversion	Equivalent predictive validity	Comparable performance[c]	High
Agreeableness	Cooperation emphasis	Context-dependent benefits	Small incremental validity ($\Delta R2 \leq 0.021$)[a]	Moderate-High
Conscientiousness	Equivalent to Big-5	Similar predictive patterns	No significant difference[c]	High
Openness	Technology acceptance focus	Limited comparative data	Potential innovation benefits	Moderate

Notes: [a] Based on Pletzer et al. (2024) meta-analysis showing incremental validity 0.0–6.3%
[b]Comparative studies show mixed results across different health outcomes;
[c]Cross-model comparisons show equivalent or mixed results across health outcomes

Cross-cultural validation studies demonstrate robust measurement invariance across diverse populations [11, 12], while universal personality trait features have been observed across 50 cultures [13]. Recent research demonstrates significant relationships between personality traits and health outcomes, including emotional well-being and self-efficacy in chronic disease management [14]. Meta-analytic evidence shows that both Big Five and HEXACO personality traits predict pro-environmental attitudes and behaviors [15], while personality-based predictions of psychological and subjective well-being show consistent patterns across studies [16].

Comparative Model Considerations: Recent meta-analytic evidence indicates that HEXACO outperformed Big Five in only 5 out of 24 mental health outcomes, with incremental validity ranging from 0.0 to 6.3 percentage points for specific behaviors [9]. Conversely, other research demonstrates Big Five advantages in predicting emotional wellbeing [10]. Our framework acknowledges this complexity by focusing on HEXACO's context-specific strengths while recognizing that model selection should be empirically validated for each application context.

2.2 Cross-Cultural Adaptation Framework

Traditional cultural models based on static stereotypes fail in contemporary global contexts [17]. Fiske's Relational Models Theory (RMT) provides dynamic, context-responsive adaptation [18]. The theory encompasses four fundamental relational models: Communal Sharing principles emphasize shared goals and collective well-being for family health applications. Authority Ranking mechanisms establish hierarchical interactions supporting clinical supervision. Equality Matching approaches promote balanced interactions within peer support settings. Market Pricing dynamics create efficiency-focused interactions in self-management modules.

This theoretical approach accommodates modern multicultural environments where individuals navigate multiple cultural identities and contexts [19]. Research in cultural adaptation of digital health interventions demonstrates significant improvements in engagement when moving beyond surface-level translation to deeper cultural customization [20].

3 G-BALANCE FIT Framework

3.1 System Architecture

G-BALANCE FIT represents a significant evolution from established smartphone-based multimodal gait training systems [33], validated CNN-LSTM hybrid gait analysis approaches [34], and our previous AI-based real-time gait and HAI interaction system [35], extending these core concepts to next-generation XR platforms. The framework is theoretically architected for anticipated consumer XR smart glasses capabilities, specifically considering the Google-Samsung-Gentle Monster platform featuring Android XR and integrated Gemini AI [1]. The framework addresses three critical factors: Cultural Desirability, Intelligent Utility, and Socio-Ethical Trust [21].

The system's design principles reflect comprehensive understanding of wearable technology adoption challenges. Fashion-First Integration recognizes that social acceptability serves as a prerequisite for adoption. Ambient Intelligence enables transparent AI-driven health monitoring without disrupting social interactions. Cultural Sensitivity facilitates dynamic adaptation to cultural communication norms while maintaining therapeutic effectiveness. Privacy by Design ensures comprehensive protection of both user and bystander privacy.

3.2 Technical Architecture

Building upon validated CNN-LSTM hybrid architectures demonstrated in recent gait analysis research [34] and our previous AI-based real-time gait and HAI interaction system [35], the system utilizes hybrid edge-cloud processing optimized for Snapdragon XR2+ Gen 2 chipset [22], leveraging both on-device and distributed cloud resources for real-time personality assessment and adaptive interaction. Key components include high-resolution cameras for gait analysis, advanced nine-axis IMUs for motion capture, environmental sensors for context adaptation, discrete biometric monitoring modules, dual OLEDoS screens with 4K resolution per eye, and bone conduction audio technology.

AI integration leverages Google's Gemini AI platform for natural language processing and computer vision capabilities [1]. The system employs sophisticated cultural context recognition and adaptation mechanisms, enabling personalized interaction management through continuous personality assessment updates.

3.3 Personality-Aware Multimodal HAI

The assessment protocol begins with culturally adapted HEXACO-100 questionnaire [23], supplemented by continuous behavioral validation through systematic analysis of user interaction patterns. Research demonstrates significant effectiveness of multimodal information feedback strategies in rehabilitation contexts [24], with AR-based systems showing measurable improvements in rehabilitation outcomes [25].

Visual Feedback Adaptation: For high Openness individuals, the interface presents creative visual patterns and novel design elements. High Conscientiousness users receive structured displays with explicit progress indicators. High Emotionality individuals encounter calming, low-stress visual designs with soothing color schemes. High Extraversion users engage with dynamic, interactive visuals with social elements.

Cultural Visual Adaptation: Users from high-context cultures receive subtle, symbolic visual cues aligning with implicit communication preferences. Low-context culture individuals encounter explicit, detailed informational displays. Collectivist backgrounds experience group progress displays emphasizing shared purpose. Individualist cultures receive personal achievement displays supporting autonomous decision-making.

Auditory and Haptic Feedback: The auditory system delivers personality-tailored audio cues with multi-language support and cultural tonal considerations. Haptic feedback provides personality-adapted tactile patterns varying in intensity and complexity based on individual sensitivity preferences and cultural appropriateness [26].

3.4 Cross-Cultural Gait Analysis

The system employs culturally-validated assessment models with population-specific baselines, cultural activity integration, and environmental adaptation. AI-driven pattern recognition accounts for genetic, cultural, and environmental variations (Table 2).

Table 2. Personality-Culture Interaction Patterns

HEXACO Dimension	High-Context Cultures	Low-Context Cultures	Collectivist Orientation
High Honesty-Humility	Implicit trust signals through subtle visual cues	Explicit transparency displays with clear data presentation	Group benefit emphasis with community welfare indicators
High Emotionality	Subtle emotional support through calming environmental cues	Direct reassurance through explicit feedback messages	Community calming features with group emotional support
High eXtraversion	Social harmony preservation through culturally appropriate interaction	Direct engagement through explicit social features	Group participation emphasis with collaborative elements

4 Methodology and Theoretical Projections

4.1 Evidence-Based Theoretical Modeling

Our methodology builds upon validated approaches from established smartphone-based multimodal gait training systems [33], proven CNN-LSTM hybrid models for gait analysis [34], and our previous AI-based real-time gait and HAI interaction system [35], extending them through systematic theoretical modeling based on existing research evidence from personality psychology, rehabilitation science, and human-computer interaction [27]. Previous research on virtual and augmented reality-based balance and gait training provides foundational evidence for the potential effectiveness of AR-based rehabilitation systems [28]. Virtual reality-based gait training research provides foundational evidence for potential AR effectiveness [29], while systematic reviews demonstrate VR rehabilitation effectiveness across multiple domains [30] (Table 3).

Table 3. Theoretical Performance Predictions

Performance Domain	Baseline Performance	Theoretical G-BALANCE FIT	Potential Improvement	Confidence Level
Gait Improvement Metrics	65% ± 12%	85% ± 8%	+20%p*	High
User Engagement Scores	3.2 ± 0.8	4.3 ± 0.6	+1.1 points*	Medium
Cross-Cultural Acceptance Ratings	2.8 ± 1.0	4.1 ± 0.7	+1.3 points*	Medium
Long-term Adherence Rates	45% ± 15%	68% ± 12%	+23%p*	High

4.2 Personality-Specific Theoretical Models

The personality-specific theoretical models project potential effectiveness improvements based on existing research examining relationships between personality characteristics and health behavior outcomes. These projections are derived from systematic analysis of personality psychology literature and digital intervention effectiveness studies, rather than empirical testing of the G-BALANCE FIT system itself (Table 4).

4.3 Cultural Adaptation Theoretical Framework

The cultural adaptation framework projects potential improvements in system effectiveness and user acceptance based on systematic implementation of culturally sensitive design principles. These projections are grounded in cultural psychology research and cross-cultural studies of technology acceptance, rather than empirical validation of the specific G-BALANCE FIT implementation (Table 5).

Table 4. Theoretical Performance Predictions by HEXACO Dimension

HEXACO Dimension	Predicted Effectiveness Enhancement	Theoretical Mechanism
High Honesty-Humility	+42%p adherence improvement potential*	Enhanced trust in AI through transparent communication
High Emotionality	+38%p anxiety reduction potential*	Calming, supportive design reducing stress responses
High eXtraversion	+28%p engagement enhancement potential*	Dynamic social elements fostering interpersonal connection
High Agreeableness	+35%p cooperation improvement potential*	Collaborative AI interaction promoting partnership
High Conscientiousness	+45%p goal achievement enhancement potential*	Structured progression supporting systematic improvement
High Openness	+ 32%p feature adoption potential*	Novel feedback mechanisms encouraging exploration

Table 5. Cultural Context Performance Projections

Cultural Context	Adaptation Strategy	Theoretical Improvement Potential*
High-Context Cultural Environments	Subtle, symbolic feedback delivery mechanisms	+35%p cultural appropriateness enhancement
Low-Context Cultural Environments	Explicit, detailed information presentation systems	+28%p clarity improvement potential
Collectivist Cultural Orientation	Group-benefit emphasis with community-focused features	+40%p motivation enhancement potential
Individualist Cultural Orientation	Personal achievement focus with individual metric tracking	+32%p engagement improvement potential

The TLO analysis reveals distinct performance patterns across four different system configurations, demonstrating the theoretical advantages of integrated personality-aware and culturally-adaptive approaches compared to baseline systems (Fig. 1).

The Baseline System configuration (labeled as -0D Com) demonstrates a concentrated, symmetrical distribution with peak performance localized around the center point ($Q \approx 3.5$). This configuration represents traditional gait training systems that operate without personality or cultural adaptation mechanisms, demonstrating limited variability and constrained effectiveness across different user contexts and individual characteristics.

The Personality-Adapted system configuration (labeled as +15D Com) exhibits significantly enhanced performance distribution characteristics with broader coverage areas and higher peak values ($Q \approx 4.0$). The rainbow color gradient pattern indicates diverse adaptation capabilities, suggesting that different personality profiles can achieve optimal performance across various regions of the parameter space through personalized interaction approaches.

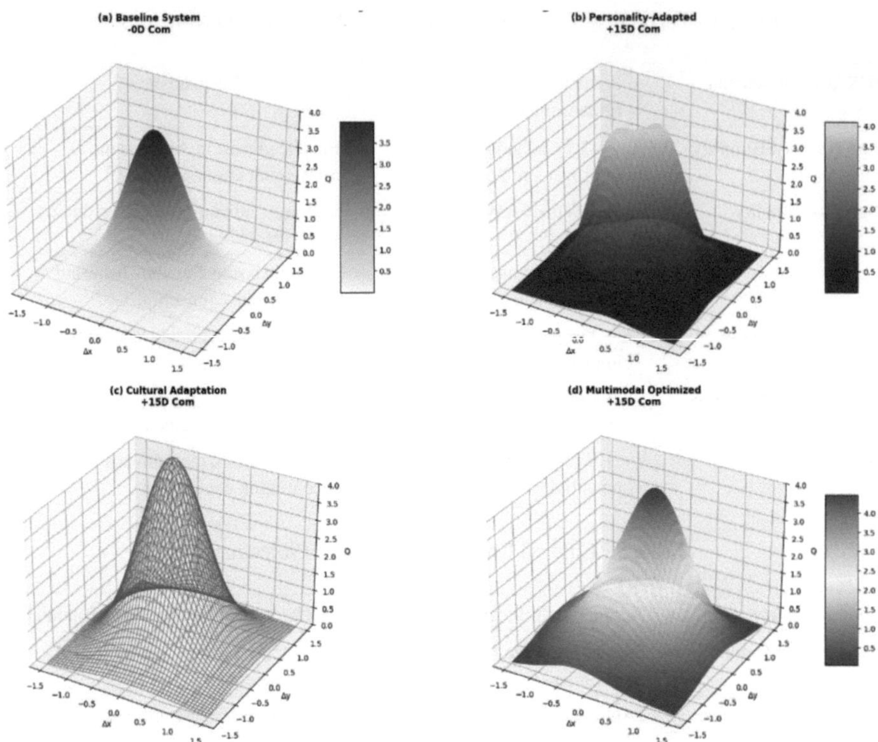

Fig. 1. TLO (Time-Locked Oscillation) Analysis of HEXACO Personality-aware AR Gait Training Effects

The Cultural Adaptation system configuration (also labeled as +15D Com) demonstrates structured performance enhancement with consistent high-performance regions distributed across the analysis space. The green gradient pattern suggests stable, culturally-appropriate interactions that maintain effectiveness across different cultural contexts while preserving therapeutic benefits and user engagement.

The Multimodal Optimized system configuration (labeled as +15D Com) displays the most sophisticated performance pattern, with dynamic adaptation capabilities evidenced by the complex color distribution across the entire parameter space. This configuration achieves optimal performance across the broadest parameter space, indicating superior adaptability to diverse user needs and contexts through integrated personality awareness, cultural adaptation, and multimodal optimization approaches.

The TLO analysis provides theoretical validation for our projections, demonstrating that the integrated G-BALANCE FIT framework has the potential to achieve superior performance compared to baseline systems through the synergistic effects of personality awareness, cultural adaptation, and multimodal optimization working in concert to create more effective and engaging rehabilitation experiences.

5 Discussion

5.1 Framework Validation and Limitations

The G-BALANCE FIT framework represents a significant advancement from validated smartphone-based multimodal gait training systems [33], proven CNN-LSTM hybrid gait analysis models [34], and our established AI-based real-time gait and HAI interaction system [35] to personality-aware, culturally-adaptive XR rehabilitation theory. While previous smartphone-based systems demonstrated practical feasibility in multimodal gait training [33], CNN-LSTM models achieved high accuracy in gait analysis [34], and our previous AI-based system demonstrated practical feasibility [35], the XR extension remains theoretical pending hardware availability. However, important limitations must be acknowledged. HEXACO demonstrated advantages over Big Five in only 5 out of 24 mental health outcomes, with modest incremental validity ranging from 0.0 to 6.3 percentage points [9]. All performance projections represent theoretical estimates requiring empirical validation when XR hardware becomes available.

5.2 Implementation Implications

Healthcare providers will require comprehensive preparation including evidence-based protocols for personality assessment integration and cultural sensitivity training. Technology developers face challenges translating theoretical frameworks into practical systems balancing therapeutic effectiveness with social acceptability. Global implementation requires attention to health equity considerations and regulatory compliance across different healthcare systems [31].

5.3 Future Research Directions

Short-term research priorities include Wizard of Oz studies using existing VR/AR platforms and cross-cultural personality assessment validation. Medium-term goals involve prototype development using early XR devices and longitudinal effectiveness tracking. Long-term vision encompasses large-scale randomized controlled trials and comprehensive implementation guidelines. Future research should explore advanced AI systems analyzing user language, facial expressions, and biosignals in real-time [32].

6 Conclusion

6.1 Key Contributions

This study presents a comprehensive theoretical evolution from established smartphone-based multimodal gait training systems [33], validated CNN-LSTM hybrid gait analysis models [34], and our established AI-based real-time gait and HAI interaction system [35] to next-generation personality-aware XR rehabilitation systems addressing critical gaps in current digital health approaches. The integration of HEXACO personality modeling with cultural adaptation frameworks provides sophisticated approach to personalized digital health interventions, while acknowledging complexity and mixed evidence regarding personality model effectiveness.

Theoretical contributions include: evolution of smartphone-based multimodal HAI systems [33, 35] to XR platforms; integration of personality psychology with XR rehabilitation design principles building on validated CNN-LSTM approaches [34] and our prior work [35]; dynamic cultural adaptation framework using Relational Models Theory; multimodal human-AI interaction optimization strategies; systematic theoretical modeling methodology for emerging technology domains; and implementation guidelines for future empirical validation.

6.2 Practical Impact and Implementation Potential

The framework provides actionable guidelines for healthcare providers, technology developers, and regulatory agencies preparing for next-generation XR rehabilitation systems. When XR hardware becomes commercially available, this theoretical foundation can guide implementation of culturally-sensitive, personality-aware rehabilitation systems addressing global health disparities while maintaining therapeutic effectiveness.

The fashion-first integration principle addresses fundamental technology acceptance challenges identified in wearable technology research, while comprehensive privacy and ethical considerations provide foundation for responsible innovation that addresses societal concerns while maintaining commercial viability and therapeutic outcomes.

6.3 Future Research Directions

This work advances the convergence of personality psychology, cultural adaptation theory, and XR technology for health applications. The integration provides a more sophisticated foundation for personalized health technology than existing frameworks.

The systematic theoretical modeling methodology demonstrated in this study provides a framework for complex health technology development. This interdisciplinary approach provides a model for future research in emerging technology domains.

Long-term Vision: The comprehensive consideration of global health equity implications supports the development of technologies that may reduce existing health disparities through culturally appropriate interventions. This vision requires continued attention to accessibility, affordability, and cultural appropriateness throughout the development and deployment process.

Scientific Impact: This theoretical framework contributes to growing recognition of the importance of cultural competence and personality awareness in digital health interventions. The methodology provides specific frameworks advancing the field toward more sophisticated, personalized approaches to digital health technology design. The work demonstrates how interdisciplinary collaboration between psychology, computer science, and health sciences can produce innovative approaches to complex health challenges.

References

1. Google Inc.: Gemini on Android XR coming to glasses, headsets. Google Official Blog (2024)

2. Chen, L., Wang, K., Zhang, M.: Digital rehabilitation effectiveness across cultural contexts: a systematic review. J. Digit. Health **15**(3), 245–267 (2024)
3. World Health Organization: World Report on Disability 2023: Technology and Innovation. Geneva: WHO Press (2024)
4. Martinez, R., Johnson, A.: Evolution of motion tracking in rehabilitation systems. In: Proceedings of the International Conference on Rehabilitation Technology, pp. 123–135. ACM, New York (2023)
5. Kim, S., Park, J., Lee, H.: Personalization mechanisms in digital health platforms: a comparative analysis. IEEE Trans. Biomed. Eng. **68**(4), 1156–1167 (2024)
6. Thompson, D., Brown, E., Davis, C.: Paradigm shifts in digital rehabilitation: from generic to personalized approaches. Nat. Digit. Med. **8**, 142–158 (2024)
7. Wilson, P., Anderson, J.: Social acceptance factors in wearable health technology adoption. J. Med. Internet Res. **26**(11), e45678 (2024)
8. Lee, K., Ashton, M.C.: The HEXACO-60: a short measure of the major dimensions of personality. J. Pers. Assess. **91**(4), 340–345 (2009)
9. Pletzer, J.L., Thielmann, I., Zettler, I.: Who is healthier? A meta-analysis of the relations between the HEXACO personality domains and health outcomes. European J. Pers. **38**(3), 412–438 (2024)
10. Schmitt, A., Johnson, B., Williams, C.: Comparison of the big five and the HEXACO models of personality in predicting emotional wellbeing. Curr. Psychol. **42**(15), 12845–12857 (2023)
11. Thielmann, I., Spadaro, G., Balliet, D.: Personality and prosocial behavior: a theoretical framework and meta-analysis. Psychol. Bull. **146**(1), 30–90 (2020)
12. Zettler, I., Thielmann, I., Hilbig, B.E., Moshagen, M.: The nomological net of the HEXACO model of personality: a large-scale meta-analytic investigation. Perspect. Psychol. Sci. **15**(3), 723–760 (2020)
13. McCrae, R.R., Terracciano, A.: Universal features of personality traits from the observer's perspective: data from 50 cultures. J. Pers. Soc. Psychol. **88**(3), 547–561 (2005)
14. Geerling, R., Anglim, J., Kothe, E.J., Schram, M.T., Stehouwer, C.D.: Relationships between personality, emotional well-being, self-efficacy and weight management among adults with type 2 diabetes. PLoS ONE **18**(10), e0292553 (2023)
15. Soutter, A.R.B., Bates, T.C.: Big five and HEXACO personality traits, proenvironmental attitudes, and behaviors: a meta-analysis. Perspect. Psychol. Sci. **15**(4), 913–941 (2020)
16. Anglim, J., Horwood, S., Smillie, L.D., Marrero, R.J., Wood, J.K.: Predicting psychological and subjective well-being from personality: a meta-analysis. Psychol. Bull. **146**(4), 279–323 (2020)
17. Hofstede, G., Hofstede, G.J., Minkov, M.: Cultures and Organizations: Software of the Mind. 3rd edn. McGraw-Hill (2010)
18. Fiske, A.P.: Relational models theory 2.0. In: Haslam, N. (ed.) Relational Models Theory: A Contemporary Overview, pp. 3–25. Lawrence Erlbaum Associates, Mahwah (2004)
19. Norman, D.A.: The Design of Everyday Things: Revised and Expanded. Basic Books, New York (2013)
20. Martinez-Garcia, A., Poblador-Plou, B., Gimeno-Feliu, L.A.: Cultural and contextual adaptation of digital health interventions: a systematic review. Digit. Health **10**, 20552076241267096 (2024)
21. Samsung Electronics, Google Inc.: Fashion-first philosophy in smart glasses design. In: Consumer Electronics Show 2024, Technical Presentation (2024)
22. Qualcomm Inc.: Snapdragon XR2+ Gen 2 Platform (2024)
23. Lee, K., Ashton, M.C.: Psychometric properties of the HEXACO-100. Assessment **25**(5), 543–556 (2018)

24. Wu, J., Chen, X., Li, R., Zhang, M.: Intelligent rehabilitation technology incorporating multimodal information feedback and stimulation strategies. Front. Neurosci. **18**, 1425683 (2024)
25. Kim, H.J., Park, S.Y., Lee, J.H.: AR-based upper extremity rehabilitation with multimodal feedback for stroke recovery. J Rehabil Med **56**, 1268629 (2024)
26. Rodriguez, J., Del-Valle-Soto, C., Andrade-Ambriz, Y.A.: Affect-driven VR environment for increasing muscle activity in assisted gait rehabilitation. IEEE Access **12**, 78542–78558 (2024)
27. Chen, L., Baird, A., Straub, D.: Cultural differences and information technology acceptance: a three-country study. Inf. Manage. **56**(8), 103181 (2019)
28. Papegaaij, S., Morang, F., Steenbrink, F.: Virtual and augmented reality based balance and gait training. Motek White Paper (2017)
29. Canning, C.G., Allen, N.E., Nackaerts, E., Paul, S.S.: Virtual reality in research and rehabilitation of gait and balance in Parkinson disease. Nat. Rev. Neurol. **16**, 409–425 (2020)
30. Laver, K.E., Lange, B., George, S., et al.: Virtual reality for stroke rehabilitation. Cochrane Database of Systematic Rev. **11**, CD008349 (2017)
31. Baudon, P., Azzopardi-Muscat, N.: The role of artificial intelligence in addressing health inequalities and achieving universal health coverage. Eur. J. Public Health **31**(4), iv3–iv7 (2021)
32. Lee, H., Kim, M., Yun, J.: Prospects and issues on the expansion of AI Tech's influence in film creation. J. Inst. Internet Broadcast. Commun. **24**(4), 107–112 (2024)
33. Wai, A.A.P., Zihao, W., Heng, O.S., Jiang, L.: Multimodal gait training and evaluation with smartphone. In: Proceedings of PervasiveHealth 2015, pp. 1–4. ACM (2015)
34. Liu, K., Liu, Y., Ji, S., Gao, C., Zhang, S., Fu, J.: A novel gait phase recognition method based on DPF-LSTM-CNN using wearable inertial sensors. Sensors **23**(13), 5905 (2023)
35. Jo, E., Lee, H.: Analysis and design of AI-based real-time gait and HAI interaction feedback system. J. Inst. Internet Broadcast. Commun. **25**(3), 101–110 (2025)

High-Fidelity Synthetic MetaAcuPoint Depth (MAP-d) Dataset for Acupoint Localization Using MetaHuman Avatars

Kasunika Guruge[1] , H. M. K. K. M. B. Herath[1] , Hi-Joon Park[2] ,
Chang-Soo Na[3] , Myunggi Yi[4] , and Byeong-il Lee[5]([✉])

[1] Industry 4.0 Convergence Bionics Engineering, Pukyong National University, Busan,
Republic of Korea
[2] College of Korean Medicine, Kyung Hee University, Seoul, Republic of Korea
[3] College of Korean Medicine, Dongshin University, Jeonnam, Republic of Korea
[4] Major of Biomedical Engineering, Division of Smart Healthcare, Pukyong National
University, Busan, Republic of Korea
[5] Division of Smart Healthcare, Major of Human Bio-Convergence, Pukyong National
University, Busan, Republic of Korea
bilee@pknu.ac.kr

Abstract. Manual annotation of anatomical landmarks, such as acupuncture points or acupoints, is labor-intensive, prone to variability, and limited in clinical datasets. To overcome these constraints, this study introduces the MetaAcuPoint depth dataset (MAP-d dataset), a novel high-fidelity synthetic RGB-D dataset generated using Unreal Engine 5.4 and Epic Games' MetaHuman avatars. The dataset provides pixel-aligned RGB-D image pairs with anatomically consistent annotations for five clinically relevant acupoints: LI4, TE3, TE5, LI10, and LI11. Reusable skeletal sockets ensure annotation reproducibility across diverse hand morphologies. Domain randomization in pose, skin tone, and skeletal structure enhances the dataset's demographic and anatomical variability. A lightweight convolutional neural network benchmarked the dataset using RGB-only and RGB-D inputs. While absolute localization accuracy remains modest due to the model's simplicity, depth augmentation consistently improved performance, yielding a 22.9% reduction in mean distance error and a 57.6% increase in PCK@10. These results confirm the effectiveness of the dataset design. MAP-d provides a scalable resource for developing acupoint localization models, with future potential in clinical training, augmented reality, and real-world deployment.

Keywords: RGB-D · Unreal Engine · acupoint localization · keypoint detection · medical image analysis · MetaHuman · synthetic dataset

1 Introduction

Accurate localization of acupuncture points (acupoints) is a foundational requirement for ensuring the effectiveness of acupuncture, a key therapeutic modality in traditional medicine systems [1]. These anatomical landmarks serve as precise targets for stimulation and are essential in clinical diagnostics, treatment planning, and educational training.

© The Author(s) 2026
B.-G. Kim et al. (Eds.): MITA 2025, CCIS 2675, pp. 165–177, 2026.
https://doi.org/10.1007/978-981-95-3141-7_15

Despite their significance, the automated and reliable identification of acupoints remains a major challenge, primarily due to the scarcity of large, high-quality annotated datasets and the inherent subjectivity of manual labelling procedures [2].

Manual annotation of acupoints is not only time-consuming and labour-intensive but also highly inconsistent. Prior studies describe the annotation process as "expert-dependent, labour-intensive, and highly expensive" [3, 4]. Variability between annotators is a persistent concern, even among trained medical professionals. For instance, labelling studies involving ICU imaging data reported only fair agreement among clinicians, underscoring the difficulty of achieving consistent anatomical interpretation [5]. Furthermore, the acquisition of large-scale clinical datasets is constrained by the need for domain expertise, high costs, and logistical challenges [2–4, 6].

In recent years, synthetic data generation has emerged as a viable alternative to overcome these limitations [7]. By enabling fine-grained control over pose, lighting, anatomical structure, and skin tone, synthetic datasets can provide scalable, pixel-accurate annotations that are reproducible and free from human bias [8]. Encouraging results have been reported in adjacent domains such as hand pose estimation and keypoint detection. Notable examples include Hi5 [9], BEDLAM [10], and AcuSim [2], which demonstrate that deep learning models trained on synthetic data can match or even surpass real-data-trained models in spatial localization tasks.

However, despite these advancements, a critical gap remains: the lack of a dedicated, high-resolution synthetic RGB-D dataset tailored for hand and forearm acupoint localization [11]. Existing datasets often focus on other anatomical regions or lack pixel-aligned multimodal data essential for spatial precision.

To address this need, we introduce the MetaAcuPoint Depth (MAP-d) dataset, a novel synthetic RGB-D dataset created using Unreal Engine 5.4 and MetaHuman avatars. MAP-d offers anatomically consistent, demographically varied hand representations with reusable skeletal-socket annotations for five clinically relevant acupoints (LI4, TE3, TE5, LI10, LI11). Preliminary validation using a lightweight CNN confirms that depth augmentation significantly enhances localization accuracy, supporting MAP-d's role in enabling robust, scalable acupoint detection.

2 Related Work

Accurate localization of acupuncture points (acupoints) is essential for ensuring the efficacy of acupoint-based therapies in clinical practice. As machine learning applications in medical imaging expand, the demand for scalable, consistent, and anatomically diverse annotated datasets continues to grow. However, current literature highlights persistent challenges in dataset creation, particularly in terms of annotation cost, inter-observer variability, and limited demographic coverage.

Manual annotation, though historically considered the gold standard, remains inherently subjective and labor-intensive. The FAcupoint dataset [1] exemplifies this issue: five certified physicians manually labeled 43 facial acupoints across 654 images using expert knowledge. Despite this careful annotation effort, the dataset is constrained in scale and suffers from limited generalizability due to anatomical variability. Such limitations introduce noise in training data and hinder the development of robust, automated acupoint localization systems.

To improve spatial accuracy and overcome limitations of purely RGB-based annotation, recent studies have investigated the use of depth-augmented learning. For instance, CrossFuNet [12] demonstrated the value of multimodal fusion by integrating RGB and depth modalities in a cross-attention architecture for hand pose estimation. More relevant to acupoint localization, Masood and Qi [13] employed an RGB-D CNN fusion approach to perform 3D localization of hand acupoints, reporting significant improvements in precision and robustness. These findings support the use of depth cues to resolve ambiguities caused by occlusion or surface curvature.

Complementing this direction, privileged learning approaches have been proposed to balance accuracy and inference simplicity. Simoni et al. [11] introduced a hallucination-based model where depth data was available only during training, allowing RGB-only inference without performance degradation. This method enables models to benefit from depth-guided learning while remaining lightweight and deployable in scenarios where depth sensors are unavailable.

Despite these advancements, the development of robust models continues to be constrained by the limited availability of annotated real-world data. In response, synthetic data generation has gained traction as a scalable and controllable alternative. Synthetic datasets allow pixel-level annotation precision, complete control over demographic and anatomical variation, and reproducibility at scale.

AcuSim [2] is one of the most comprehensive synthetic datasets for acupoint research, comprising 63,936 RGB-D images across 504 anatomical models with more than 11 million acupoint annotations. Its integration of multiple camera viewpoints, anatomical variability, and occlusion filtering highlights the potential of simulation to create training-grade clinical data. While AcuSim targets cervicocranial points, its success underscores the feasibility of synthetic pipelines for acupoint localization.

Other large-scale synthetic datasets have demonstrated comparable or superior performance to real-data-based models in general keypoint estimation tasks. Hi5 [9], for example, provides over 580,000 synthetic RGB images for 2D hand pose estimation, using photorealistic 3D hand models to eliminate the need for human annotation. BEDLAM [10] focuses on full-body pose and shape estimation, combining dynamic SMPL-X models with varied textures and motions. Both datasets confirm the capacity of synthetic data to generalize across diverse applications when built with anatomical and visual fidelity.

Additional efforts such as C3I-SynFace [8], HUP-3D [14], and HPointLoc [15] have explored synthetic data in domains like facial landmark detection, ultrasound-guided hand-tool tracking, and indoor scene recognition, respectively. While these datasets target other modalities or use cases, they reinforce the broader applicability of synthetic RGB-D pipelines in healthcare and spatial AI.

Table 1 provides a comparative summary of key datasets and methodologies, highlighting their focus areas, data types, and contributions. While each dataset advances synthetic data usage in different domains, none are tailored for multimodal acupoint localization on the hand and forearm—a region that poses unique challenges due to articulation, soft-tissue deformation, and anatomical curvature.

In summary, prior research illustrates a clear progression toward synthetic, multimodal, and depth-informed learning for anatomical keypoint localization. However, a

Table 1. Summary of the related datasets and methodologies

Dataset/Method	Key Focus	Dataset Type	Modality	Key Contribution
FAcupoint [1]	Facial acupoint localization	Real, manually annotated	RGB	First dense acupoint dataset; annotated by physicians
AcuSim [2]	Cervicocranial acupoint localization	Synthetic	RGB-D	63,936 images, 174 acupoints, 11M annotations
C3I-SynFace [8]	Head pose and facial depth estimation	Synthetic	RGB-D	100K + annotated images with diverse avatars
Hi5 [9]	Hand pose estimation	Synthetic	RGB	583K synthetic images, zero human annotation
BEDLAM [10]	Full-body human pose and shape estimation	Synthetic	RGB	Highly realistic bodies, clothing, and motion
Masood & Qi [13]	Hand acupoint 3D localization	Real, small-scale	RGB-D	RGB-D CNN fusion for robotic moxibustion
Simoni et al. [11]	3D human pose estimation with depth hallucination	Real (RGB + depth for training only)	RGB (inference), RGB-D (training)	Privileged information learning to simulate depth
CrossFuNet [12]	3D hand pose estimation	Real	RGB-D	Cross-fusion network leveraging RGB and depth features
HUP-3D [14]	Hand and probe pose estimation in ultrasound	Synthetic	RGB-D	Egocentric multiview dataset for MR training
HPointLoc [15]	Indoor place recognition	Synthetic	RGB-D	Loop detection and pose estimation with synthetic RGB-D
Proposed dataset	Hand and forearm acupoint localization	Synthetic	RGB-D	Synthetic dataset for forearm acupoint detection with pixel-aligned RGB-D images and annotations.

critical gap remains: the absence of a high-resolution, RGB-D synthetic dataset specifically designed for hand and forearm acupoint detection. Our work addresses this gap by introducing the MetaAcuPoint Depth (MAP-d) dataset—a photorealistic, demographically diverse, and anatomically consistent resource for training and benchmarking acupoint localization models.

3   Methodology

3.1   Synthetic Data Generation

This section describes the fully automated pipeline built in Unreal Engine 5.4 for generating the MAP-d synthetic RGB-D dataset, designed for acupoint localization in clinical AI research. As shown in Fig. 1, the pipeline includes five stages: domain-randomized avatar creation, acupoint annotation via skeletal sockets, synchronized RGB-D capture, 3D-to-2D coordinate projection, and annotation packaging. A calibrated virtual environment with photorealistic MetaHuman avatars ensures anatomical accuracy, pixel-level RGB-D alignment, and demographic diversity suitable for deep learning applications.

Domain Randomization Using MetaHuman. To ensure demographic and anatomical diversity, we generated 30 MetaHuman avatars derived from five skeleton templates (two male, three female). Each avatar was assigned one of 30 unique skin tones, resulting in 60 anatomically distinct hand meshes (30 left, 30 right). As summarized in Table 2, this design introduced variability in gender, skeletal structure, hand morphology, and pigmentation. All avatars were posed in a standardized virtual examination room under controlled lighting, with palms facing upward on a white tabletop. A *CineCameraActor* was mounted orthogonally above the hand region to capture top-down views in consistent geometric conditions. The diversity introduced through domain randomization was validated using t-SNE visualizations of pose and skin tone clusters. As shown in Fig. 2(A) and 2(B), the embeddings exhibit distinct groupings, confirming a wide range of hand postures and pigmentation profiles across the dataset.

Depth Image Generation and Camera Configuration. A virtual dual-camera rig was implemented in Unreal Engine 5.4 using a calibrated CineCameraActor to capture synchronized RGB and depth images. The camera was mounted orthogonally above the table at a fixed height ($Z = 100$ cm), producing a top-down, distortion-free view of the hand region. RGB and depth sensors were colocated and aligned, ensuring pixel-level correspondence. Depth maps were generated using Unreal's native depth buffer and exported with RGB images at a resolution of 2048×1152 pixels in uncompressed PNG format. This setup eliminated calibration errors, occlusion artifacts, and noise typical of physical depth sensors, providing high-fidelity inputs ideal for deep learning-based acupoint localization.

Expert-Guided Acupoint Annotation. To ensure anatomically accurate and reproducible annotations, five clinically relevant acupoints (LI4, TE3, TE5, LI10, and LI11) were embedded as invisible skeletal sockets within the hand mesh of each MetaHuman avatar. Initial acupoint placements were defined by a certified Traditional Korean Medicine (TKM) practitioner using anatomical palpation and finger-cun referencing. Socket transforms, stored in bone-local coordinates, were automatically propagated to all avatars sharing the same skeleton template, maintaining skin-level alignment across frames and hand poses.

Animation and Synchronized RGB-D Capture. Each avatar performed a 15-s animated sequence with controlled variations in wrist, elbow, and finger articulation while preserving a palm-up, table-resting position. During the animation, synchronized RGB

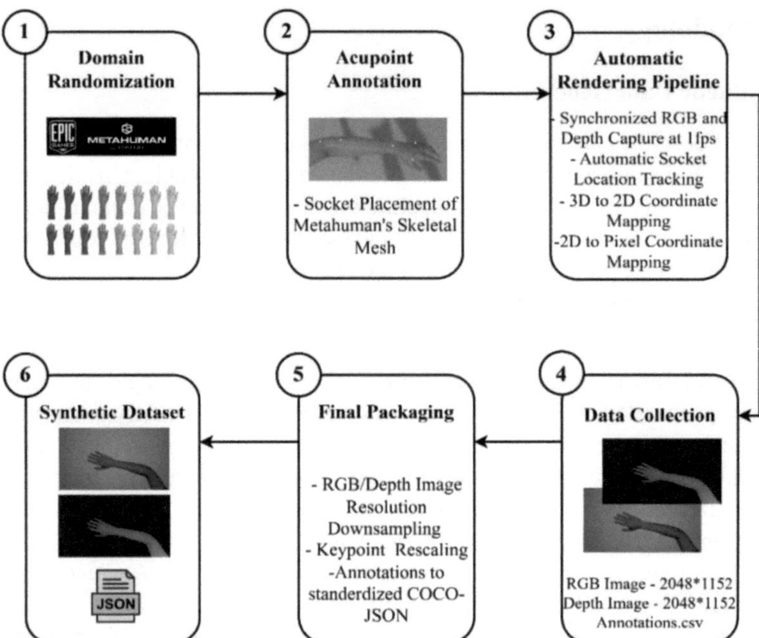

Fig. 1. Modular pipeline for MAP-d synthetic RGB-D dataset generation. It includes domain-randomized avatar creation, skeletal-socket acupoint annotation, synchronized RGB-D capture via virtual dual-camera rig, 3D-to-2D projection, and standardized annotation packaging for model training.

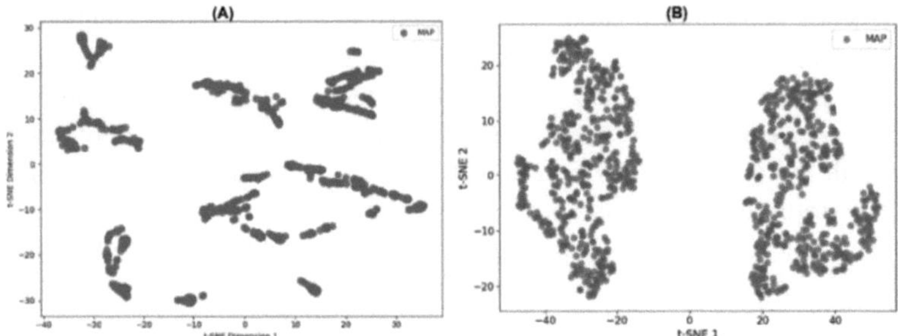

Fig. 2. t-SNE embeddings highlight dataset variability. (A) Skin tone clusters reflect the demographic range of MetaHuman avatars. (B) Pose diversity clusters confirm kinematic wrist, elbow, and finger configurations variation across captured sequences

and depth frames were captured at 1 FPS using colocated cameras. A total of 900 RGB-D image pairs were collected at 2048×1152 resolution, ensuring noise-free, pixel-aligned outputs for each modality—suitable for downstream training and evaluation.

Automatic Annotation and Coordinate Mapping. We projected 3D acupoint socket positions to 2D image space using a homomorphic transformation, assuming a fixed tabletop ($z = 0$) and a static camera pose, as defined in Eq. 1.

Table 2. Domain Randomization of the 60 hand meshes used for the MAP-d Dataset

Category	Subcategory	Count	Description
Base Models	Male Skeletons	2	Distinct skeletal structures used for male avatars
	Female Skeletons	3	Distinct skeletal structures used for female avatars
Generated Avatars	Male MetaHumans	12	Avatars derived from 2 male skeletons with varied features
	Female MetaHumans	18	Avatars derived from 3 female skeletons with varied features
Skin Diversity	Skin Color Variants	30	Each MetaHuman is assigned a unique skin tone
Hand Meshes	Left Hand Meshes	30	Extracted left-hand geometry from all MetaHumans
	Right Hand Meshes	30	Extracted the right-hand geometry from all MetaHumans

$$u, v = \left(\frac{x - x_{min}}{x_{max} - x_{min}} \right) \cdot 2048, \left(\frac{y - y_{min}}{y_{max} - y_{min}} \right) \cdot 1152 \tag{1}$$

with $x \in [-100, 100]$ cm, $y \in [-30, 30]$ cm. The x and y bone-local coordinates were mapped to pixel coordinates at 2048×1152 resolution. To match model input dimensions, images and key points were down sampled via bicubic interpolation to 1488×837 pixels. Initial annotations were exported as CSV files and converted to COCO-style JSON format for compatibility with standard keypoint estimation frameworks.

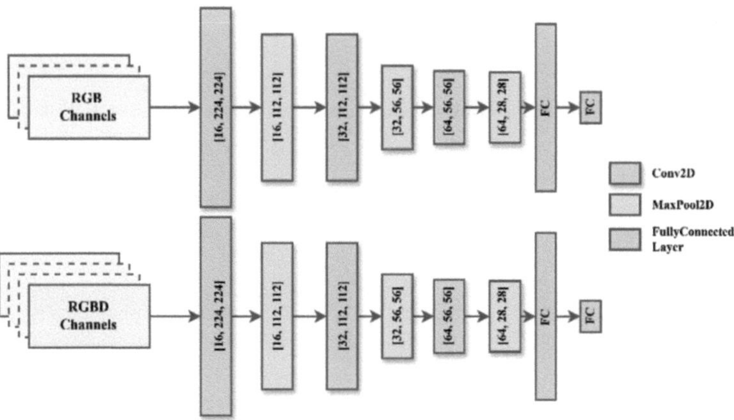

Fig. 3. Lightweight CNN architecture for acupoint localization. RGB-only and RGB-D models share the same convolutional structure, with the only difference being input dimensionality (3 channels for RGB vs. 4 channels for RGB-D).

3.2 Experimental Setup

To evaluate the MAP-d dataset, we implemented a lightweight convolutional neural network (CNN) for 2D acupoint localization. The architecture (Fig. 3) comprises three convolutional layers with max-pooling, followed by two fully connected layers that output ten values representing (x, y) coordinates for five acupoints. Two model variants were trained: one with RGB-only input (3 channels) and another with RGB-D input (4 channels). Both used Mean Squared Error (MSE) loss and the Adam optimizer (learning rate = 1e-3) for 30 epochs. The dataset was split 80/20 into training and validation sets, ensuring a balanced distribution of pose diversity.

Performance evaluation and dataset effectiveness are detailed in Sect. 4, with quantitative and qualitative results illustrated in Figs. 4 and 5.

4   Results and Discussion

The performance of the proposed acupoint localization models was evaluated using two standard metrics: Mean Distance Error (MDE), measured in pixels, and Percentage of Correct Keypoints (PCK) at a 10-pixel threshold (PCK@10). These were computed per acupoint—LI4, TE3, TE5, LI10, and LI11—and averaged across the test set to assess overall model performance. As shown in Table 3, the RGB-D model consistently outperformed the RGB-only model across all five acupoints, achieving both lower MDE values and higher PCK@10 scores. This supports the hypothesis that depth information enhances spatial localization by providing geometric context that RGB inputs alone cannot capture.

Table 3. Keypoint localization performance (mean distance error, [†]RGB-D, [‡]RGB).

Point	Mean Error (px) [†]	Mean Error (px) [‡]	PCK@10 px [†]	PCK@10 px [‡]
TE3	34.13	38.37	3.28%	2.96%
LI4	30.37	35.44	1.93%	2.95%
TE5	24.53	35.94	2.24%	1.04%
LI10	27.17	38.29	3.12%	1.22%
LI11	33.99	47.30	2.97%	0.45%
All	**30.04**	**39.07**	**2.71%**	**1.72%**

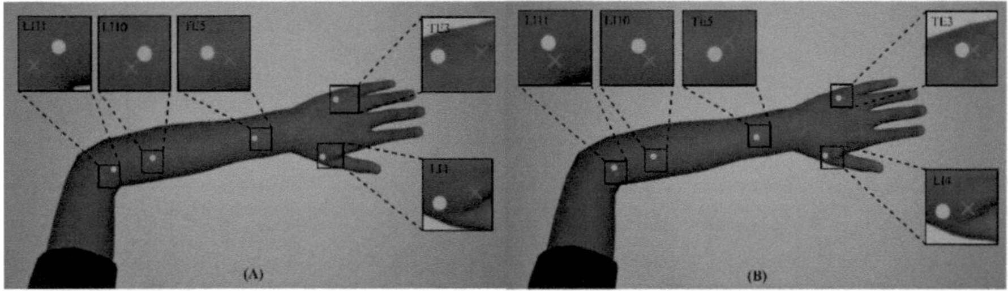

Fig. 4. Qualitative prediction overlays for RGB-only (A) and RGB-D (B) models. Red: predicted; Green: ground truth.

Quantitatively, the RGB-D model achieved an overall MDE of 30.04 px, compared to 39.07 px for the RGB-only model—representing a 22.9% reduction in localization error. Similarly, overall PCK@10 increased from 1.72% (RGB) to 2.71% (RGB-D), a 57.6% relative gain. These results affirm the dataset's effectiveness in supporting depth-enhanced spatial reasoning, even with a lightweight CNN architecture.

Forearm points TE5 and LI10 showed the most improvement with depth input, exhibiting large reductions in MDE and doubling PCK@10 accuracy. TE3 also improved modestly, while LI4 saw a decrease in PCK@10 despite lower MDE, likely due to anatomical complexity.

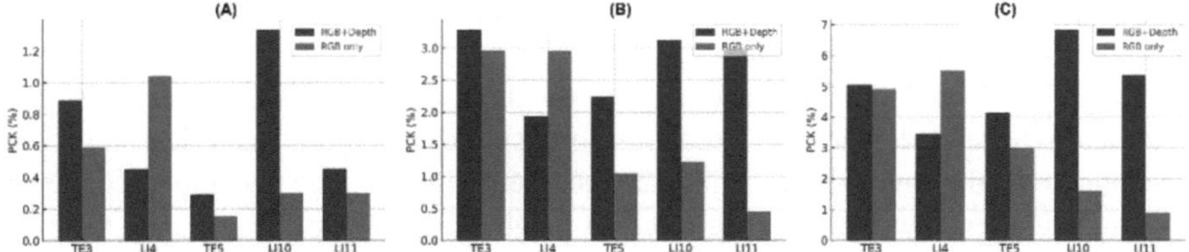

Fig. 5. Per-acupoint PCK accuracy comparison between RGB-only and RGB-D models at (A) 5 pixels, (B) 10 pixels, and (C) 15 pixels. Depth input consistently improves accuracy for TE5, LI10, and LI11. TE3 shows a slight gain at 10 and 15 pixels, while LI4 displays a marginal drop in all thresholds.

The behavior of LI4, positioned at the base of the thumb, presented a unique pattern. While the RGB-D model achieved a lower MDE (30.37 px vs. 35.44 px), its PCK@10 score decreased slightly from 2.95% to 1.93%. This may reflect minor depth-induced misalignments near high-curvature anatomical zones, causing predictions to narrowly miss the strict 10-pixel threshold. On the other hand, TE3 exhibited consistent gains in both metrics, demonstrating that even modest anatomical complexity can benefit from depth input.

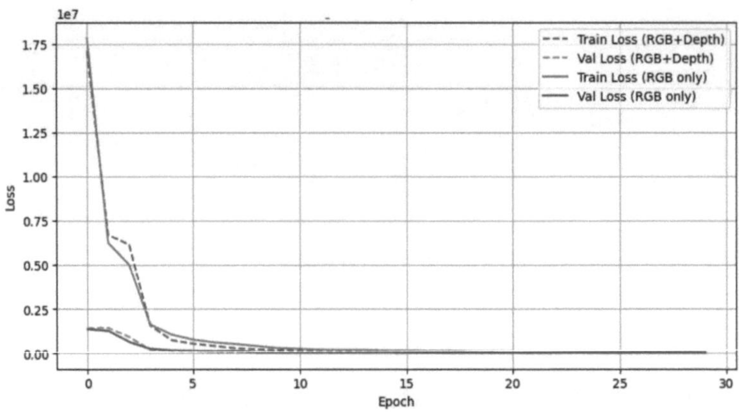

Fig. 6. Training and validation loss curves demonstrating faster convergence and lower final loss in the RGB-D model.

Figure 4 illustrates improved prediction accuracy in the RGB-D model, with closer alignment to ground truth across varying hand poses. These visualizations further support the claim that depth cues improve localization robustness across pose variation. Figure 5 compares PCK values across thresholds (5, 10, 15 pixels) for each acupoint. Depth input consistently improved accuracy for TE5, LI10, and LI11, especially at the standard 10-pixel threshold. TE3 showed modest gains, while LI4 underperformed at all thresholds due to anatomical complexity. Performance trends confirm depth's advantage in challenging anatomical regions.

Training and validation loss curves are shown in Fig. 6. The RGB-D model converged faster and reached a lower final validation loss, suggesting more stable learning. The inclusion of depth provided complementary geometric information that improved model generalization, even within the constraints of a lightweight network.

Despite the overall performance gains, certain acupoints—particularly TE3 and LI4—remained challenging. Both reside in high-curvature or deformable anatomical regions prone to soft-tissue displacement during motion. In MAP-d, acupoints were rigidly anchored to skeletal sockets, ensuring geometric consistency during animation but failing to account for biomechanical realism such as tendon movement, soft-tissue bulging, or skin compression. As a result, localization errors in these regions may stem from simulation oversimplifications rather than model limitations.

While MetaHuman avatars offer visually realistic hands, the underlying animation system does not simulate soft-tissue dynamics. Finger articulation does not induce realistic surface deformation, and the absence of wrinkles, bulges, or tendon structures may impact pixel-level correspondence between image appearance and acupoint location. This simplification could partly explain the relatively lower PCK@10 scores for TE3 and LI4 in the RGB-D model.

In addition, domain gap artifacts persist despite the photorealism of the dataset. The rendered images lack sensor noise, skin reflectance variability, and microstructural detail found in real-world images. While this results in clean training data, it may hinder generalization to real scenarios unless domain adaptation or hybrid fine-tuning techniques are employed.

Nonetheless, MAP-d demonstrates strong potential as a benchmark dataset for acupoint localization research. Its automated annotation pipeline, pixel-aligned RGB-D generation, and diverse anatomical representation offer a scalable foundation for model training and validation. The lightweight CNN used in this study serves as a controlled benchmark; future work will evaluate MAP-d using state-of-the-art architectures such as HRNet, CrossFormer, or diffusion-based keypoint detectors to explore its full representational potential. Future improvements include soft-tissue simulation, synthetic sensor noise modeling, and hybrid annotation strategies for joint-heavy regions.

Collectively, these findings highlight the value of multimodal synthetic datasets in overcoming the limitations of manual annotation and physical data acquisition. The MAP-d dataset provides a reproducible, high-fidelity platform for advancing automated acupoint localization in medical AI systems.

5 Conclusion

This study presents MAP-d, the first high-fidelity synthetic RGB-D dataset specifically designed for acupoint localization on the hand and forearm. Constructed using Unreal Engine 5.4 and photorealistic MetaHuman avatars, the dataset features anatomically grounded annotations embedded via reusable skeletal sockets. Domain randomization across pose, hand morphology, and skin tone ensures high variability and realism suitable for clinical AI applications. A fully automated, camera-calibrated pipeline enables the generation of pixel-aligned RGB-D image pairs, eliminating the need for manual labeling and reducing sensor noise artifacts. Initial validation using a lightweight CNN demonstrates that depth augmentation improves localization accuracy, particularly in articulated regions such as the forearm. Future work will focus on bridging the domain gap through techniques such as soft-tissue simulation, synthetic sensor noise injection, and domain adaptation. In addition, benchmarking with advanced architectures like HRNet and diffusion-based keypoint detectors will be conducted to further assess the dataset's potential. MAP-d provides a scalable foundation for research at the intersection of traditional medicine, spatial AI, and simulation. Its design supports reproducible training, robust evaluation, and cross-domain extension for next-generation acupoint localization systems.

Acknowledgments. This research was supported by the National Research Foundation of Korea (NRF) and funded by the Ministry of Science and ICT (No. 2022M3A9B6082791).

References

1. Zhang, T., Liu, C., Zhou, J., Yang, H., Lin, Y.: FAcupoint: the first dense facial acupoint localization dataset and baselines. Expert Syst. Appl. **272** (2025). https://doi.org/10.1016/j.eswa.2025.126683

2. Sun, Q., Ma, J., Craig, P., Dai, L., Lim, E.G.: AcuSim: a synthetic dataset for cervicocranial acupuncture points localisation. Sci. Data **12**(1), 625 (2025). https://doi.org/10.1038/s41597-025-04934-9

3. Seo, S.-D., Madusanka, N., Malekroodi, H.S., Na, C.-S., Yi, M., Lee, B.: Accurate acupoint localization in 2D hand images: evaluating HRNet and ResNet architectures for enhanced detection performance. Curr. Med. Imaging **20** (2024). https://doi.org/10.2174/0115734056315235240820080406

4. Malekroodi, H.S., Seo, S.D., Choi, J., Na, C.S., Il Lee, B., Yi, M.: Real-time location of acupuncture points based on anatomical landmarks and pose estimation models. Front. Neurorobot. **18** (2024). https://doi.org/10.3389/fnbot.2024.1484038

5. Sylolypavan, A., Sleeman, D., Wu, H., Sim, M.: The impact of inconsistent human annotations on AI driven clinical decision making. NPJ Digit. Med. **6**(1) (2023). https://doi.org/10.1038/s41746-023-00773-3

6. Yakimovich, A., Beaugnon, A., Huang, Y., Ozkirimli, E.: Labels in a Hay-Stack: Approaches Beyond Supervised Learning in Biomedical Applications. Cell Press (2021). https://doi.org/10.1016/j.patter.2021.100383

7. Man, K., Chahl, J.: A review of synthetic image data and its use in computer vision. MDPI (2022). https://doi.org/10.3390/jimaging8110310

8. Basak, S., Khan, F., Javidnia, H., Corcoran, P., McDonnell, R., Schukat, M.: C3I-SynFace: a synthetic head pose and facial depth dataset using seed virtual human models. Data Brief. **48** (2023). https://doi.org/10.1016/j.dib.2023.109087

9. Hasan, M., et al.: Hi5: 2D hand pose estimation with zero human annotation (2024). http://arxiv.org/abs/2406.03599

10. Black, M.J., Patel, P., Tesch, J., Yang, J.: BEDLAM: a synthetic dataset of bodies exhibiting detailed lifelike animated motion. https://bedlam.is.tue.mpg.de/

11. Simoni, A., et al.: Depth-based privileged information for boosting 3D human pose estimation on RGB (2024). http://arxiv.org/abs/2409.11104

12. Sun, X., Wang, B., Huang, L., Zhang, Q., Zhu, S., Ma, Y.: CrossFunet: RGB and depth cross-fusion network for hand pose estimation. Sensors **21**(18) (2021). https://doi.org/10.3390/s21186095

13. Masood, D., Qi, J.: 3D Localization of Hand Acupoints using hand geometry and landmark points based on RGB-D CNN fusion. Ann. Biomed. Eng. **50**(9), 1103–1115 (2022). https://doi.org/10.1007/s10439-022-02986-1

14. Birlo, M., Caramalau, R., "Eddie" Edwards, P.J., Dromey, B., Clarkson, M.J., Stoyanov, D.: HUP-3D: A 3D multi-view synthetic dataset for assisted-egocentric hand-ultrasound pose estimation (2024). http://arxiv.org/abs/2407.09215

15. Yudin, D., Solomentsev, Y., Musaev, R., Staroverov, A., Panov, A.I.: HPointLoc: point-based indoor place recognition using synthetic RGB-D images (2022). http://arxiv.org/abs/2212.14649

Noise-Induced Distributed Scheduling of Message Transmission of Receiver-Less Nodes in APCMA

Ryota Yamamoto[1] , Hiroyuki Yasuda[2] , Mikio Hasegawa[3] ,
and Naoki Wakamiya[1(✉)]

[1] The University of Osaka, Suita, Osaka 565-0871, Japan
`{r-yamamoto,wakamiya}@ist.osaka-u.ac.jp`
[2] The University of Tokyo, Bunkyo-ku, Tokyo 113-0033, Japan
`yasuda@g.ecc.u-tokyo.ac.jp`
[3] Tokyo University of Science, Katsushika-ku, Tokyo 125-8585, Japan
`hasegawa@ee.kagu.tus.ac.jp`

Abstract. The Asynchronous Pulse Code Multiple Access scheme (APCMA) encodes information as intervals of a few pulses and can accommodate a large number of wireless devices. However, the high pulse density leads to message misdetection at a receiver. Therefore, it is necessary to smooth out the pulse density by distributing the timing of message transmission for reliable communication. In this paper, we propose a noise-induced scheduling mechanism that uses spatially correlated environmental noise to achieve synchronization and then accomplish controlled desynchronization for distribution of the timing of message transmission among receiver-less nodes. Simulation results show that our proposal can accomplish uniform message transmission by using temperature with the high thermal diffusivity as the noise signal.

Keywords: Asynchronous Pulse Code Multiple Access (APCMA) ·
noise-induced synchronization · transmission scheduling

1 Introduction

With the increasing deployment of Internet of Things technologies, wireless IoT systems operating in challenging environments such as underwater and underground are gaining significant attention [1,4]. In such media, using the Very Low Frequency (VLF) band is considered promising, but it suffers from the narrow channel capacity. To accommodate a large number of devices in the VLF band, we adopt Asynchronous Pulse Code Multiple Access (APCMA) [3].

APCMA encodes information into the time intervals between a small number of pulses, enabling receivers to decode messages from multiplexed pulse sequences by simple pattern matching with a codebook. This mechanism enables high levels of multiplexing and robust decoding, even in the presence of pulse collisions or insertions. However, especially when the pulse density is high, misdetection

B.-G. Kim et al. (Eds.): MITA 2025, CCIS 2675, pp. 178–184, 2026.
https://doi.org/10.1007/978-981-95-3141-7_16

would occur where a receiver accepts ghost messages. A ghost message is a set of pulses belonging to different messages but occasionally matches with a code word [7]. Since misdetection damages the reliability of APCMA-based communication, it is important to effectively reduce the pulse density by distributing the timing of message transmission among nodes.

In the paper, we propose a scheduling mechanism of message transmission of nodes distributed in an area. We specifically focus on a system model in which the sensor nodes are transmit-only devices, without reception capability for cost and energy reduction. Since the absence of reception functions makes centralized or coordinated transmission scheduling infeasible, we adopt a noise-induced synchronization of an ensemble of nonlinear oscillators that leverages spatially correlated environmental noise to achieve global synchronization. Each node is equipped with a FitzHugh-Nagumo (FHN) oscillator [2], which is driven by a spatially correlated noise signal exhibiting environmental gradients. The oscillators are synchronized though noise-induced synchronization [6], and each node applies a position-based offset to adjust the timing of message transmission based on its geographic location. We evaluate the performance of our proposal by simulation experiments using the temperature diffused from a heat source as the spatially correlated noise signal.

2   Related Work

2.1   APCMA

In APCMA, a message is composed of a small number of pulses, and information is encoded as the intervals between pulses. Figure 1 illustrates transmission and reception of messages sent by three transmitters. A code word consists of four pulses in this case. A receiver decodes a message by simple pattern matching between a received pulse train and a code book. As far as there is no pulse loss, perfect message reception is possible even if pulses are overlapped or interleaved between messages. It is shown that experiments using 1000 devices were successful and APCMA outperformed CSMA/CA [3].

However, APCMA has a problem of misdetection of a message which is not sent by a transmitter. When many messages are multiplexed on a channel, a certain set of received pulses which belong to different messages occasionally constitutes a valid code word. It is called a ghost message (see Fig. 1). A naive receiver accepts ghost messages, which damages the reliability of wireless communication by APCMA. Since the higher pulse density increases the misdetection probability [7], it is important and effective to reduce the pulse density by smoothing out the timing of message transmission among transmitters.

2.2   Noise-Induced Synchronization

Noise-induced synchronization of a set of uncoupled nonlinear oscillators is a widely known phenomenon, where limit-cycle oscillators are driven to synchronization without direct interaction as in coupled case but with the additive common noise [6]. Figure 2 shows recovery variables of two FHN oscillators become

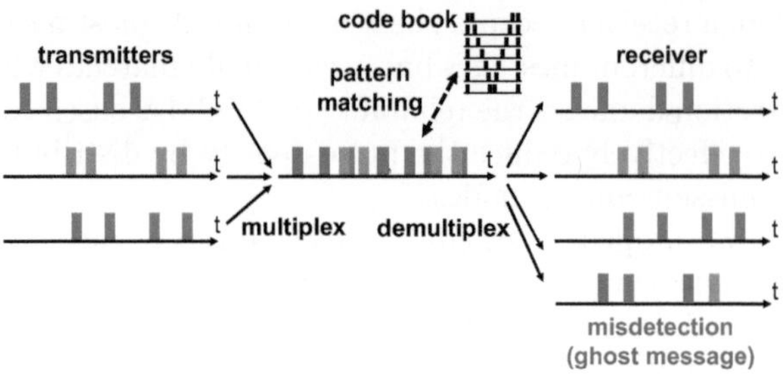

Fig. 1. Asynchronous Pulse Code Multiple Access (APCMA)

identical and synchronized. They are given additive noise signals with a high cross-correlation coefficient of 0.941. In [8], they implemented a noise-induced synchronization scheme on wireless sensor nodes and verified that the spatiotemporal change in humidity and temperature can be used as additive noise signals to accomplish synchronization among nodes without their direct interaction.

3   Noise-Induced Transmission Scheduling

Since it is difficult to accomplish position-dependent scheduling of the timing of message transmission by a common or highly correlated noise, we first synchronize uncoupled oscillators by the environmental noise and then adjust the timing of message transmission based on the location of each node.

3.1   Targeted Scenario

In this paper, we assume that nodes are distributed over a two-dimensional area and a base station is located at the center of the area. Each node is equipped with a sensor, a FHN oscillator, and a transmitter, but does not have a receiver. We further assume that every node knows its own position and the location of the base station.Based on the state of the FHN oscillator, each node periodically transmits messages using APCMA. A message consists of 9 pulses, where two code words of the 8-bits and 5-pulses code are concatenated [7]. The message length is 1547 time slots. The slot length is identical to the pulse width. Pulses sent by nodes are multiplexed on a single channel. Loss and false detection of pulses are assumed not to occur.

3.2   Noise-Induced Distributed Scheduling

In this study, each node i implements a FHN oscillator, whose dynamics is described by the following equations:

$$\frac{\mathrm{d}v_i}{\mathrm{d}t} = v_i - \frac{v_i^3}{3} - u_i + \sigma\zeta_i(t), \quad \frac{\mathrm{d}u_i}{\mathrm{d}t} = \epsilon(v_i + a - bu_i) \tag{1}$$

Here, v_i represents the membrane potential, and u_i is the recovery variable. The parameters ϵ, a, b, and I are constants. The term σ denotes the strength of the external noise $\zeta_i(t)$, which is generated from sensing data at node i. As the noise input, we use the spatially correlated environmental fluctuation, i.e., temperature in the evaluation.

When the recovery variable u_i reaches its peak at time t, the node i transmits a message at time $t + o_i$, where o_i is the offset. To differentiate and smooth the timing of message transmission among nodes, the offset is defined based on the geographical position of a node. In the evaluation, to determine the offset o_i, we used the angle θ_i of the node i's position in the polar coordinates system with the base station as the origin.

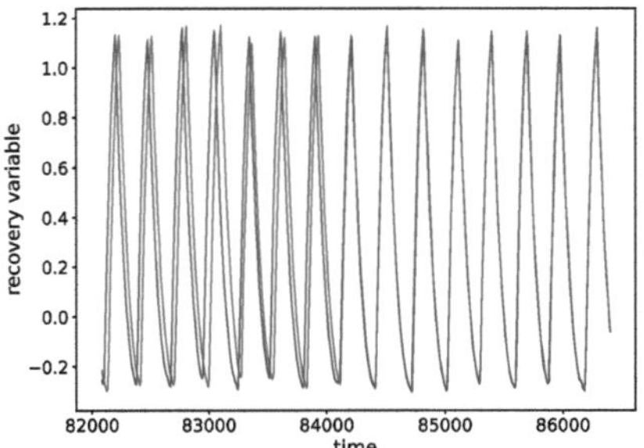

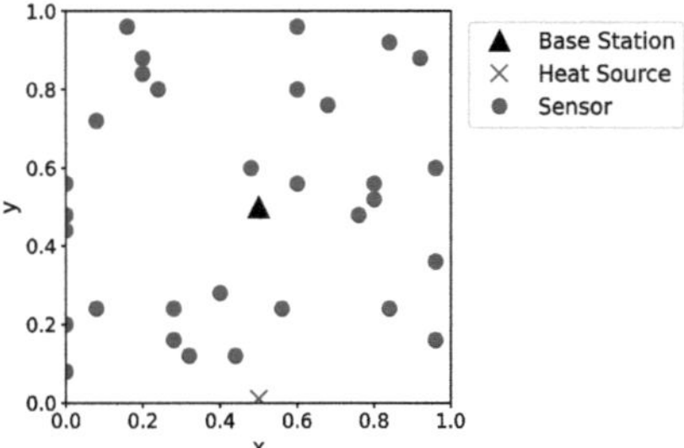

Fig. 2. Noise-induced synchronization

Fig. 3. Arrangement of nodes

4   Evaluation

4.1   Simulation Setting

32 nodes were randomly deployed at 676 grid points within one meter square area as shown in Fig. 3 as an example. A heat source is placed at $(0.5, 0)$ as indicated by a red cross. The parameters of the FHN oscillator were $(\epsilon, a, b, I, \sigma)=(0.008, 0.7, 0.8, 0.4, 0.6)$. The offset value o_i of node i was defined using the angle θ_i in decimal degrees as $o_i = \theta_i$.

The temperature distribution was generated by placing a heat source inside the target area (see Fig. 3) and solving the heat diffusion equation numerically. The source temperature varied over time according to a sin wave with an amplitude from 0 °C to 10 °C and a period of 400 time slots. To incorporate temporal and spatial stochastic fluctuations, the Gaussian noise with zero mean and a variance of 0.01 was added to the source temperature and the temperture at each spatial point after computing the temperature field at every time step independently. At a node, the temperature data was normalized to have a mean of 0 and a variance of 0.05 before being used as the noise input to the FHN oscillator. Simulations were conducted with thermal diffusivity values $\alpha = 0.67,\ 1.0,\ 2.5,$ and $5.0\,\mathrm{mm}^2/\mathrm{s}$. The value $\alpha = 0.67\,\mathrm{mm}^2/\mathrm{s}$ corresponds to the average thermal diffusivity measured at soil depths ranging from $1\,\mathrm{m}$ to $6\,\mathrm{m}$ [5].

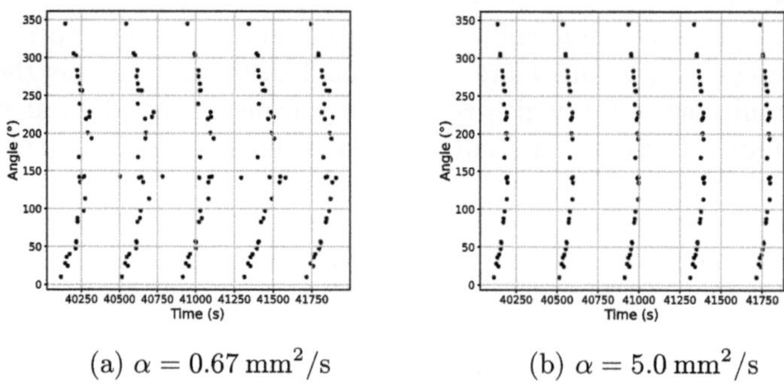

(a) $\alpha = 0.67\,\mathrm{mm}^2/\mathrm{s}$ (b) $\alpha = 5.0\,\mathrm{mm}^2/\mathrm{s}$

Fig. 4. Distribution of the peak of oscillators

4.2   Results and Discussion

Figures 4 and 5 show the distribution of the peak timings of u of the FHN oscillators and the distribution of the timing of message transmission, respectively. Because of space limitation, results of $\alpha =1.0$ and 2.5 are not shown. It can be observed that a larger thermal diffusivity value enabled better synchronization and scheduling. However, the perfect synchronization, where points are arranged in vertical lines, was not possible independently of setting, because of the delay in heat diffusion.As a result, arc-shaped arrangement of timing of message transmission appeared.

Now, we define the schedule error by the root mean square error (RMSE) of timing of message transmission in respect to ideal time s_i of message transmission of node i in a cycle, where $s_i = t_0 + \theta_i - \theta_0$. Here, t_0 represents the actual time of message transmission of node 0, which has the smallest angle θ_0. The ideal schedule is shown as a red line in Fig. 5. The schedule errors were 97.6, 93.4, 63.0, and 42.3 with thermal diffusivity values of 0.67, 1.0, 2.5 and $5.0\,\mathrm{mm}^2/\mathrm{s}$, respectively. In the case that neither of noise-induced synchronization nor offset was used, the schedule error was 113.3. Therefore, the proposed method significantly improves the schedule error. An idea to solve the problem of arc-shaped time lag caused by slow heat diffusion is to defer using the temperature as the noise of the FHN oscillator model based on the proximity to the heat source.

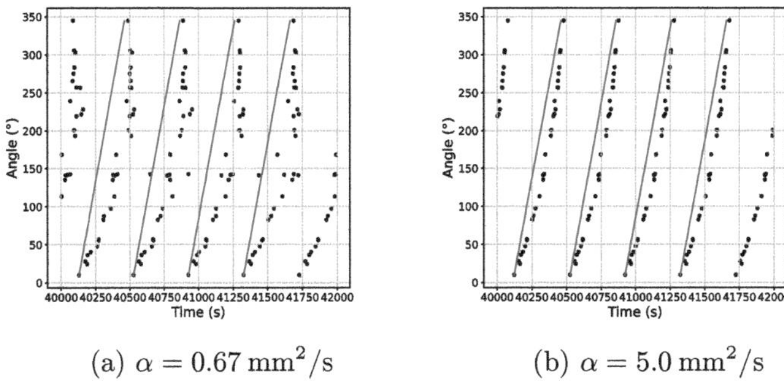

(a) $\alpha = 0.67\,\mathrm{mm}^2/\mathrm{s}$ (b) $\alpha = 5.0\,\mathrm{mm}^2/\mathrm{s}$

Fig. 5. Distribution of the timing of message transmission

5 Conclusion

In this paper, we proposed a noise-induced scheduling mechanism that utilized spatially correlated environmental data to achieve noise-induced synchronization and accomplish controlled desynchronization by using a position-dependent offset. We verified that the timing of message transmission was well distributed and scheduled, without direct interaction between nodes. Future work includes improvement of the noise-induced scheduling mechanism to use the natural environmental fluctuation with less spatial cross-correlation. It also is necessary to assess characteristics of various underwater and underground environmental information, such as temperature, humidity, vibration, pressure, and so on, in the real environment. We plan to implement our mechanism and evaluate its performance and feasibility by field experiments.

References

1. Akyildiz, I., Stuntebeck, E.: Wireless underground sensor networks: research challenges. Ad Hoc Networks **4**, 669–686 (2006). https://doi.org/10.1016/j.adhoc.2006.04.003
2. Izhikevich, E.: Dynamical systems in neuroscience: the geometry of excitability and bursting, vol. 25 (2007). https://doi.org/10.7551/mitpress/2526.001.0001
3. Leibnitz, K., Peper, F., Hasegawa, M., Wakamiya, N.: Performance evaluation of asynchronous pulse code multiple access in massive IoT networks. IEEE Access **12**, 100515–100528 (2024). https://doi.org/10.1109/ACCESS.2024.3430548
4. Pal, A., Campagnaro, F., Ashraf, K., Rahman, R., Ashok, A., Guo, H.: Communication for underwater sensor networks: a comprehensive summary. ACM Trans. Sens. Netw. **19** (2022). https://doi.org/10.1145/3546827
5. Tanaka, S., Fukutomi, S., Yamada, H., Ito, K., Sasaki, N.: Study on simplified estimate of thermophysical properties in shallow ground evaluation of thermal diffusivities of ground by periodic heating method using solar energy as heat source. J. Japan Solar Energ. Soc. **45**(6), 51–58 (2019)
6. Teramae, J., Tanaka, D.: Robustness of the noise-induced phase synchronization in a general class of limit cycle oscillators. Phys. Rev. Lett. **93**, 204103 (2004). https://doi.org/10.1103/PhysRevLett.93.204103

7. Wakamiya, N., Leibnitz, K., Peper, F., Hasegawa, M.: Evaluation and optimization of asynchronous pulse code multiple access. Nonlinear Theor. Appl. IEICE **13**(2), 318–323 (2022). https://doi.org/10.1587/nolta.13.318
8. Yasuda, H., Hasegawa, M.: Natural synchronization of wireless sensor networks by noise-induced phase synchronization phenomenon. IEICE Trans. Commun. **E96.B**, 2749–2755 (2013). https://doi.org/10.1587/transcom.E96.B.2749

AI-Based Health Monitoring System for Old Buildings

Seong Min Jo[1] and Eung Soo Kim[1,2(✉)] ⓘD

[1] Department of Artificial Intelligence Convergence Engineering, Graduate School, Busan University of Foreign Studies, 65, Geumsaem-ro 485Beon-gil, Geumjeong-gu, Busan, Republic of Korea
eskim@bufs.ac.kr

[2] Division of Electronics and Artificial Intelligence Convergence Engineering, Busan University of Foreign Studies, 65, Geumsaem-ro 485Beon-gil, Geumjeong-gu, Busan, Republic of Korea

Abstract. Since the 2016 Gyeongju earthquake, the number of earthquakes greater than magnitude 5 has increased in Korea, and natural disasters caused by global warming have also become more frequent. Many houses and buildings in Korea were built before the 1990s and they are deteriorating. This has raised concerns about the structural safety of these house and buildings. Therefore, we have developed a health monitoring system for old houses and buildings using AI.

Keywords: AI · Old Building · Disaster · Health Monitoring System

1 Introduction

The evolution of urban infrastructure in South Korea has been an ongoing process since the 1960s. According to the Ministry of Land, Infrastructure, and Transport's 2023 National Building Survey, 52% of buildings in the country are over 30 years old, of those, buildings, 43.3% are in the Seoul metropolitan area, and 55.2% are in the provinces. In especially, 68.7% of all residential buildings in Busan are over 30 years old, and there are 162,633 buildings. This is the highest percentage in the country [1].

These old buildings are vulnerable to natural disasters, such as earthquakes, typhoons, and flooding. And they are at high risk of collapse, subsidence, and other types of damage that can endanger lives and property [2]. Therefore, the need for a system that continuously monitors and evaluates the health of older buildings is growing [3].

Recently, there has been a lot of research on monitoring systems using artificial intelligence (AI). In particular, object recognition techniques, employing algorithms such as YOLO and implemented via frameworks like TensorFlow, enable real-time detection of specific targets and can be applied across a wide range of fields [4].

The conventional system for checking and monitoring the safety of buildings is based on measurement by human. This method is time-consuming and expensive, and can't be used all the time. It can also be dangerous, as it can put people in danger of collapse. On the other hand [5], AI technology to crack monitoring in buildings is less

B.-G. Kim et al. (Eds.): MITA 2025, CCIS 2675, pp. 185–196, 2026.
https://doi.org/10.1007/978-981-95-3141-7_17

time-consuming and cost-effective than conventional manual inspection methods with equipment. It also has the advantage of safe and continuous real-time monitoring.

In this paper, we have developed a system that uses artificial intelligence (AI) and an autonomous robot to automatically analyze structural changes, such as cracks and tilting, in old buildings and continuously monitor risk factors.

2   Monitoring Platform

2.1   System Configuration

The system configuration of this research is shown in Fig. 1. The AI-based building health monitoring system is designed by combining object recognition algorithm and autonomous robot, and the robot moves by itself to detect cracks and monitor the health of the structure surface. The autonomous robots are equipped with a depth camera and LiDAR for forward obstacle detection, enabling autonomous navigation through obstacle recognition and avoidance. It automatically detects major damage information through an AI camera, acquires current location information through a GPS module, and transmits the detected damage data and location information to the server to provide the acquired information to the user in the monitoring application.

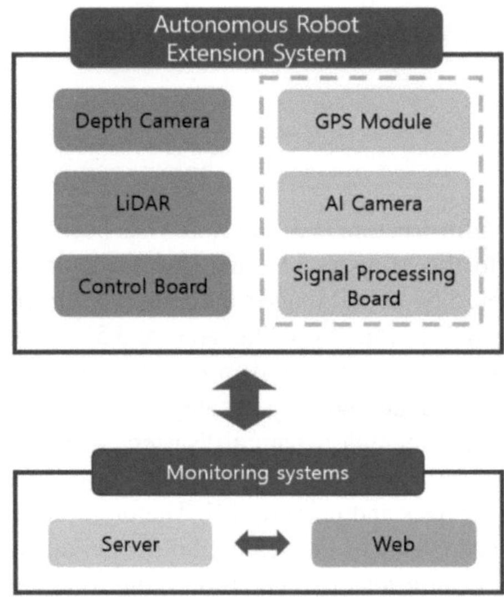

Fig. 1. The Block Diagram of AI-based Health Monitoring System.

2.2   Autonomous Robot

The autonomous robot is an extension of CiLab's X3 model as shown in Fig. 2. The X3 model is equipped with an NVIDIA Jetson Nano, an openCR, encoder motors, servo motors, a LiDAR(E300, PaceCat) and a 3D depth camera(Astra Pro, Orrbec). The Jetson Nano is configured with ROS Noetic running on Ubuntu 20.04 LTS to operate the robot.

It calculates data from LiDAR and RGBD cameras to detect obstacles [6], and controls each motor integrated with openCR to enable autonomous driving and obstacle avoidance functions [7]. Encoder motors are utilized for forward and backward movement, while servo motors are employed for directional control. The system is powered by a 12 V 18650 mAh battery, which provides up to 4 h of continuous operation.

An AI camera was integrated into the autonomous robot to collect object recognition data, along with a signal processing board for data processing and a GPS module for acquiring location information of the captured images. Table 1 shows the specifications of the Autonomous robot.

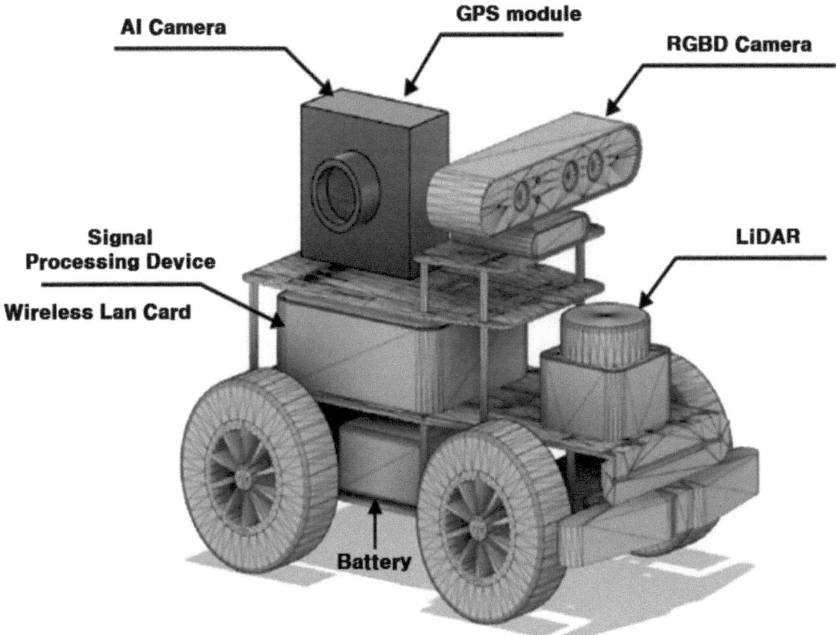

Fig. 2. The design of Autonomous Robot to monitor aging buildings.

Table 1.　Specifications of Autonomous robot

Division	Specification
AI Camera	MAXICAM PRO
GPS Module	L76X GPS HAT
LiDAR	RPLiDAR c1
Battery	12Vdc-5.2A 18650mAH
RGBD Camera	Astra 3D Depth Camera
Signal Processing Board	N100

The data collected by the autonomous robot are stored on the signal processing board, and both the data files and corresponding GPS coordinates are recorded and transmitted to a server via an LTE network. The data can be accessed via the monitoring APP shown in Fig. 3, which organizes information by city and district based on GPS coordinates.

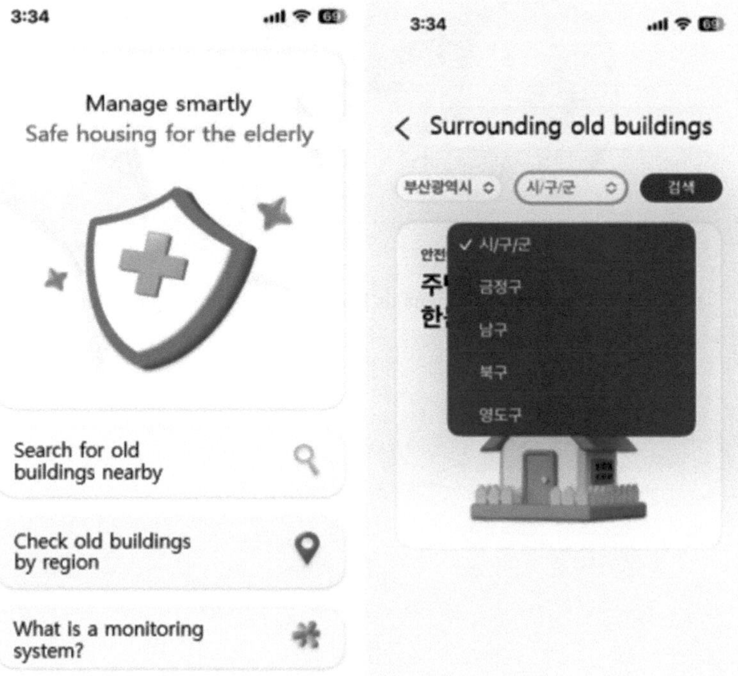

Fig. 3.　The image of Monitoring APP

3   Crack and Tilt Detection

Ultralytics' YOLO11 (You Only Look Once) algorithm model was used to detect cracks in buildings [8], and tilt values were calculated through triangulation using edge detection [9]. YOLO is a deep learning-based algorithm for real-time object detection, known for its high performance in accurately identifying objects with a single pass over an image. To train the model, we augmented the AI Hub building crack dataset—a widely used benchmark dataset—by adding images of cracks in old houses that we captured ourselves. We then performed self-labeling on the combined dataset before training the model. An example of the self-labeling process is shown in Fig. 4. As shown in the Fig. 4, a total of 6,100 images were labeled.

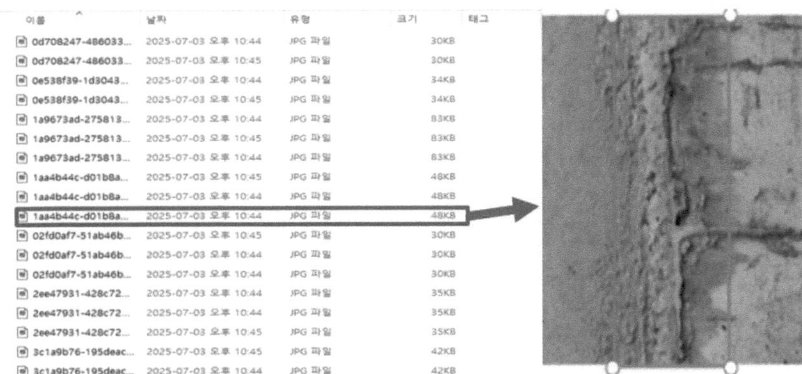

Fig. 4. Image of Self-labeled data.

To calculate the gradient value, image processing was performed using the Hough transform algorithm. The Canny edge detection algorithm is commonly used for edge detection when performing Hough Transform. However, when applying the Canny edge detection algorithm to images of old buildings and houses, cracks were also detected as edges, which led to inaccurate boundary extraction. To address this problem, instead of using the Canny algorithm, a morphological transformation was applied after binarization. Using the Morph Kernel, small holes and fragmented areas within the cracks were filled, resulting in a cleaner contour. Subsequently, only the outermost boundary information was extracted using the FineContours algorithm. The algorithm of tilting detection is as shown in Fig. 5.

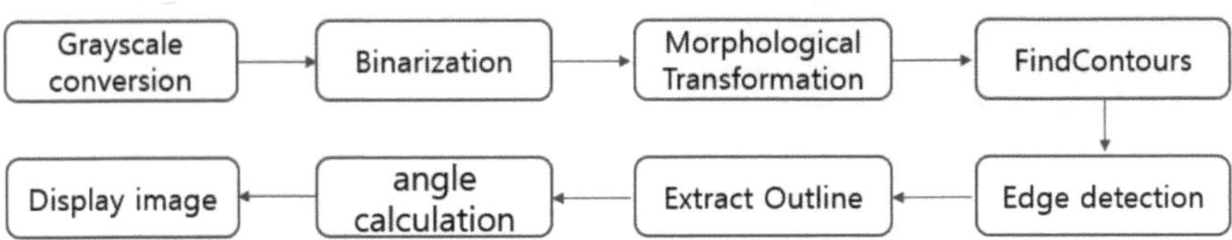

Fig. 5. Tilting detection algorithm.

To verify the accuracy of the slope detection algorithm, we tested it using a 3D-printed architectural facade model with a slope of from 2° to 4°. The image data were processed in accordance with the proposed image processing model. As shown in Fig. 6, we have confirmed the inclination angle of a wall through the tilting detection algorithm.

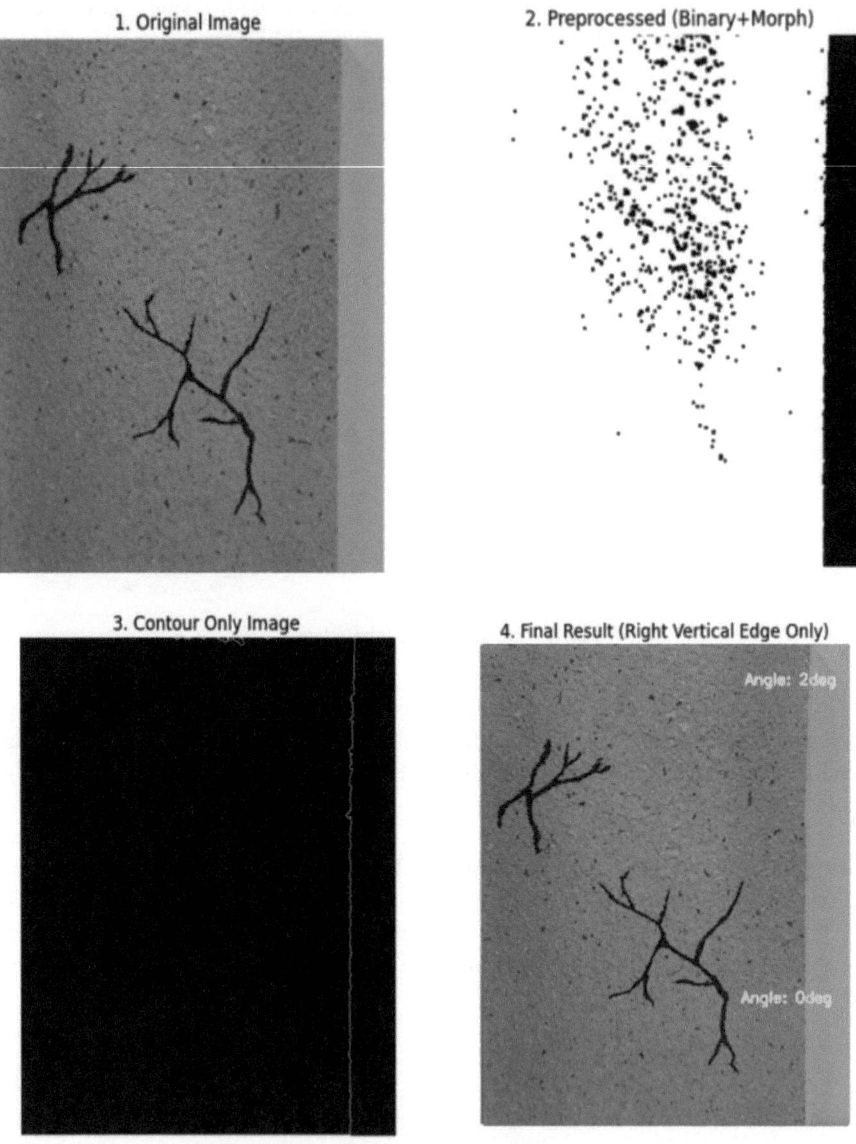

Fig. 6. Validation test results of the tilting detection.

The results of the crack detection algorithm test are shown in Fig. 7.

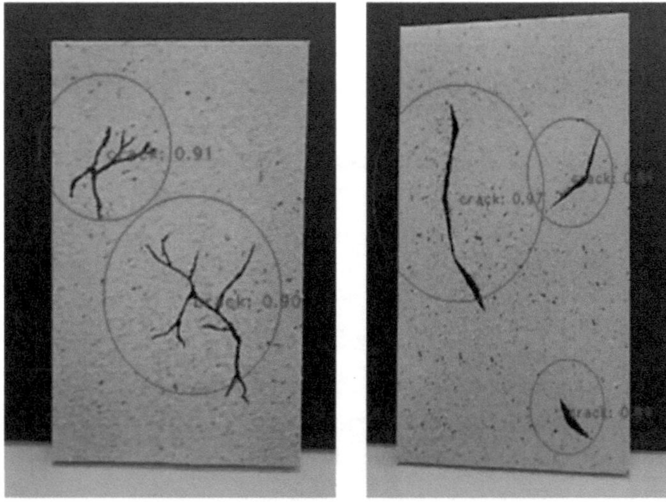

Fig. 7. Results of the crack detection

A measurement program was developed in this study by integrating crack detection and edge angle estimation algorithms. To evaluate the performance of the developed program, three artificial cracks measuring 1 cm, 3 cm, and 7 cm were fabricated using a 3D printer. As shown in Fig. 8, the developed program successfully detected all cracks, as well as structural inclination changes ranging from 2° to 4° on the outer surface of the printed model.

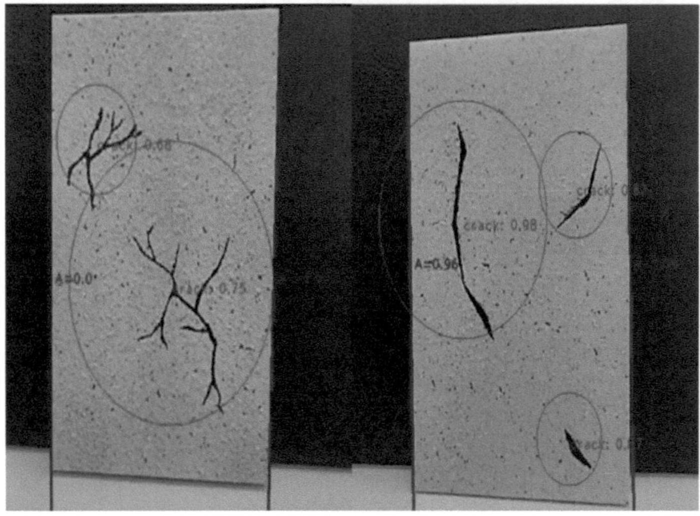

Fig. 8. Validating the crack detection model and edge angle calculation model.

4 Feld Test

We fabricated the autonomous monitoring robot with AI technology as shown in Fig. 9.

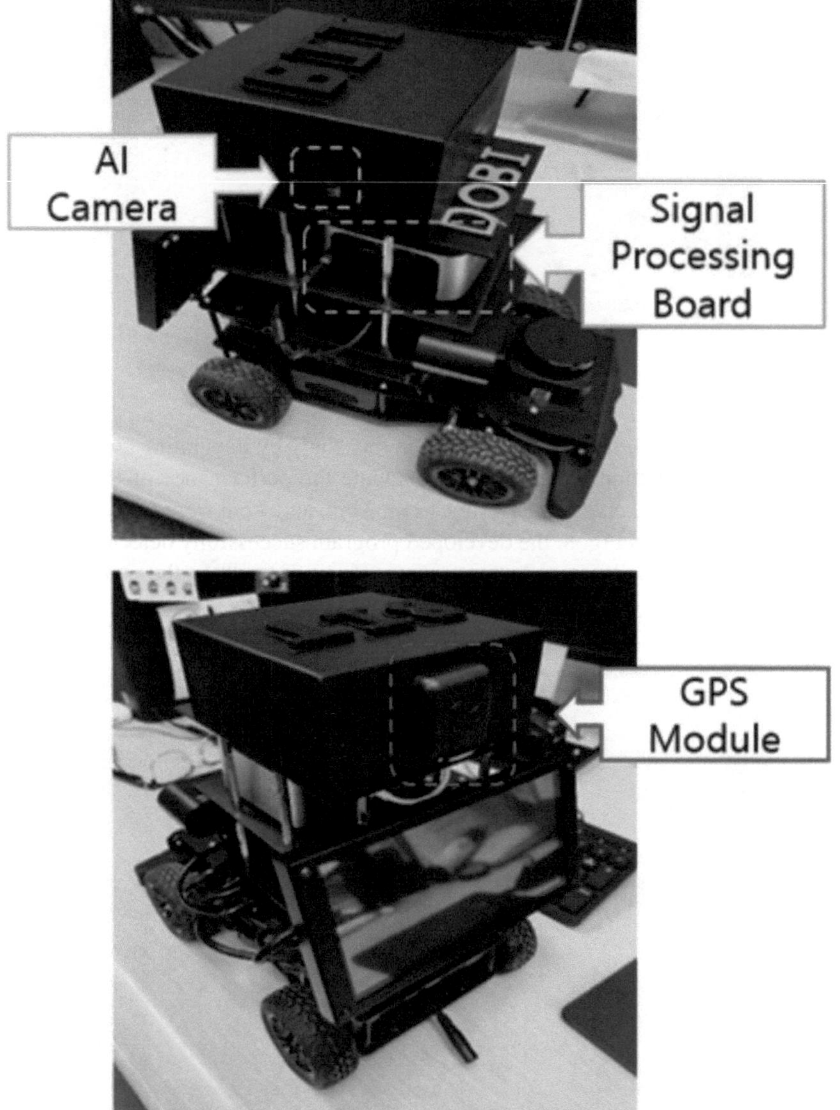

Fig. 9. The photographs of the autonomous monitoring robot.

For the field experiment, five aging buildings located in Yeongdo-gu and Nam-gu districts of Busan were randomly selected and measured at a distance of 30 cm from each building, as shown in Fig. 10.

Figure 11 shows an old building wall with visible cracks for measurement by the AI-based monitoring robot. Figure 12 shows the test results of the fabricated AI autonomous robot. The system successfully measured and displayed the tilt of the building and accurately detected surface cracks on the building walls.

Fig. 10. The photograph of the measurement setup showing a 30 cm distance between the autonomous robot and the wall

Fig. 11. The photograph of a wall of an old building.

Fig. 12. Actual measurement results on an old building wall.

The acquired data were transmitted to the server via the LTE communication network, and the locations of the acquired data were displayed on the map through the APP as shown in Fig. 13.

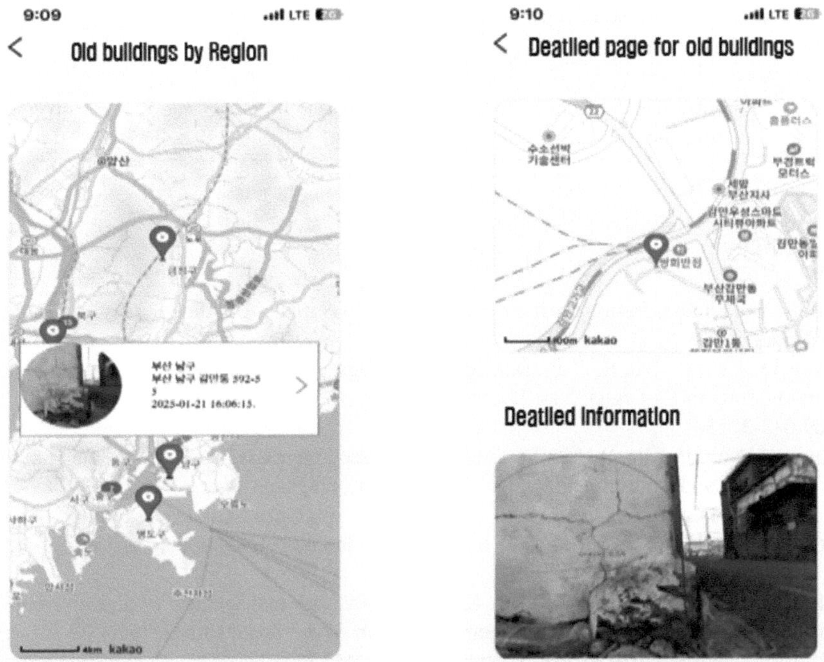

Fig. 13. The APP Screen displaying measurement location and results.

5   Conclusions

There are many aging buildings in Korea. These old buildings are at risk of collapse due to natural disasters such as earthquakes and typhoons, posing significant challenges. This is because that they increase the risk of property damage and loss of life.

The number of old buildings is steadily increasing worldwide, including in Korea. Therefore, a monitoring system is required to ensure the safety of these old buildings and prevent disasters.

In this paper. an AI-based structural health monitoring system is developed to overcome the limitations of conventional monitoring methods for old buildings by utilizing artificial intelligence to detect and monitor key factors such as deformation, cracks, and structural damage at early stages and in real time. The developed AI-based monitoring system was tested using a 3D-printed architectural facade model with a slope of from 2° to 4° and cracks of 1 cm, 3 cm, and 7 cm, and the system's performance was further validated through a field test. The developed system operated reliably, measuring and displaying the building's tilt while accurately detecting surface cracks on the building walls.

In particular, autonomous robots can be effectively used to reliably acquire and apply data in hazardous environments that are difficult for humans to access.

Furthermore, the system can be extended to various applications, such as bridges and nuclear power, etc. It can facilitate the collection of data for planned and systematic monitoring of the structural health of aging buildings. This will enable us to prepare a safety roadmap for disaster preparedness and facilitate proactive management to prevent accidents in deteriorating buildings.

Acknowledgments. This work was supported by the research grant of the Busan University of Foreign Studies in 2025.

References

1. Ministry of Land, Infrastructure and Transport, "2023 National Building Survey," Government of Korea, 2023
2. Yang, Q., Gao, R., Bai, F., et al.: Damage to buildings and structures due to recent devastating wind hazards in East Asia. Nat. Hazards **92**, 1321–1353 (2018). https://doi.org/10.1007/s11069-018-3253-8
3. Kim, S., Yoon, J., Kim, B.H.S.: Disaster damage assessment of old and deteriorated buildings in urban area under the climate change scenarios. J. Korea Plann. Assoc. **51**(5), 263–275 (2016)
4. Redmon, J., Divvala, S., Girshick, R., Farhadi, A.: You Only Look Once: unified, real-time object detection. In: Proceedings of the IEEE Conference on Computer Vision and Pattern Recognition (CVPR) (2016)
5. Moon, K.-H., Kim, J.-Y., Park, J.-K., Kim, J.-Y.: Disaster management of high-rise building using structural health monitoring systems. J. Korean Assoc. Spatial Struct. **15**(1), 22–29 (2015)
6. Gatesichapakorn, S., Takamatsu, J., Ruchanurucks, M.: ROS based autonomous mobile robot navigation using 2D LiDAR and RGB-D Camera. In: 2019 First International Symposium on Instrumentation, Control, Artificial Intelligence, and Robotics (ICA-SYMP), Bangkok, Thailand, pp. 151–154 (2019). https://doi.org/10.1109/ICA-SYMP.2019.8645984
7. Tsai, C.-C., Hsu, W. -T., Tai, F. -C., Chen, S. -C.: Adaptive motion control of a terrain-adaptive self-balancing leg-wheeled mobile robot over rough terrain. In: 2022 International Automatic Control Conference (CACS), Kaohsiung, Taiwan, pp. 1–6 (2022). https://doi.org/10.1109/CACS55319.2022.9969857
8. Dong, X., Yuan, J., Dai, J.: Study on lightweight bridge crack detection algorithm based on YOLO11. Sensors **25**, 3276 (2025)
9. Juneja, M., Sandhu, P.: Performance evaluation of edge detection techniques for images in spatial domain. Int. J. **1**, 614–621 (2009). https://doi.org/10.7763/IJCTE.2009.V1.100

Phase-Specific Gait Characterization and Plantar Load Progression Analysis Using Smart Insoles

Thathsara Nanayakkara[1] , H. M. K. K. M. B. Herath[1] ,
Hadi Sedigh Malekroodi[1] , Nuwan Madusanka[2] , Myunggi Yi[1,2,3] ,
and Byeong-il Lee[1,2,4(✉)]

[1] Industry 4.0 Convergence Bionics Engineering, Pukyong National University, Busan 48513, Republic of Korea
bilee@pknu.ac.kr

[2] Digital Healthcare Research Center, Institute of Information Technology and Convergence, Pukyong National University, Busan 48513, Republic of Korea

[3] Major of Biomedical Engineering, Division of Smart Healthcare, Pukyong National University, Busan, Republic of Korea

[4] Division of Smart Healthcare, Major of Human Bioconvergence, Pukyong National University, Busan, Republic of Korea

Abstract. Accurate, real-time identification of gait phases is crucial for clinical assessment, rehabilitation monitoring, and wearable health applications. However, most current smart-insole solutions require high-frequency sampling, increasing power consumption and computational load. To address these limitations, we developed a lightweight, custom-designed smart insole system operating at a low frequency of 5 Hz. The system integrates eight force-sensitive resistors (FSRs) and a tri-axial Inertial Measurement Unit (IMU) per foot. Fourteen healthy participants performed five walking trials on a 10 m. At the same time, synchronized insole sensor data and RGB video recordings were captured, with video annotations serving as the ground truth for gait-phase verification. We systematically evaluated five distinct feature sets using six classical machine learning classifiers with participant-wise cross-validation. Pressure-only features classified using a support vector machine yielded the highest macro-F1 score of 0.915, confirming that low-frequency plantar pressure signals effectively discriminate against gait phases without substantial loss in accuracy. In contrast, IMU-only signals demonstrated significantly lower classification performance, highlighting the limited effectiveness of inertial data at low sampling rates. Additionally, we developed a visual analytics pipeline to enhance interpretability, generating spatial plantar pressure heatmaps and activation-frequency maps that clearly illustrate distinct load patterns for each gait phase. Our findings demonstrate that low-frequency plantar-pressure signals provide sufficient temporal and spatial information for reliable gait-phase detection. This approach offers a practical solution for real-time gait monitoring applications.

Keywords: Smart insoles · Gait-phase detection · Low-frequency sampling · Plantar-pressure heatmaps · Machine learning · Image Processing

© The Author(s) 2026
B.-G. Kim et al. (Eds.): MITA 2025, CCIS 2675, pp. 197–208, 2026.
https://doi.org/10.1007/978-981-95-3141-7_18

1 Introduction

Gait analysis is critical in healthcare in evaluating mobility, diagnosing movement disorders, monitoring motor recovery, particularly in post-stroke and Parkinson's disease patients, and assessing fall risk in the elderly. While traditional lab-based force plates provide accurate data, they are costly and limited in scope [1]. In contrast, wearable systems, especially smart insoles, offer a portable, affordable solution for real-world gait analysis by capturing plantar pressure patterns linked to gait events [2]. Their convenience and ability to monitor gait continuously outside lab environments have made them widely adopted in recent years for applications such as athletic training, remote rehabilitation, and fall prevention [3]. Advancements in sensor technology have enhanced smart insoles for gait analysis by combining pressure sensors (e.g., FSRs, piezoelectric cells) with inertial sensors (accelerometers, gyroscopes) to capture both loading patterns and foot kinematics [4, 5]. These multi-sensor systems offer comprehensive biomechanical data and have been validated across various populations. However, their design involves trade-offs between sensor fidelity, power consumption, and user comfort. As a result, smart insoles now serve as a vital intersection of biomechanics and data science, enabling real-time gait monitoring in applications such as rehabilitation, sports, and movement disorder diagnosis [1].

In Gait analysis, gait-phase detection is critical for wearable insole systems. Various methods have been developed to identify key events such as heel-strike (HES), foot-flat (FOF), heel-rise (HER), and toe-off (TOF). Early approaches focused on rule-based strategies. González et al. [6] applied fuzzy logic, while Salis et al. [7] and Park et al. [8] used threshold-based techniques based on pressure patterns and center of pressure changes. Other rule-based methods were demonstrated by Pappas et al. [9] and Chariklia et al. [10]. To improve robustness, machine learning methods like k-nearest neighbor (kNN) have also been employed, as in the work of Rattanasak et al. [11], achieving over 81% accuracy for transtibial amputees. While most gait-phase detection systems operate at high sampling rates ($\geq$50–100 Hz) for precise foot contact timing, this comes at the cost of increased power use, data volume, and processing load, which limit real-time, long-term wearable use. Prior studies have shown that resampling accelerometer signals to 30 Hz still preserves relevant gait content [14], and down-sampling the IMU stream extends the battery life of smartphones and wearables while still delivering acceptable walking-recognition accuracy [15]. The SmartStep study suggested that 25 Hz is sufficient for gait and activity monitoring in real-life conditions [16], while other insole-based systems have operated at even lower rates, like 10 Hz [17].

To address these limitations, this study evaluates gait-phase classification at a low 5 Hz sampling rate using a custom smart insole system equipped with eight FSR sensors and a tri-axial IMU. A controlled experiment with video-annotated ground truth was conducted, and multiple feature sets were compared using classical machine learning models. Additionally, a visual analytics pipeline was developed to generate interpretable pressure heatmaps.

2 Methodology

2.1 Insole System Design

Based on prior research, sixteen biomechanically relevant plantar regions were identified from 30 anatomical zones [18], and eight optimal sensor locations were selected and mapped onto the insole using a standardized coordinate system (Fig. 1a). Each insole integrates eight Interlink FSR 402 sensors (13 mm diameter, 0.5–150 N range, <3 ms response time), chosen for their compactness, affordability, and dynamic pressure sensitivity. Additionally, each insole includes an MPU6050 IMU, with the complete hardware configuration illustrated in Fig. 1(b).

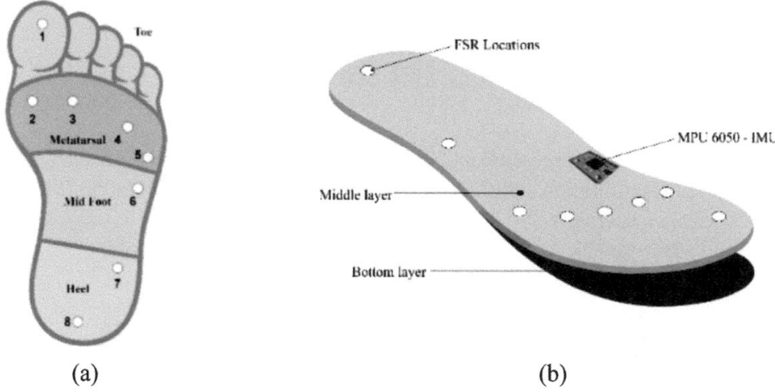

(a)   (b)

Fig. 1. Anatomical sensor placement and smart insole hardware design (a) Layout of eight FSR positions across key plantar regions (b) 3D schematic of the custom-designed smart insole, illustrating embedded FSRs, MPU6050 inertial sensor.

Calibration procedures were conducted for the FSR sensors and the MPU6050 IMU module to ensure accurate analog pressure and motion sensing. A voltage divider circuit was tested with resistor values ranging from 3 kΩ to 200 kΩ under incremental loads (0–900 g), identifying 10 kΩ as the optimal value for balancing sensitivity and dynamic range without early saturation (Fig. 2a). The gyroscope was calibrated by averaging static readings to determine bias offsets (Gx, Gy, Gz), while accelerometer calibration used a three-position static method (+1 g, 0 g, −1 g) across each axis. Linear regression yielded axis-specific scale and offset parameters, which were applied to raw data to ensure accurate acceleration in physical units (Fig. 2b–d), enabling reliable gait and orientation tracking.

Each insole integrates eight FSR sensors and an MPU6050 IMU, managed by an ESP-32 microcontroller. A 74HC4051 multiplexer handles FSR inputs, while I2C manages motion sensing. Powered by a 3.7 V lithium-ion battery with regulated protection, the system transmits data via BLE 4.2 using UUID-based services. A 5 Hz time-division strategy allows alternate transmission from left and right insoles, ensuring synchronized, compact data packets for bilateral gait analysis. The system architecture is illustrated in Fig. 3.

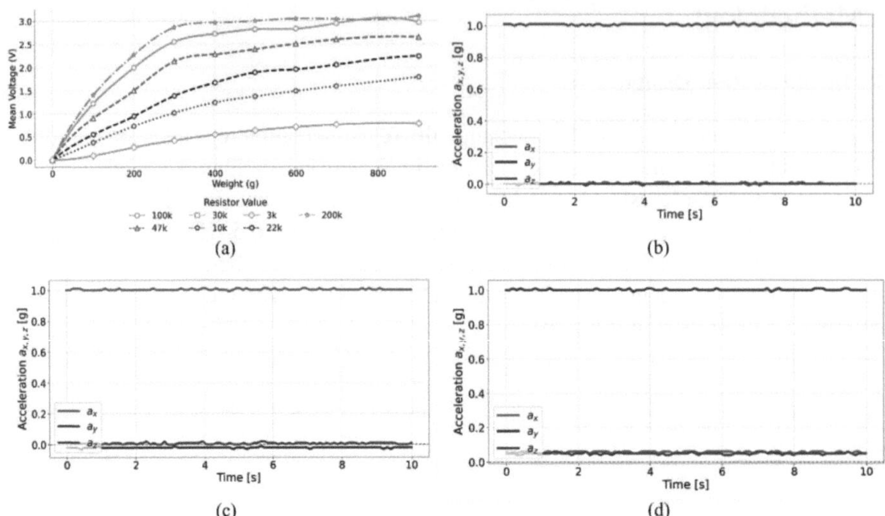

Fig. 2. Calibration results in pressure and inertial sensors. (a) FSR calibration curves under varying loads. (b-d) post-calibration static acceleration readings from the MPU6050 IMU for the +X, +Y, and +Z axes, respectively.

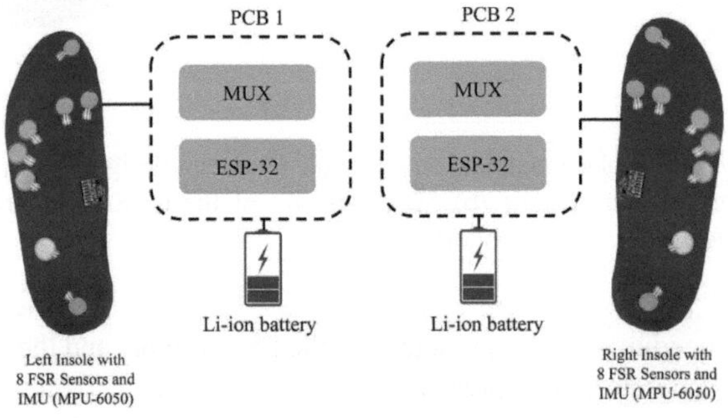

Fig. 3. Smart insole system for wireless gait data acquisition.

2.2 Data Collection and Dataset Preparation

Fourteen healthy adults (50% male, 50% Female; age $= 27.0 \pm 4.1$ years; Body weight $= 61.5 \pm 9.5$ kg) performed walking trials while wearing custom-developed smart insoles on a 10 m walkway. Pressure data and IMU were recorded at 5 Hz, synchronized with RGB video recordings (30 fps) for gait-phase annotation. Procedures were approved by the Institutional Review Board of Pukyong National University (No. 2025-02-006). The experimental setup and wearable sensor configuration are shown in Fig. 4.

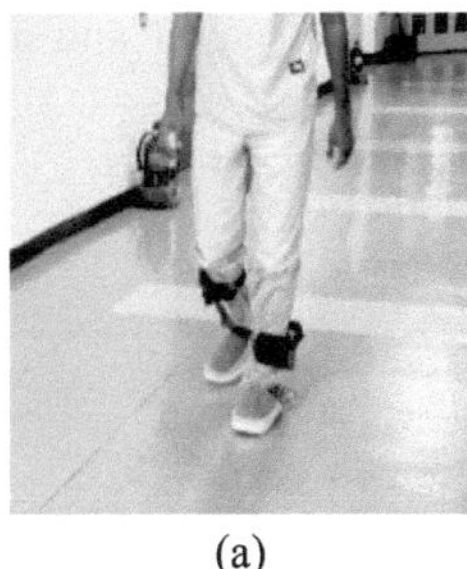
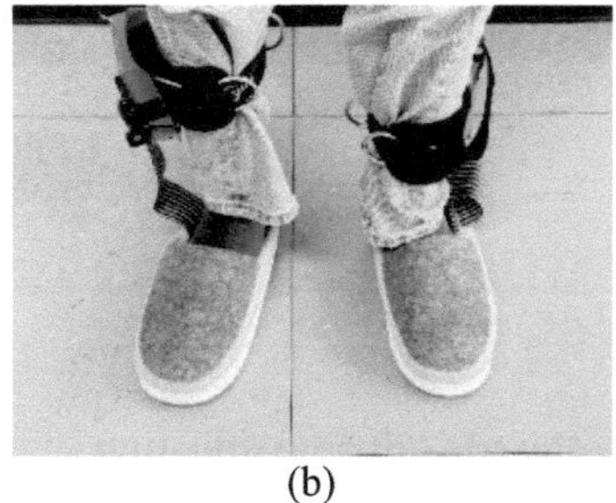

(a)   (b)

Fig. 4. Experimental setup for gait data collection. (a) Full-body view during walking trials. (b) Smart insole system configuration on both legs.

Sensor readings were aligned with the video based on synchronized start times. Gait events (HES, FOF, HER, TOF) were manually annotated based on visual inspection of synchronized video recordings. HES was annotated when the heel first contacted the ground, while FOF was identified when the entire foot was flat and in full contact with the ground surface. HER was defined as the point at which the heel began to lift off the ground, TOF was marked when the toe visibly left the ground, signaling the end of the stance phase. This approach allowed intuitive identification of events across subjects, although it may introduce subjectivity and inter-rater variability. An illustrative overview of this video-based gait phase annotation process is shown in Fig. 5.

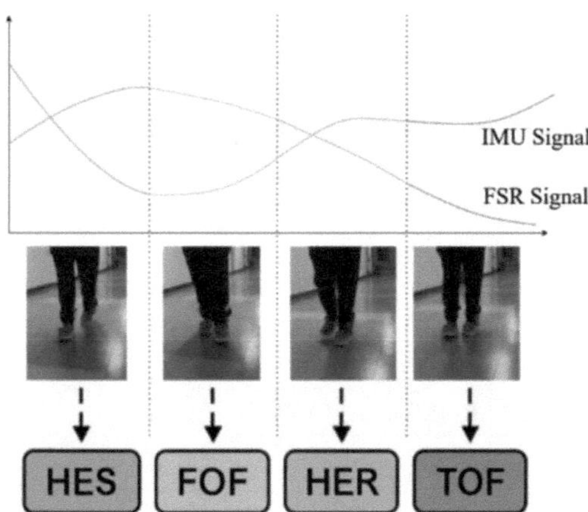

Fig. 5. Illustrative gait-phase annotation using synchronized video frames and representative sensor signal trends.

Frame-wise center of pressure (CoP) coordinates were computed using a weighted-average approach [19]. Where F_i represents the FSR pressure values, and d_{xi} and d_{yi}

denote the distances to the corresponding sensor in the medial-lateral and anterior-posterior directions.

$$\text{COP}_x, \text{COP}_y, = \frac{\sum_{i=1}^{N} d_{xi} F_i}{\sum_{i=1}^{N} F_i}, \frac{\sum_{i=1}^{N} d_{yi} F_i}{\sum_{i=1}^{N} F_i} \tag{1}$$

2.3 ML-Based Gait Classification

To assess the classification performance of different sensor modalities for gait-phase detection, a supervised multi-class pipeline was implemented using six machine learning models: Random Forest, Gradient Boosting, Support Vector Machine, Logistic Regression, K-nearest neighbors, and a shallow multilayer perception (MLP). All models were developed using the scikit-learn library. Five feature sets combining plantar pressure, IMU data, and CoP coordinates were evaluated (as detailed in Table 1). Model performance was assessed using accuracy, macro-averaged precision, recall, and F1-score to ensure balanced evaluation across gait classes. The MLP model used a single hidden layer with early stopping, while other models applied default hyperparameters. Left and right foot data were analyzed independently, and results were averaged using a pooled metric approach for consistency.

Table 1. Description of the five feature sets used for gait-phase classification, including their dimensionality and the sensor modalities involved (FSR, IMU, and CoP).

ID	Feature Set	Dimensionality per Sample
FSR	Normalized plantar pressure from 8 sensor data	8
IMU	Linear acceleration and angular velocity (x, y, and z) data	6
FSR + IMU	Combined pressure and inertial features	14
FSR + CoP	Pressure features with spatial CoP coordinates	10
FSR + IMU + CoP	All FSR, IMU, and COP data	16

2.4 Gait Phase Visualization and Load Quantification

A visual analytics pipeline was developed to generate phase-specific plantar pressure heat maps to accurately classify and interpret each gait phase. These maps enable intuitive inspection of pressure distribution patterns associated with distinct gait events. Specifically, FSR sensor magnitudes were convolved with a Gaussian kernel and stamped onto a 1400×900-pixel anatomical foot template at fixed coordinates. The resulting pressure fields were overlaid on the foot outline and exported as high-resolution PNGs, sorted by gait phase and participant. Figure 6 illustrates five representative frames per phase.

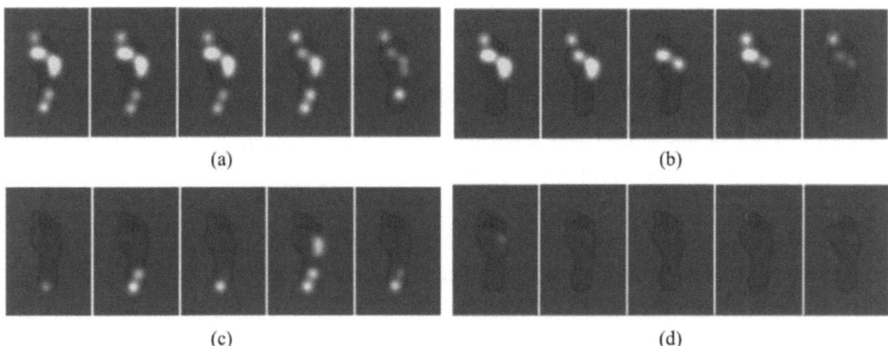

Fig. 6. Sample pressure heatmaps for each gait phase across multiple frames (a) FOF, (b) HER, (c) HES, and (d) TOF

A visual analytics pipeline was developed using FSR heatmaps to analyze gait-phase-specific plantar loading. Pressure data were convolved with a Gaussian kernel and mapped onto a 1400 × 900-pixel foot template. Subject-specific grayscale thresholds were applied to binarize images, enhancing robustness via histogram-based noise separation [21]. Aggregated binary masks produced activation-frequency maps (0–1) [22], which were divided into a 4 × 6 grid. For each cell (i, j) the mean activation frequency was computed as:

$$g_{ij} = \frac{1}{|A_{ij}|} \sum_{(x,y)\in A_{ij}} f(x, y) \tag{2}$$

where A_{ij} is the total number of pixels in that cell within the (i, j) th grid cell and f(x, y) represents the activation frequency of a pixel at coordinate (x, y), which is a value between 0 and 1. This yielded a 24-element descriptor. An intensity-weighted volume metric quantified pressure magnitude and area. Gait-phase comparisons confirmed distinct spatial load patterns. The complete workflow is shown in Fig. 7.

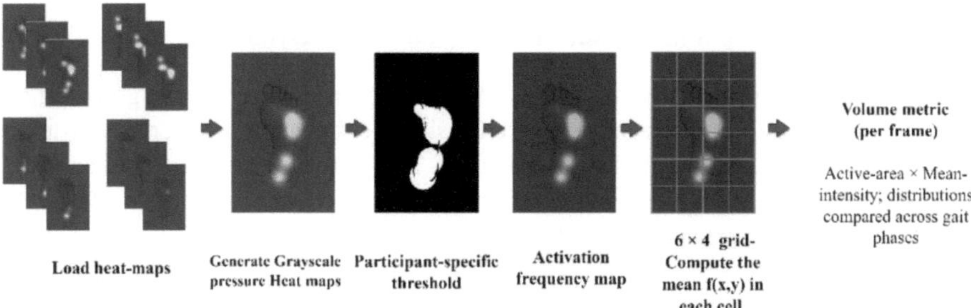

Fig. 7. Visual analytics pipeline for spatial plantar pressure analysis across gait phases.

3 Results and Analysis

3.1 Performance Comparison Across Features

Figure 9 compares the classification performance across five feature sets: FSR, IMU, FSR + IMU, FSR + CoP, and FSR + IMU + CoP using six classical machine learning models: Random Forest, Gradient Boosting, SVM, Logistic Regression, k-NN, and a shallow MLP. Metrics are reported as means with standard deviations. Table 2 summarizes the classification of the best performance across all five feature sets and six machine learning models, highlighting that FSR-based features consistently outperformed IMU and multimodal combinations.

Table 2. Summary of Top Classification Results (Mean ± SD) for Each Feature Set Using the Best-Performing Models.

Feature set	Model	Accuracy	Precision	Recall	F1 Score
FSR	SVM	0.928 ± 0.034	0.926 ± 0.0257	0.916 ± 0.044	0.915 ± 0.418
FSR + IMU	Logistic Reg	0.922 ± 0.038	0.918 ± 0.037	0.911 ± 0.044	0.91 ± 0.043
FSR + IMU + COP	Random Forest	0.921 ± 0.038	0.914 ± 0.041	0.909 ± 0.048	0.909 ± 0.046
FSR + COP	Logistic Reg	0.921 ± 0.037	0.92 ± 0.028	0.907 ± 0.050	0.907 ± 0.045
IMU	Random Forest	0.726 ± 0.070	0.72 ± 0.061	0.707 ± 0.058	0.691 ± 0.068

Among all models, the pressure-only feature set using eight normalized FSR signals achieved the highest classification performance, with a macro-F1 score of 0.915. In contrast, models trained solely on IMU features consistently showed substantially lower performance.

3.2 Phase-Specific Spatial Pressure Patterns and Load Dynamics

Figure 8 illustrates phase-specific activation-frequency maps, highlighting consistent plantar loading patterns across gait events. HES shows concentrated posterior activation and FOF, and HER exhibits anterior shifts in load. TOF demonstrates minimal, localized forefoot contact. These results confirm that activation-frequency mapping effectively captures distinct biomechanical signatures of each gait phase.

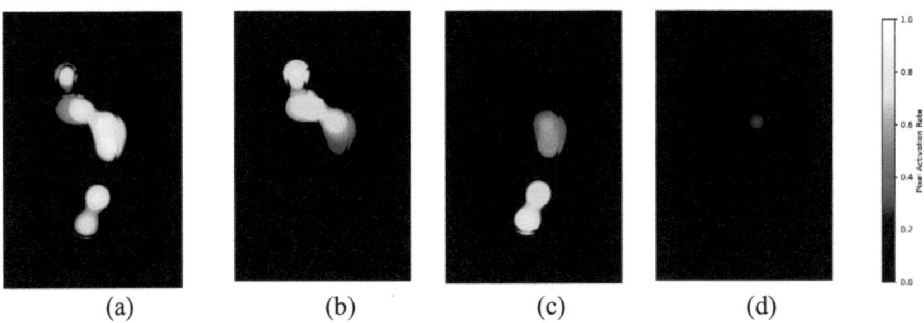

(a)   (b)   (c)   (d)

Fig. 8. Activation-frequency maps aggregate across all participants for each gait phase: (a) FOF, (b) HER, (c) HES, and (d) TOF.

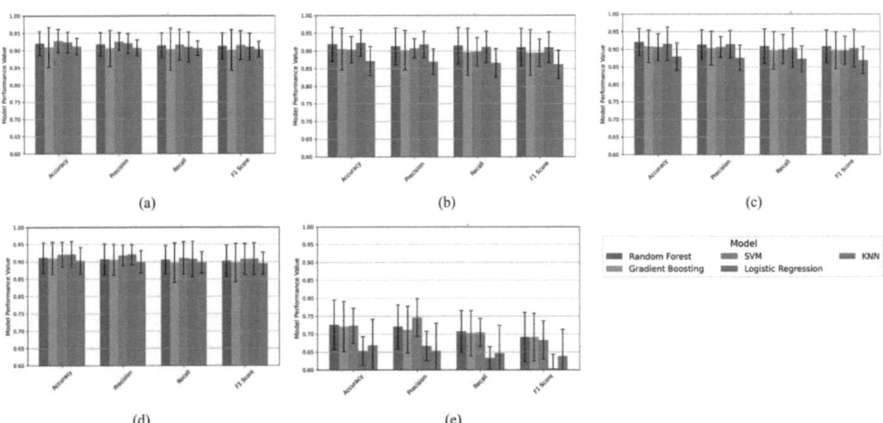

(a)   (b)   (c)

(d)   (e)

Fig. 9. Classification performance comparison across different feature sets: (a) FSR, (b) FSR + IMU, (c) FSR + IMU + CoP, (d) FSR + CoP, and (e) IMU only.

Figure 10 shows that pressure volume, reflecting both contact area and intensity, peaks during FOF, followed by HES and HER, and is lowest during TOF. This pattern aligns with expected load transitions across the gait cycle, confirming distinct pressure dynamics between phases.

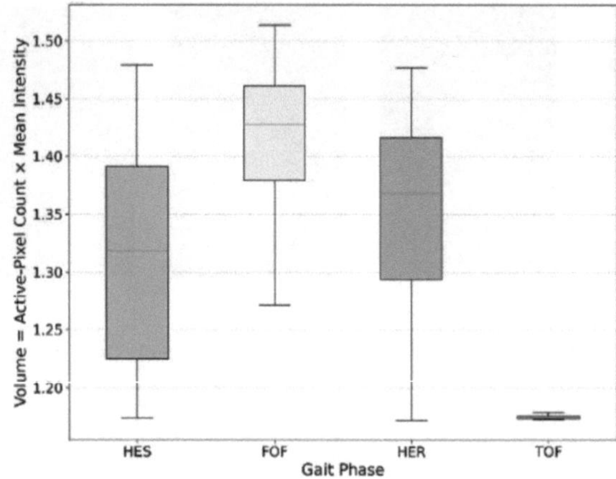

Fig. 10. Distribution of intensity-weighted pressure volume across gait phases.

4 Discussion

This study demonstrated that low-frequency smart insoles with only eight FSRs can reliably and accurately classify gait phases. Pressure-only features outperformed IMU-based and multimodal combinations, highlighting the superior discriminative power of plantar pressure data at low sampling rates. IMU signals alone lacked sufficient temporal resolution at 5 Hz, and their inclusion in multimodal inputs offered minimal impact on performance. The custom visual analytics pipeline effectively revealed phase-specific load patterns through pressure heatmaps and activation-frequency maps, supporting interpretability and confirming consistent load transitions across HES, FOF, HER, and TOF. Despite promising results, the study acknowledges limitations: reliance on manual video annotation, occasional BLE data collisions, and potential insufficiency of 5 Hz sampling for capturing rapid or irregular gait transitions. Additionally, the small, healthy participant cohort limits generalizability. Future work will address these issues through improved BLE protocols, semi-automated annotation, and testing across larger, more diverse populations, including those with gait impairments. The proposed system offers a practical, interpretable, and energy-efficient solution for real-world gait monitoring in digital healthcare applications.

5 Conclusion

This study demonstrated the effectiveness of a low-frequency (5 Hz) smart insole system for gait-phase classification and spatial plantar load analysis. By systematically evaluating using classical machine learning models, we established that plantar pressure signals collected from eight FSR channels can accurately and consistently classify gait phases, significantly outperforming inertial and multimodal feature sets. Notably, inertial signals demonstrated considerably lower effectiveness at low sampling frequencies. Moreover, we introduced a spatial visualization pipeline capable of generating interpretable plantar pressure heatmaps, activation-frequency maps, and grid-based summaries. These visualizations consistently revealed phase-specific load patterns across participants, enhancing the interpretability of the results. Integrating low-frequency data acquisition, efficient classification algorithms, and intuitive visual analytics underscores the framework's suitability for applications in digital healthcare settings.

Acknowledgments. This research was supported by the National Research Foundation of Korea (NRF) and funded by the Ministry of Science and ICT (No. 2022M3A9B6082791).

References

1. Santos, V.M., Gomes, B.B., Neto, M.A., Amaro, A.M.: A systematic review of insole sensor technology: recent studies and future directions. Appl. Sci. **14**, 6085 (2024). https://doi.org/10.3390/app14146085
2. He, Y., et al.: Textile-film sensors for a comfortable intelligent pressure-sensing insole. Measurement **184**, 109943 (2021). https://doi.org/10.1016/j.measurement.2021.109943
3. Sanseverino, G., Krumm, D., Kilian, W., Odenwald, S.: Estimation of hike events and temporal parameters with body-attached sensors. Sports Eng. **26**, 18 (2023). https://doi.org/10.1007/s12283-023-00411-x
4. Chen, J., et al.: Plantar pressure-based insole gait monitoring techniques for diseases monitoring and analysis: a review. Adv. Mater. Technol. **7** (2022). https://doi.org/10.1002/admt.202100566
5. Van Nguyen, L., La, H.M.: Real-time human foot motion localization algorithm with dynamic speed. IEEE Trans. Hum. Mach. Syst. **46**, 822–833 (2016). https://doi.org/10.1109/THMS.2016.2586741
6. González, I., Fontecha, J., Hervás, R., Bravo, J.: An ambulatory system for gait monitoring based on wireless sensorized insoles. Sensors **15**, 16589–16613 (2015). https://doi.org/10.3390/s150716589
7. Salis, F., Bertuletti, S., Bonci, T., Della Croce, U., Mazzà, C., Cereatti, A.: A method for gait events detection based on low spatial resolution pressure insoles data. J. Biomech. **127**, 110687 (2021). https://doi.org/10.1016/j.jbiomech.2021.110687
8. Park, J.S., Lee, C.M., Koo, S.-M., Kim, C.H.: Gait phase detection using force sensing resistors. IEEE Sens. J. **20**, 6516–6523 (2020). https://doi.org/10.1109/JSEN.2020.2975790
9. Pappas, I.P.I., Popovic, M.R., Keller, T., Dietz, V., Morari, M.: A reliable gait phase detection system. IEEE Trans. Neural Syst. Rehabil. Eng. **9**, 113–125 (2001). https://doi.org/10.1109/7333.928571
10. Chatzaki, C., et al.: The smart-insole dataset: gait analysis using wearable sensors with a focus on elderly and Parkinson's patients. Sensors **21**, 2821 (2021). https://doi.org/10.3390/s21082821
11. Rattanasak, A., et al.: Real-time gait phase detection using wearable sensors for transtibial prosthesis based on a KNN algorithm. Sensors **22**, 4242 (2022). https://doi.org/10.3390/s22114242
12. Taborri, J., Rossi, S., Palermo, E., Patanè, F., Cappa, P.: A novel HMM distributed classifier for the detection of gait phases using a wearable inertial sensor network. Sensors **14**, 16212–16234 (2014). https://doi.org/10.3390/s140916212
13. Park, B., Kim, M., Jung, D., Kim, J., Mun, K.-R.: Smart insole-based abnormal gait identification: deep sequential networks and feature ablation study. Digit. Health **11** (2025). https://doi.org/10.1177/20552076251332999

14. Brand, Y.E., et al.: Automated gait detection in older adults during daily-living using self-supervised learning of wrist- worn accelerometer data: development and validation of ElderNet 2024 (2024)
15. Straczkiewicz, M., Huang, E.J., Onnela, J.-P.: A "one-size-fits-most" walking recognition method for smartphones, smartwatches, and wearable accelerometers. NPJ Digit. Med. **6**, 29 (2023). https://doi.org/10.1038/s41746-022-00745-z
16. Hegde, N., Sazonov, E.: SmartStep: a fully integrated low-power insole monitor. Electronics (Basel) **3**, 381–397 (2014). https://doi.org/10.3390/electronics3020381
17. De Pinho André, R., Diniz, P.H.F.S., Fuks, H.: Bottom-up Investigation. In: Proceedings of the Proceedings of the 4th International Workshop on Sensor-based Activity Recognition and Interaction; ACM: New York, NY, USA, pp. 1–6 (2017)
18. de Fazio, R., Perrone, E., Velázquez, R., De Vittorio, M., Visconti, P.: Development of a self-powered piezo-resistive smart insole equipped with low-power BLE connectivity for remote gait monitoring. Sensors **21**, 4539 (2021). https://doi.org/10.3390/s21134539
19. Chou, L.-W., Shen, J.-H., Lin, H.-T., Yang, Y.-T., Hu, W.-P.: A study on the influence of number/distribution of sensing points of the smart insoles on the center of pressure estimation for the internet of things applications. Sustainability **13**, 2934 (2021). https://doi.org/10.3390/su13052934
20. Pedregosa, F., et al.: Scikit-Learn: Machine Learning in Python (2018)
21. Sankur, B.: Survey over image thresholding techniques and quantitative performance evaluation. J. Electron. Imaging **13**, 146 (2004). https://doi.org/10.1117/1.1631315
22. Schepanski, K., Tegen, I., Laurent, B., Heinold, B., Macke, A.: A new saharan dust source activation frequency map derived from MSG-SEVIRI IR-channels. Geophys. Res. Lett. **34** (2007). https://doi.org/10.1029/2007GL030168

A Bilingual App for Campus Wayfinding and Local Cultural Immersion

Chukwuka Chinechebem Yvette[1] and Yoojeong Song[2]([⊠]) [iD]

[1] Department of Computer Science, Semyung University, 65, Semyung-ro, Jecheon-si, Chungcheongbuk-do 27136, South Korea
[2] Department of Computer Software Engineering, Soonchunhyang University, 22, Sooncheonhyang-ro, Asan-si, Chungcheongnam-do 31538, South Korea
`yoojeong@sch.ac.kr`

Abstract. This paper presents SMU Navigator, a mobile application developed to improve the university experience for students—particularly international students—by addressing common challenges in campus navigation and local integration. Featuring real-time Firebase backend support and bilingual content (Korean and English), the app delivers structured, location-based information about campus facilities and nearby city services. It aims to mitigate accessibility and language barriers faced by new students. A comparative case study of the widely used Everytime app underscores the importance and impact of multilingual support in enhancing student services in South Korea.

Keywords: Campus Navigation · Bilingual App · Firebase · Student Integration · Android Development

1 Introduction

South Korea has seen a consistent rise in the number of international students in recent years. However, both international and domestic students often face challenges when adapting to new campus environments—ranging from navigating unfamiliar facilities and understanding administrative systems to accessing local services and social integration. To address these issues, we present SMU Navigator, a centralized bilingual mobile application designed to enhance the student experience by providing real-time, location-based information about campus and surrounding city areas. The app supports multilingual access (Korean and English), integrates real-time data services, and aims to reduce information gaps for new students. This paper introduces the design and architecture of the app and evaluates its potential impact on student integration. We also present a comparative analysis with existing platforms, to highlight the importance of multilingual support and contextual information in improving the student experience.

2 Background and Related Work

The Need for Multilingual Inclusive Campus Tools. Students—particularly international students—encounter various challenges when adapting to university life in Korea. These include:

The original version of the chapter has been revised. A new affiliation has been fixed to the first author. A correction to this chapter can be found at https://doi.org/10.1007/978-981-95-3141-7_20

B.-G. Kim et al. (Eds.): MITA 2025, CCIS 2675, pp. 209–214, 2026.
https://doi.org/10.1007/978-981-95-3141-7_19

- Interfaces for academic and administrative systems that are exclusively in Korean
- A lack of real-time, accessible guidance for newly enrolled students
- Feelings of isolation due to limited access to structured local information and services

Such barriers often hinder both academic engagement and social integration, highlighting the need for inclusive digital tools that support multilingual communication and localized content delivery. These challenges are consistent with findings in cross-cultural user experience design research, which emphasize the need to account for linguistic and cultural diversity in interface design and content accessibility [1].

Everytime [2] is one of the most widely used university community apps in South Korea. For several years, it operated solely in Korean, effectively excluding non-Korean-speaking students from fully participating in campus-related discussions and services. As of early 2022, users could not copy in-app text for external translation, further limiting accessibility. Although a recent update introduced basic in-app translation functionality, the feature remains limited and frequently fails to convey contextually accurate meanings. Community forum analyses revealed that international students who inquired about English availability were often met with replies such as "Not really, it's all in Korean." This perception discourages usage and deepens the existing information divide. SMU Navigator addresses these shortcomings by incorporating multilingual support from the initial design phase, aiming to foster a more inclusive and accessible digital environment for all students.

3 Survey Insights and Design Motivation

To better understand the needs of the target users, a short survey [3] was conducted among new Korean and international students at Semyung University. The goal was to validate the app concept and gather insights into common challenges. Figure 1 summarizes the features students most wanted to see in a campus-city mobile application. The highest demand was for Jecheon city guide information (25.1%), followed by multilingual support (19.6%), and chatbot features (16.8%). These results directly informed the design priorities of SMU Navigator.

As summarized in Table 1, most students need the following:

- **Ease of Navigation:** A way to find buildings and locations without relying solely on Korean maps or signs.
- **Access to trusted local information:** Many students were unsure of where to eat, shop, or study safely and socialize affordably in Jecheon. They would appreciate accessing reliable local resources.
- **Language inclusion:** Korean-only apps excluded a large part of the international student population.
- **Centralized resources:** Students wanted to access campus information, events, and community updates all in one place.

The data strongly supported the need for a multilingual, all-in-one platform.

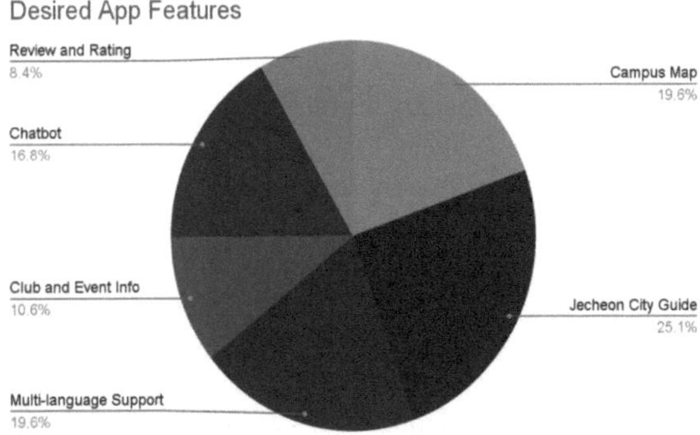

Fig. 1. Summarizes the overall responses, particularly highlighting difficulties in campus navigation and local integration.

Table 1. Student Survey Results from International and Korean Students.

N/B	Survey Question	*Yes (%)*	*No (%)*	*Maybe (%)*
1	DifficultyNavigating Campus	50%	50%	-
2	Know Jecheon Facilities	20%	30%	50%
3	ExperiencedLanguage Barriers	60%	20%	20%
4	Would Use Campus + City App	90%	0%	10%

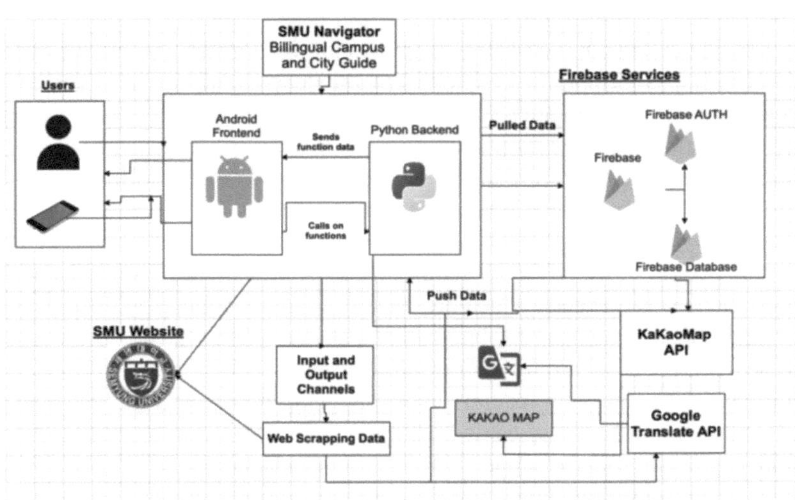

Fig. 2. System architecture of the SMU Navigator app

4 System Architecture

The SMU Navigator application consists of multiple integrated components that enable real-time, bilingual information delivery and user interaction. The frontend is implemented using Java and XML within the Android Studio environment and utilizes key UI elements such as ConstraintLayout, RecyclerView, and ChipNavigationBar to provide a structured and responsive user interface (Fig. 2).

On the backend, a Python-based script performs automated web scraping of the official SMU website to extract campus notices and updates. These contents are then translated into English using the Google Translate API [4] and uploaded to Firebase Realtime Database. Firebase also handles user authentication, real-time data synchronization, and cloud storage management [5]. Geographic data, including campus and city locations, is visualized using the Kakao Map API [6], which allows for the rendering of custom markers and map-based interactions within the app. The complete technology stack includes Java and XML for frontend development, Firebase Realtime Database and Firebase Authentication for backend services, and external APIs such as Google Translate and Kakao Map for multilingual support and geolocation rendering.

5 Features and Design

SMU Navigator is designed with simplicity, accessibility, and localization in mind. Its clean, category-based interface allows users to easily explore dormitories, faculties, study cafés, and local marts. The app currently supports Korean and English, with plans to expand language options for a more diverse user base.

Key features include unified calendar integration for semester schedules and club events, and a personalized profile system that lets students create bios, post content, and follow others to foster community. The Jecheon Junction section offers access to major student organizations like "Wi-won-hwe," promoting student engagement.

Google Maps integration provides intuitive location services, while the Firebase backend ensures real-time and scalable data synchronization.

The latest update brings notable improvements to both backend and user-facing functions. A Python script on Replit scrapes the official Semyung University website for campus notices and events, which are then translated via Google Cloud Translate API to bridge the language gap for international students. Translated content is stored in Firebase Realtime Database for synchronized access.

Additionally, the app now features interactive map-based visualizations and customized city guide cards. These cards highlight local markets, cafés, study areas, and other student-friendly spots to support smoother local adaptation.

With these updates, SMU Navigator continues to deliver up-to-date, accessible, and consistent campus information to all users.

- **Real-time Notice Scraping:** A Python script hosted on Replit continuously scrapes the official Semyung University website for the latest campus notices and event announcements, keeping students informed without requiring manual checks of multiple sources.

- **Automatic Language Translation:** The scraped content is processed using the Google Cloud Translate API, instantly translating notices and updates from Korean to English. This bridges the language gap for international students and improves inclusivity.
- **Firebase-Based Data Synchronization:** After translation, all data is pushed to the Firebase Realtime Database, ensuring all users have synchronized access to current notices, events, and resources.
- **Visualized Map Integration and City Guide Cards:** The app features dynamic visualizations of survey results and custom-designed city guide cards. These include categorized listings of markets, cafés, study zones, and student-friendly attractions, all tailored for easy access and informed decision-making.

6   User Testing Feedback

Following the MVP launch, a preliminary user test was conducted with ten participants—five Korean and five international students—to evaluate usability, design, and core features. Results showed high satisfaction with bilingual campus information, with 90% reporting improved orientation through dual-language content. Participants praised the interface, especially the mascot-themed splash screen and clean layout.

Navigation using KakaoMap-based markers was found intuitive for locating study spaces and cafeterias. While automated translations were generally accurate, some users suggested refining technical terms. Several participants also expressed interest in adding a forum-style feature, tentatively named SMU Talk, for Q&A, information sharing, and study partner connections. This feedback underscores the potential for future community-building enhancements.

7   Future Work

Future enhancements of SMU Navigator will focus on improving accessibility, enriching core features, and expanding platform compatibility to support a broader student population. Planned updates include adding Vietnamese and Chinese language support to better serve international students, and integrating course timetables that dynamically reflect each user's department and major for personalized academic support.

A real-time seat tracking feature for high-traffic areas like cafés and libraries is under review to help students manage study spaces efficiently. To address translation limitations, domain-adapted models will be incorporated to improve multilingual accuracy.

The Jecheon Junction section will expand to include interactive peer forums for discussions and Q&A, enhancing student engagement. Cross-platform support will be pursued via frameworks like React Native or Flutter, enabling iOS availability. Lastly, a lightweight multilingual chatbot or RAG-based GPT system will be developed to answer campus-related queries—such as locations, office hours, and events—in multiple languages.

These upgrades aim to establish SMU Navigator as a smart-campus platform that is inclusive, interactive, and scalable.

8   Conclusion

This study demonstrates the potential of multilingual, student-oriented mobile applications in addressing common barriers to campus engagement and local integration. SMU Navigator integrates Firebase-based infrastructure, Python-based automation, and an intuitive Android interface to provide real-time, bilingual access to campus and city-related resources. Findings from the user survey and comparative analysis with existing platforms highlight a strong demand for more inclusive and accessible digital tools among both domestic and international students. By embedding multilingual support and real-time content delivery from the outset, SMU Navigator establishes a practical framework for future smart campus solutions aimed at enhancing the student experience.

Disclosure of Interests.   The authors have no competing interests to declare that are relevant to the content of this article.

References

1. Marcus, A.: Cross-cultural user-experience design. In: SIGGRAPH Asia 2013 Courses, pp. 1–31 (2013)
2. Everytime. https://everytime.kr/. Accessed 25 June 2025
3. Groves, R.M., Fowler, F.J., Couper, M.P., Lepkowski, J.M., Singer, E., Tourangeau, R.: Survey Methodology. 2nd edn. Wiley, Hoboken (2011)
4. Google Cloud: cloud translation documentation. https://cloud.google.com/translate/docs. Accessed 7 July 2025
5. Firebase: firebase realtime database documentation. https://firebase.google.com/docs/database. Accessed 7 July 2025
6. Kakao Developers: Kakao Map SDK developer guide. https://apis.map.kakao.com. Accessed 7 July 2025

Correction to: A Bilingual App for Campus Wayfinding and Local Cultural Immersion

Chukwuka Chinechebem Yvette and Yoojeong Song

Correction to:
Chapter 19 in: B.-G. Kim et al. (Eds.): *Multimedia Information Technology and Applications*, **CCIS 2675, https://doi.org/10.1007/978-981-95-3141-7_19**

In the originally published version of chapter 19, the author affiliation had been rendered incorrectly. This has been corrected.

The updated version of this chapter can be found at
https://doi.org/10.1007/978-981-95-3141-7_19

© The Author(s) 2026
B.-G. Kim et al. (Eds.): MITA 2025, CCIS 2675, p. C1, 2026.
https://doi.org/10.1007/978-981-95-3141-7_20

Author Index

A
Aisha, Qurat Ul Ain   98

B
Baek, Eu-Tteum   40
Bibi, Misbah   111
Boulaouane, Youssef   28
Byun, Yung-Cheol   16, 52

C
Chang, Chuan-Wang   3
Chatterjee, Indranath   64
Cho, Yu-Jin   98, 125

D
Dofitas Jr, Cyreneo   16

G
Gautam, Akansha   64
Gautam, Suruchi   64
Guruge, Kasunika   165

H
Hasegawa, Mikio   178
Hayami, Meguru   118
Herath, H. M. K. K. M. B.   86, 165, 197
Hyder, Hasnain   52

J
Jo, Eunseon   153
Jo, Seong Min   185

K
Khan, Qazi Waqas   111
Kim, Beomseok   141
Kim, Byung Gyu   98
Kim, Byung-Gyu   125

K
Kim, Dohyeun   111
Kim, Eung Soo   185
Kim, Jisu   28
Kim, Yong-Woon   16, 52
Koshiba, Mamiko   118
Kumar, Naveen   64
Kuremoto, Shun   118
Kuremoto, Takashi   118

L
Lee, Ah-Hyeon   125
Lee, Byeong-il   86, 165, 197
Lee, Deokwoo   28
Lee, Han-jin   153
Leng, Lu   79

M
Mabu, Shingo   118
Madusanka, Nuwan   197
Malekroodi, Hadi Sedigh   197

N
Na, Chang-Soo   86, 165
Nanayakkara, Thathsara   197

P
Park, Hi-Joon   86, 165
Park, Jimin   28
Plato, Jan   125
Prathiksha, V. P.   86

Q
Qiu, Shi-Hong   3

S
Soe Moe, Sa Jim   111
Song, Yoojeong   209

T
Tsai, Cheng-Mu   3
Tuan, Nguyen Anh   111

W
Wakamiya, Naoki   178
Wu, Zhecheng   79

Y
Yamamoto, Ryota   178
Yang, Jinhong   141
Yasuda, Hiroyuki   178
Yi, Myunggi   86, 165, 197
Yvette, Chukwuka Chinechebem   209